Achieving Literacy Success with English Language Learners

Insights · Assessment · Instruction

*This book is dedicated
to young English language learners
and to the teachers who enrich their learning.*

Reading Recovery Council of North America (RRCNA)
500 W. Wilson Bridge Road, Suite 250
Worthington, OH 43085

www.readingrecovery.org

All children's names used throughout this book are pseudonyms.

Library of Congress Control Number   2008941083

ISBN   978-0-9763071-6-7

First published 2009; Reprinted 2011

Principal photographer: Charles Baxter, Baxter Photography, Argyle, Texas
Additional photography: Greg Blomberg, Greg Blomberg, Inc., Dallas, Texas
Design and production: Vicki S. Fox, RRCNA publications manager

Printed in the United States of America on acid-free paper

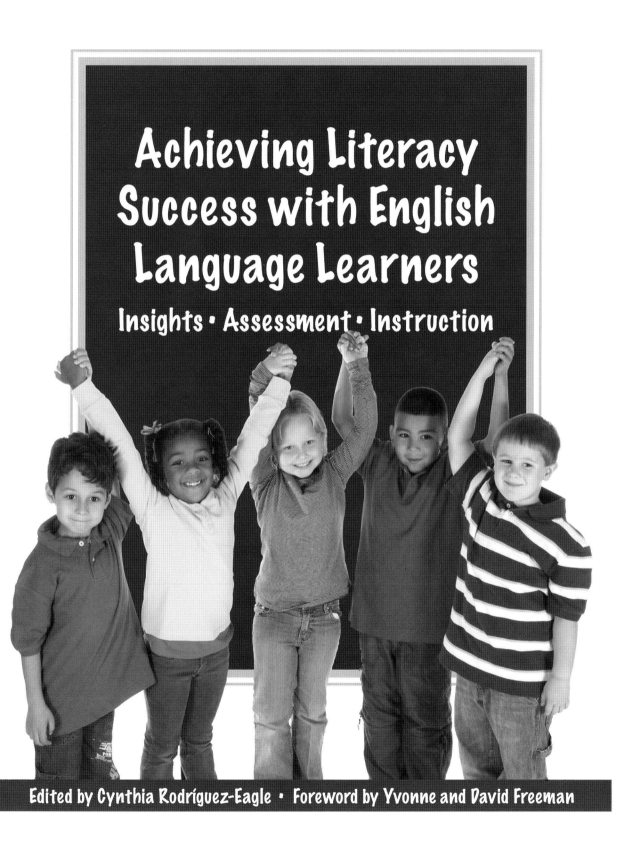

Achieving Literacy Success with English Language Learners

Insights · Assessment · Instruction

Edited by Cynthia Rodríguez-Eagle · Foreword by Yvonne and David Freeman

Contents

Acknowledgements

The editor would like to recognize Jady Johnson and the staff of the Reading Recovery Council of North America for their hard work in producing this book. A special acknowledgement must be made to Vicki Fox, technical editor. Her impeccable and timely work made the development of this text and our job of editing all the easier.

Special thanks are extended to Charles Baxter of Baxter Photography. His beautiful photos added immensely to the quality of this publication. His patience and kindness during the photo shoots are much appreciated!

Special thanks to the administration of the Denton (Texas) Independent School District, especially the personnel of the Tomás Rivera Elementary School. Principal Robert González, Assistant Principal Roshanda Thomas, Curriculum Coordinator Melanie Mitchell, and all the staff and children welcomed us into their school and allowed us to conduct 2 days of photo shoots. Their generosity and welcoming spirit is a true reflection of the school and the entire district.

The support and encouragement of my colleagues in the Reading Department at Texas Woman's University was motivating and inspirational. Their kindness and collegiality are much appreciated.

Thanks so much to each of the contributing authors. It was, after all, their manuscripts that made the production of this book possible. Their work no doubt will impact schools and classrooms nationwide. It has been a pleasure and an honor to work with each of them. I truly appreciate their professionalism, hard work, and valuable contributions.

This book would not have been possible without having been so enthusiastically embraced by my friend and collaborator, Dr. Billie Askew. Her patient guidance and mentoring were invaluable. Billie allowed me the opportunity to work with her side-by-side from the initial conception of this book all the way through final publication. The scholarly presentation and overall quality of this professional text are greatly enhanced because of the depth of her knowledge, her generosity, and her willingness to share. It has been an educational journey for us both that began over lunch and continued through many phone calls and meetings at her kitchen table. I have learned so much from her, and I am immensely grateful.

Finally, to my family. My husband, Shawn Eagle, who is endlessly supportive and encouraging of each and every professional project I undertake. I appreciate and love him more than I can say. And to our amazing 1-year-old son, Robbie. He's already teaching me more than ever about language learning, as he's developing into a bilingual toddler. I am certain he will be the subject of many future publications!

Many students in U.S. schools struggle with reading and writing. In particular, English language learners (ELLs) face a daunting challenge as they attempt to develop literacy in a new language. Most younger ELLs do not read or write in their first language. As a result, they need to learn to read in a language they may only be beginning to speak and understand. This is a formidable task.

Achieving Literacy Success with English Language Learners: Insights, Assessment, Instruction provides needed information for teachers trying to help ELLs develop literacy. A common focus that runs through the chapters is the need to help ELLs understand that reading should make sense. With the current emphasis in early reading on decoding, particularly in schools following the mandates of Reading First, ELLs may conclude that reading in English consists of simply saying the words. Once these students can decode, instruction shifts to fluency with the result that ELLs may decide that good readers are the ones who can pronounce all the words very fast.

The National Reading Panel report (National Institute of Child Health and Human Development, 2000), which provided the research base for Reading First programs, concluded that instruction in phonemic awareness and phonics in the early grades was an important factor for later reading success. The summary of the research results and the publications sent to schools, such as *Put Reading First,* (Armbruster & Osborn, 2001), claimed that phonemic awareness and phonics are essential for reading success. These claims, which went well beyond the evidence presented in the report itself, had a strong influence on teaching practices. Despite critiques of the National Reading Panel report (Coles, 2000; Garan, 2002), schools got the message that decoding was what counted in early reading instruction.

Recently, we were observing a student teacher working with a young English language learner. They were reading a story together. The student teacher asked the child questions designed to help him interact with the text and to make connections between the story

Foreword

Yvonne and David Freeman

and his life. Even though the student teacher was doing a good job, the young reader seemed to ignore her. He plowed through the story as quickly as he could, pronouncing most of the words correctly. The bell rang to end the period, and the boy stood up and announced, "I'm a good reader. I read fast." Unfortunately, this is the message that many ELLs have received. Good readers read fast. They can say all the words. Comprehension is something that will come later.

The National Reading Panel report did not include studies that included English language learners in the sample population. A follow-up study conducted by the National Literacy Panel (August & Shanahan, 2006) synthesized studies that looked at how ELLs develop as readers and writers. An important finding from that report was that "second language readers are more likely to achieve adequate performance (defined as performance that either is equivalent to that of monolinguals or meets local education standards) on measures of word recognition and spelling than on measures of reading vocabulary, comprehension, and writing" (Snow, 2006). The studies reviewed by the National Literacy Panel showed that ELLs need instruction in developing word-level skills; however, their finding that ELLs develop these skills quickly but fall behind in comprehension suggests that teachers should focus much more on comprehension than they do in many schools.

The authors of *Achieving Literacy Success* all keep the focus on comprehension. As Judith Neal states in her chapter, "Only adults enamored of a sophisticated analysis of reading mechanics would propose we denigrate children with code-only emphasis for their reading instruction." Neal and the other authors of this book present a balanced approach to literacy instruction. For example, Neal discusses three practices commonly used in Reading Recovery that are particularly appropriate for ELLs. These practices are guided reading, interactive writing, and reading aloud. Using these three practices on a regular basis, teachers can differentiate instruction to meet the needs of ELLs at different levels of English proficiency.

Often, teachers are told that best practices for all students are also best practices for ELLs. While it is true that ELLs benefit from these best practices, there is a danger in thinking that providing instruction that works well for native English speakers will completely meet the needs of ELLs. In fact, ELLs need these good practices plus additional help since they are not only learning to read and write but also learning English.

Several of the authors address the specific needs of ELLs. Neal, for example, points out that four common literacy challenges for ELLs are unknown concepts, unfamiliar vocabulary, abstract ideas, and a lack of familiarity with English sentence structures. In her chapter, Neal provides concrete suggestions for meeting each of these challenges.

Other chapters also help readers understand the additional knowledge teachers of ELLs need to work effectively with ELLs. For example, Harper and de Jong outline several points the experienced English as a second language teachers they surveyed reported that mainstream teachers should know to teach ELLs effectively. These include understanding language and cultural differences and understanding second language acquisition. The authors provide specific examples of ways teachers can put this specialized knowledge into practice in classes with ELLs.

Other chapters in *Achieving Literacy Success* focus on other areas that teachers need to consider when working with ELLs. In her chapter, Yoon explains the importance of recognizing how 'teacher talk' positions students and affects students' 'identity formation.' As Cummins (1996) points out, school is a place where students, especially ELLs, negotiate identities. In their chapter, Escamilla and her colleagues describe specific techniques teachers can use with Spanish-speaking ELLs to help them make cross-language connections. Williams and Haag discuss ways teachers can draw on students' knowledge of their first language to improve their writing in English.

Each chapter in this book gives teachers ideas for ways to help their ELLs achieve literacy success. The authors help teachers understand how to provide the kind of literacy instruction students need to comprehend and write texts in English. Teachers who follow the ideas presented in *Achieving Literacy Success* can move their ELLs beyond simply being word callers and help them become engaged readers and writers.

References

Armbruster, B., & Osborn, J. (2001). *Put reading first: The building blocks for teaching children to read*. Washington, DC: U.S. Department of Education.

August, D., & Shanahan, T. (Eds.). (2006). *Developing literacy in second-language learners: Report of the National Literacy Panel on language minority children and youth*. Mahwah, NJ: Lawrence Erlbaum Associates.

Coles, G. (2000). *Misreading reading: The bad science that hurts children*. Portsmouth, NH: Heinemann.

Cummins, J. (1996). *Negotiating identities: Education for empowerment in a diverse society*. Ontario, CA: California Association of Bilingual Education.

Garan, E. (2002). *Resisting reading mandates*. Portsmouth, NH: Heinemann.

National Institute of Child Health and Human Development (2000). *Report of the National Reading Panel. Teaching children to read: An evidence-based assessment of the scientific research literature on reading and its implications for reading instruction*. (NIH Publication No. 00–4769). Washington, DC: U.S. Government Printing Office.

Snow, C. (2006). Cross-cutting themes and future research directions. In D. August & T. Shanahan (Eds.), *Developing literacy in second-language learners: Report of the national literacy panel on language-minority children and youth* (pp. 631–651). Mahwah, NJ: Lawrence Erlbaum Associates.

Introduction

In my previous position as a bilingual and English as a second language teacher, I was always seeking resources to assist me in addressing the unique needs of English language learners (ELLs). My colleagues and I spent a great deal of time problem solving the needs of these students. We knew the importance of planning instruction that would value their contributions while building their understandings of reading, writing, and speaking in English. I carried this challenge with me to my current role as a university trainer of Reading Recovery and Descubriendo la Lectura (Reading Recovery in Spanish) teacher leaders.

Teachers and administrators work diligently to be knowledgeable about effective practices for all students in their classrooms and schools. In addition to the ever-changing landscape of literacy instruction, the student population is also evolving. This book takes a close look at ELLs and suggests ways to prepare these students to become successful readers and writers through appropriate literacy instruction. The information shared by recognized leaders in the field is targeted to support classroom teachers, specialist teachers, literacy coaches, facilitators, and administrators.

Dr. Marie Clay's work helped me develop a deeper understanding of the complex nature of literacy learning and to remain tentative and flexible in my understandings. Her emphasis on individual learners who take different paths to common outcomes reinforced the notion that what works for one student might not work for another and that, as teachers, we need to be open to trying something different.

Clay's emphasis on oral language and the reciprocal nature of reading and writing has also guided my work with children. "It is useful to assume that working effectively in one activity will help with working in the other. …they affect each other reciprocally, and…oral language is a further rich resource for both those activities" (Clay, 2005, p. 2).

Teachers of ELLs are challenged to develop oral language while also teaching reading and writing in the new language. This is the challenge that has driven the development of this book. It is intended as a resource for teachers that will provide (a) multiple perspectives of ELLs and their teachers, (b) a variety of ways to assess these learners, and (c) suggestions for effective teaching and learning in all school settings.

Editor's Note: Throughout the book, two terms are used to describe the population of students for whom English is not the first language: English language learners (ELLs) and English learners (ELs).

After a thorough review of current research and educational trends, it was determined that both of these terms are used interchangeably and refer to the same population of students. Therefore, the author's choice of terms was honored.

Part 1 centers on three fundamental and overarching perspectives. First, Rudy Rodríguez shares foundational information and describes challenges related to the influx of immigration and the influence of policies. Bogum Yoon focuses on the attitudes and participation of ELLs in classrooms, suggesting ways in which teachers can build active and successful learner engagement. In the final chapter in this section, Candace Harper and Ester de Jong suggest ways that experienced teachers who work with ELLs can share their knowledge and expertise with mainstream teachers.

Part 2 focuses on assessing and teaching English language learners. The first three chapters are written by Reading Recovery trainers who have worked with ELLs in one-to-one lessons and have applied their experiences in other school settings. In my chapter, I consider how the lessons I have learned from ELLs in Reading Recovery could apply to classroom teachers. Pat Kelly explores underlying principles of Reading Recovery and how those principles transferred into effective literacy assessment and practice in a kindergarten classroom. Judith Neal suggests helpful and practical ways to support English learners, with specific attention to comprehension and language development.

The remaining four chapters also target assessment and classroom practices for ELLs. Lori Helman focuses on literacy assessments that guide instruction, suggesting ways teachers can use assessments to observe patterns in literacy learning. Turning a close lens on the importance of developing essential vocabulary for ELLs, Susan O'Leary suggests vocabulary strategies that will contribute to students' self-perception and quality of thought. Kathy Escamilla and her colleagues propose ways to build cross-language connections from Spanish to English, providing some concrete ideas for teachers to use. In the final chapter, Joan Williams and Claudia Haag share exciting ideas for teachers to encourage active engagement as they build academic language.

It is my hope that this book will help untangle confusions and propose some new understandings about effective literacy practices for English language learners. The foundational and practical information shared in each chapter will undoubtedly strengthen the quality of teaching ELLs. It is critical for these students to build a strong foundation in English literacy in order to be successful learners and eager contributors to our society. I applaud your hard work and your commitment to make this an attainable goal for all of your students.

— Cynthia Rodríguez-Eagle, editor

Reference

Clay, M. M. (2005). *Literacy lessons designed for individuals part one: Why? when? and how?* Portsmouth, NH: Heinemann.

Achieving Literacy Success with English Language Learners

Insights • Assessment • Instruction

Educators today are facing seemingly insurmountable obstacles in meeting the needs of an increasingly diverse student population. These are students who, for the most part, are the most vulnerable and at risk of school failure. The huge enrollment surge over the past 2 decades, especially of poor and non-English-speaking immigrant children, coupled with a national movement toward greater school accountability, has exacerbated the challenge and placed even greater pressure on the schools.

Who are these children and adolescent learners? What are their language and cultural attributes and needs? What are desirable behaviors and attitudes of teachers in responding to the language and cultural diversity challenge within the context of an expanding system of rigid school reform?

Understanding the Challenge of Educating Immigrant English Language Learners in Today's Schools

Rudy Rodríguez
University of North Texas

Although change in public education and in response to language minority students has been underway since the mid-1960s, in more recent years school personnel have had to reshape past practices and approaches. This is to accommodate a new generation of learners different in many ways from those populations served by the earlier models of bilingual and English as a second language (ESL) education and other special programs. Any discourse about issues and perspectives associated with the education of culturally diverse learners—specifically new immigrant groups—should begin with an understanding of social policy, the shifts in U.S. demographics, and their effects on education.

Policy Influences and Immigration Influx from Third World Nations

The 1965 Immigration Law signed by President Lyndon B. Johnson marked a radical break with previous policy and helped provide the

Table 1
Growth Pattern of Foreign-Born Population (thousands)

Population	Share of All Immigrants	Total	Pre-1980	1980–89	1990–99	2000–07	Share of Post-2000 Arrivals
All Latin America	54.6%	20,372	3,443	4,442	6,467	6,015	58.7%
Mexico[2]	31.3%	11,671	1,788	2,408	3,890	3,583	34.9%
Caribbean	9.1%	3,379	886	752	960	781	7.6%
South America	7.3%	2,725	492	585	852	796	7.8%
Central America	7.0%	2,597	277	697	765	855	8.3%
East/Southeast Asia	17.6%	6,558	1,233	1,720	1,922	1,682	16.4%
Europe	12.5%	4,646	2,007	538	1,187	914	8.9%
South Asia	5.5%	2,044	249	388	680	727	7.1%
Middle East	3.5%	1,310	344	398	324	244	2.4%
Sub-Saharan Africa	2.8%	1,030	130	155	349	396	3.9%
Canada	1.9%	699	309	90	184	116	1.1%
Not given/Oceana	1.7%	621	158	122	180	161	1.6%
Total	100.0%	37,280	7,873	7,853	11,293	10,258	100.0%

Year of Entry[1]

[1] Indicates the year immigrants said they came to the U.S.

[2] Includes 100,000 persons who indicated they are foreign born, Hispanic, Mexican, but who did not indicate a country of birth.

SOURCE: Center for Immigration Studies analysis of March 2007 Current Population Survey

U.S. Census data show that the first half of the 2000–2010 decade was the highest period of immigration in U.S. history.

impetus for profound demographic changes in the United States. What the 1965 policy did was suppress immigration from traditional areas in Europe and opened up immigration from Third World nations. Since 1970, the foreign-born, non-European population has increased rapidly due to large-scale immigration (Ovando, Combs, & Collier, 2006). U.S. Census data also show that the first half of the 2000–2010 decade was the highest period of immigration in U.S. history with nearly half estimated to be undocumented immigrants.[1] Although immigrants have come to this country from practically every corner of the world, one country, Mexico, and one region, Spanish-speaking Latin America, have come to dominate U.S. immigration during the same time period (Camarota, 2005). For more information on the significance and growth pattern of the foreign-born population during the present decade, see Table 1.

Some Considerations and Concepts
Regarding the Education of Immigrant Students

The Language Diversity Factor

A report by the Pew Hispanic Center reveals new patterns of immigrant settlement beyond the traditional and mainly urban areas of Texas, New York, and California. Metropolitan and rural areas of six southern states—Arkansas, Alabama, Georgia, North Carolina, South Carolina, and Tennessee—have had rapid increases in their immigrant population. The largest growth in each of these areas has been in the Latino population (Kochhar, Suro, & Tafoya, 2005).

The impact of Latinos has been especially felt in public education — a group which accounts for the largest enrollment increase in the schools since the early 1990s. These are children who are largely limited or non-English-speaking and account for the greatest number of English language learners (ELLs)[2] in such special programs as bilingual and ESL education (Batalova, 2006). While Spanish is the mother tongue of three in four English learners in bilingual/ESL programs, other languages spoken by elementary and secondary students include Vietnamese, Hmong, Cantonese, Korean, Haitian, Creole, Arabic, Urdu, Tagalog, Mandarin, Serbo-Croatian, Lao, Japanese, Armenian, Polish, and Hindi (Crawford, 2004). See Figure 1 for the significance of the ELL enrollment growth in comparison to the general K–12 enrollment over a 10-year period.

As illustrated in Table 2, recent immigrant students and the growing number of first-generation immigrant ELLs in bilingual and ESL

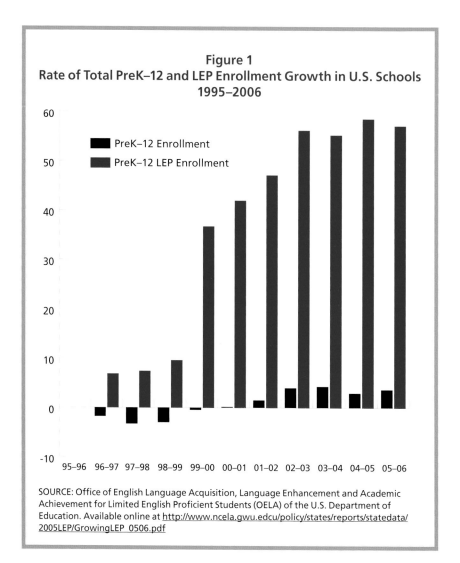

Figure 1
Rate of Total PreK–12 and LEP Enrollment Growth in U.S. Schools 1995–2006

SOURCE: Office of English Language Acquisition, Language Enhancement and Academic Achievement for Limited English Proficient Students (OELA) of the U.S. Department of Education. Available online at http://www.ncela.gwu.edcu/policy/states/reports/statedata/2005LEP/GrowingLEP_0506.pdf

Table 2
English Language Proficiency Levels Among Recent Immigrants
and First-Generation Immigrant Students and Families

Descriptor	Proficiency Level
Recent immigrant ELL with previous formal education	Immigrant students with prior schooling in their home countries tend to have the cognitive foundation (i.e., CALP á la Cummins, 1991) necessary for them to cope with the academic demands of U.S. schools. These students are, therefore, able to transfer concepts learned in first language to second language with greater ease and less time than recent immigrants who have not attended schools in their countries of origin.
Recent immigrant ELL without previous formal education	These students typically do not have the cognitive/academic skills underlying literacy in their first language, much less English. Even children who come to the U.S. as toddlers or are born in the U.S. of recent immigrants who are poor and illiterate, experience adjustment and learning difficulties in American schools.
First generation immigrant	According to Ovando, et al. (2006) these students may be more proficient in English than their heritage (home) language. They may be fairly balanced in proficiency in both languages or, in some cases, more proficient in the heritage language than in English (e.g., Farsi, Urdu, Spanish, Korean, Vietnamese). For most immigrants, however, as fluency in English increases across generations, so too does the regular use of English by students. Literacy skill development in English shows a similar trend (Hakimzadeh & Cohn, 2007).

programs present distinctive challenges to educators and instructional planning based on their differing levels of English language proficiency (Batalova, 2006; Compton-Lilly, 2008). The degree of success of ELLs in learning of academic content is, according to Cummins (1991), related to the learner's strength in *cognitive/academic language proficiency* (CALP). The stronger the ELL is in native-language CALP, for example, the greater his/her chances for success in acquiring a second language (i.e., English) and understanding cognitively demanding subject material. [3]

Recent immigrant students with little or no exposure to formal schooling in their home countries, on the other hand, would be severely lacking in the cognitive/academic language and critical skills needed to transfer to an all-English class setting with no special language support. These students would require extended instruction in developing the social/survival language (i.e., Basic Interpersonal Communication Skills or BICS) and preliterate skills as a prerequisite to development of the language necessary for them to compete in the more rigorous English-only academic program. A 2003 report by the President's Advisory Commission on Educational Excellence for Hispanic Americans documents the importance of acquisition of preliterate and vocabulary skills as a foundation for success in the critical content areas of the curriculum. The report further emphasizes that students who read more, know more. "They also have larger vocabularies, write better, and spell better" (p.14).

Economic and Social Factors

Poverty is the most common factor that pushes immigrants out of economically depressed countries and opportunity pulls them into the United States (Noboa-Polanco, 1991). Central American and Mexican immigrants, in particular, have come to the U.S. in large numbers to escape impoverished conditions or political conflict in their home countries. In a series of personal interviews with 133 Central American children living in Houston, Texas, for example, Rodríguez and Urrutia-Rojas (1990) found that 114 (86 percent) had personally experienced a traumatic event because of social or government crisis before migrating to America.

Another factor that adds to the complexity of the language minority population is the presence of immigrants admitted as political refugees. These are individuals who have resettled in this country from some of the African nations, the Middle East, Southeast Asia, and other politically unstable regions of the world. Many have suffered the traumatic psychological effects of war and persecution.

Also, at a time of aggressive activity by the U.S. government to repatriate undocumented immigrants, children in school live with the constant fear that they may not find their parents when they come home. The stress and insecurity felt by immigrant children of not knowing who will care for them because of a missing parent or loved one may be difficult to endure and all-consuming physically and emotionally. These are concerns that weigh heavily on entire families — many of whom have lived in the United States for many years and with children who were born in this country.[4]

Immigration status, language diversity, the poverty factor, and refugee experience of families and children, taken together, no doubt challenge the professional acumen and cultural sensitivities of educators. How to attend to the basic charge of educating students to their highest potential becomes problematic when there are a myriad of complex issues interfering with the process of teaching and learning.

Solidifying our Commitment to the Core Values of the Profession

Where do we start in dealing with the critical issues extant in today's multicultural schools? The inspirational words of one of my early graduate school professors reminds us of those traditional core values that make our profession unique and provide the foundation for good teaching in multiple school contexts. The following captures the salience of his message and appreciation of the ardor of the teacher:

> We are, by history… an optimistic profession. No group in our society has been more dedicated to the American Dream than the teacher. We not only believe in the ultimate triumph of free-

Highly qualified teachers are especially urged to embrace the diversity of languages and cultures of immigrant and non-immigrant students as a positive and valuable contribution in the classroom, rather than view them as deficits or liabilities.

dom and democracy, we have tried to convince the American people that regardless of the problems we face, education holds the solutions.… . Especially we have held that education is the escalator that moves people from lower-class poverty and misery to middle-class affluence and comfort. (Melby, 1968, p.2)

There is considerable research evidence demonstrating that teachers in today's classrooms who subscribe to these basic values tend to be more successful in impacting student learning. [See, for example, Reyes, Scribner, & Scribner (1999); and the 2000 report by the Texas Education Agency (TEA) on the Texas successful school study; also see, Walker-Dalhouse & Risko (2008).] These are teachers who have a focus and a clear vision built on high expectations for learning. They naturally assume a greater personal and professional responsibility for making sure that children learn (Dembo & Gibson, 1985). Very significantly, these teachers are able to perform successfully even during a time of increasing demands from state and federal bureaucrats to raise achievement levels for all students (TEA, 2000).

Within the rigid constraints of the back-to-basics movement, "highly qualified" teachers are especially urged to embrace the diversity of languages and cultures of immigrant and nonimmigrant students as a positive and valuable contribution in the classroom, rather than view them as deficits or liabilities. According to Fayden (2005), in programs that are built on the deficit approach, students perceived as not fitting the mainstream cultural norm are regarded as academically incapable, and thus, often receive literacy instruction that is not "adequate, unauthentic, de-contextualized, and irrelevant." The mission of the school then becomes one of changing the so-called "disadvantaged" students so they will be able to fit within the larger sociocultural milieu. These types of emotionally stressful school environments are counterproductive and greatly reduce the student's ability to learn.

Another view that can be equally detrimental to language minority students is one influenced by what García (2002) calls *el pobrecito* approach, as characterized by "Oh, you poor thing… non-English-speaking immigrant; we sympathize with your circumstances and lower our expectations for what you might be able to learn" (p. 55). Educators committed to quality programs for ELLs make no assumptions about why students can't learn. Instead, they have a high estimate of each individual student's ability to achieve.

In her paper on toughness and caring, Hoffman (2001) believes that it is possible for educators to make a difference in schools confronted with over-regulation from government and increasing enrollments of ELLs and economically disadvantaged children.[5] It will require, she argues, a "no excuses," tough love approach to teaching and learning. There are instances, for example, when teachers who are tenacious in their demands for excellence and high performance face accusations from students and parents as being too difficult or unfair. In extreme cases, these same talented and dedicated teachers may be accused of being

> Educators committed to quality programs for ELLs make no assumptions about why students can't learn. Instead, they have a high estimate of each individual student's ability to achieve.

racist because of what parents perceive as grading practices that favor other students, or unjust demands on their "minority" child because of poor work ethic and shabby performance. Teachers who practice "pedagogic caring," according to Hoffman, resist pressures to water (or dumb) down the curriculum and soften their learning expectations, however harsh and intimidating. They stay the course, appealing to the parents to partner in this special effort reminding them always that caring and love for their son or daughter means supporting those teachers who are genuinely committed to their children and their success in school.

Concluding Remarks

The challenges presented by a growing population of newly arrived and more-established immigrant students in our schools are varied and complex. Clearly, these are not places for educators who are tentative in their commitment to education, emotionally fragile, and unable to understand cultural diversity and the poor or children of the poor. Instead, these new and evolving schools require creative and efficacious teachers who operate from a sense of optimism, a respect for cultural differences, and care for all students. These teachers don't blame social conditions for student failure. They abhor educational laxness and are unyielding in their high expectations for learning.

Endnotes

[1] Undocumented immigrant is the preferred term to "illegal alien," "illegal immigrant," or "illegal(s)." This term describes the immigration status of people who do not have the federal documentation to show they are legally entitled to work, visit or live in the United States. Undocumented children, however, are allowed "free access to public education" based on the U.S. Supreme Court's 1982 decision in *Plyler v. Doe.*

[2] Many educators prefer the more-neutral and more-positive term English language learner (ELL) over the traditional limited-English-proficient (LEP) label. According to Ovando, Combs, and Collier (2006), LEP reflects a focus on what "the child cannot do rather than on what he or she can do" (p. 10).

[3] The study by Collier and Thomas (2002) examines various models of bilingual and ESL education and length of time needed for ELLs (also, language minority students) to learn academic English. A related goal of the study was to determine which of the models was most effective in closing the achievement gap for English learners.

[4] This observation is based on experiences shared with me by my wife who recently retired as the school social worker for the Denton (Texas) Independent School District. Her 22 years of community service included assisting economically disadvantaged families and children, many of whom were immigrants from Latin America.

[5] There is research critical of the current reform movement that argues that the solution to successful schools for Latinos is not more competitive pressure stemming from high-stakes testing. McNeil (2004) in her study of the Texas reform program, for example, reports that highly regulatory state policies purported to eliminate inequities in educational services provided poor and minority students are instead creating "perverse incentives" that widen the achievement gap for language minority children and others.

> Schools require creative and efficacious teachers who operate from a sense of optimism, a respect for cultural differences, and care for all students.

References

Batalova, J. (2006). *Spotlight on limited English proficient students in the United States.* Washington, DC: Migration Policy Institute.

Camarota, S. A. (December, 2005). *Immigrants at mid-decade: A snapshot of America's foreign-born population in 2005.* Washington, DC: Center for Immigration Studies.

Collier, V. P., & Thomas, W. P. (2002). *A national study of school effectiveness for language minority students' long-term academic achievement final report: Project 1.1.* Santa Cruz, CA: Center for Research on Education, Diversity and Excellence (CREDE). Available online at www.crede.org/research/llaa.1.1_final.html

Compton-Lilly, C. (2008). Teaching struggling readers: Capitalizing on diversity for effective learning. *The Reading Teacher, 61*(8), 668–672.

Crawford, J. (2004). *Educating English learners: Language diversity in the classroom* (5th ed.). Los Angeles: Bilingual Educational Services, Inc.

Cummins, J. (1991). Interdependence of first- and second-language proficiency in bilingual children. In E. Bialystok (Ed.). *Language and processing in bilingual children* (pp. 70–89). Cambridge: England. Cambridge University Press.

Dembo, M., & Gibson, S. (November, 1985). Teachers' sense of efficacy: An important factor in school improvement. *Elementary School Journal, 86*(2), 173–184.

Fayden, T. (Ed.) (2005). *How children learn: Getting beyond the deficit myth.* Boulder, CO: Paradigm Publishers.

García, E. (2002). *Student cultural diversity: Understanding and meeting the challenge.* (3rd ed.). New York: Houghton Mifflin Co.

Hakimzadeh, S., & Cohn, D. (2007). *English usage among Hispanics in the United States.* Washington, DC: Pew Hispanic Center.

Hoffman, N. (2001). Toughness and caring: To teach for higher standards, we'll need both. *Education Week, 20*(28), 40–42.

Kochar, R., Suro, R., & Tafoya S. (2005). *The new Latino south: The context and consequences of rapid population growth.* Washington, DC: Pew Hispanic Center.

McNeil, M. M. (2004). Faking equity: High stakes testing and the education of Latino youth. In A. Valenzuela (Ed.), *Leaving children behind: How "Texas-style" accountability fails Latino youth* (pp. 57–111). Albany, NY: SUNY Press.

Mebly, E. O. (1968, October). The community school: A school imperative. In C. M. Campbell (Ed.), *NCSEA News, VII*(2). Newsletter by the National Community School Education Association.

Noboa-Polanco, J. (1991). *They come to learn: Hispanic immigrant students in Texas.* San Antonio, TX: The Tomás Rivera Center.

Ovando, C. J., Combs, M. C., & Collier, V. P. (2006). *Bilingual and ESL classrooms: Teaching in multicultural contexts* (4th ed.). Boston: McGraw-Hill.

Plyler v. Doe, 457 U.S. 202, 102 S. Ct. 2382 (1982).

President's Advisory Commission on Educational Excellence for Hispanic Americans. (2003, March 31). *From risk to opportunity: Fulfilling the educational needs of Hispanic Americans in the 21st century.* A report commissioned by President George W. Bush under Executive Order No.13230, Washington, DC.

Reyes, P., Scribner, J. D., & Scribner, A. P. (1999). *Lessons from high performing Hispanic schools: Creating learning communities.* New York: Teachers College Press.

Rodríguez, N. P., & Urrutia-Rojas, X. (1990). *Undocumented and unaccompanied: A mental health study of unaccompanied, immigrant children from Central America.* Houston, TX: University of Houston Institute for Higher Education, Law and Governance.

Texas Education Agency. (2000, August). *The Texas successful school study: Quality education for limited English proficient students.* A report by the Program Evaluation Unit, Office of the Education of Special Populations, Texas Education Agency, Austin. Available online at http://www.ncela.gwu.edu/pubs/tea/tsss.pdf

Walker-Dalhouse, D., & Risko, V. J., (2008). Learning from literacy successes in high-achieving urban schools. *The Reading Teacher, 61*(5), 422.

"I am not an ESL teacher. Is it my responsibility to teach English language learners?"

"Why do we need to understand the cultural and social needs of ELLs?"

"What do these needs have to do with the students' language and literacy learning?"

I frequently hear questions like these from preservice and inservice teachers with whom I work in teacher education programs. The basic assumption underlying these questions is that teaching English language learners (ELLs) is the job of the English as a second language (ESL) teacher, rather than that of all of the teachers. Also, ELLs are often viewed only from a linguistic perspective — they just need English language instruction. That view ignores *cultural* and *social* human beings who construct and reconstruct their identities while they interact with their teachers and peers in the classroom. This linguistic-only focus is incomplete because it can prevent us from seeing the complexities of ELLs' literacy learning processes (Gutiérrez & Orellana, 2006); yet it has been prevalent in research and practice with regard to ELLs.

English Language Learners in Classrooms: Valued Members or Uninvited Guests

Bogum Yoon
Texas Woman's University

In this chapter I attempt to answer the questions above by arguing that teachers should view ELLs from cultural and social aspects to support their engagement in language and literacy learning. My rationales are grounded in two theoretical perspectives: *positioning theory* and *culturally relevant pedagogy.* These perspectives give us useful lenses to look at ELLs' cultural and social identities and teachers' approaches to engage their learning. After presenting the theoretical framework, I offer suggestions for effective teaching of ELLs in their classrooms. Suggestions are based on the findings of my studies (Yoon, 2004, 2007, 2008) which focused on ELLs' participatory behaviors and teachers' teaching approaches.

Positioning Theory and Culturally Relevant Pedagogy

Two relevant theoretical perspectives can help us understand English language learners' cultural and social needs and their identities. It is important for teachers of ELLs to know their roles in positioning their students for successful literacy learning and in positioning themselves to support *all* students in their classrooms.

> It is often difficult to reposition oneself in an unequal society where hidden power relations are continuously at work (Walsh, 1991). This is particularly true for English language learners.

1. Positioning theory helps teachers understand the importance of positioning ELLs in ways that empower their learning and build a positive identity for the students.
2. Culturally relevant pedagogy helps teachers understand the importance of how they position themselves and their students in classroom settings.

Positioning Theory

Positioning is a metaphorical term originally introduced to analyze interpersonal encounters (Hollway, 1984). It has a specific meaning in the analysis of interactions between people and, in the technical sense, it has an effect on the possibilities for interpersonal and intergroup action. Positioning is relational and reciprocal; it is an active and discursive practice.

People position others (*positioning*) and the others position them back (*repositioning*). While positioning and repositioning each other, power relations are always imbedded in action. In short, positioning focuses on the characteristics of dynamic power relationships. People can reposition themselves by challenging the ways others position them. It is, however, often difficult to reposition oneself in an unequal society where hidden power relations are continuously at work (Walsh, 1991). This is particularly true for ELLs.

People not only position others, they also position themselves; this is called *reflexive positioning* (Davies & Harré, 1990, p. 48). We all view the world from a certain position that guides the way in which we act and think about our roles, assignments, and duties in a given context. Certainly, teachers' views of their roles help to explain how they position themselves in the classroom. For example, some teachers might position themselves as the teachers for all students and others might position themselves as content teachers focusing on general education students. Whatever positions teachers take up, that positioning guides their interactive approaches to students in classroom settings.

Peter Johnston (2004) argues that ". . . children should leave school with a sense that if they act, and act strategically, they can accomplish their goals. I call this feeling a sense of agency. Some teachers are very good at building a sense of agency in children . . ." (p. 29). Children who believe in their own agency tend to work harder, attend better, build interest in their studies, and are less likely to give up when the tasks become difficult (Skinner, Zimmer-Gembeck, & Connell, 1998).

The way in which children position themselves is important for their sense of competence, well-being, and performance (Johnston, 2004). The same child might act and position herself differently in different contexts. She can be silent in a given context and vocal in another context. The same child might position herself as powerful in a given situation and as powerless in another situation. Children actively negotiate and achieve their multiple identities as they are positioned by others and as they position themselves in different contexts (Greenwood, 1994).

Individuals create and re-create their own identities and actively achieve their identities. Interactive positioning "in which what one person says positions another" (Davies & Harré, 1990, p. 48) indicates that positioning occurs in relation to others. In this view, positioning a child in certain ways can limit or extend what that child can say and do (Adams & Harré, 2001) and can inhibit or provide the options of choice of speaking forms, actions, and thoughts (Harré & van Langenhove, 1999). Positioning children as deficient may deny them the right to correct their cognitive performance (Harré & Moghaddam, 2003) and positioning them as intelligent may allow them the possibility to improve performance.

How does positioning influence a child's identity? An individual's identity is dynamically created and re-created through positioning, and it changes through positioning in social interactions (Tan & Moghaddam, 1995). As people position each other, they assign rights, duties, and obligations. How children construct a positive identity is largely dependent on how they are positioned by others. The way in which teachers position ELLs is a major factor in the positive identity of these children. If they are positioned as powerful, the positioning helps them form their identity as powerful. If children are positioned as powerless, they are not likely to construct a positive identity.

The notion of identity has been represented in many ways such as voice, self-identity, social identity, and cultural identity (Miller, 1999). Many scholars (e.g., Miller, 1999; Norton, 2000) agree that identity is a complicated concept that cannot be defined in one simple phrase. Two relevant perspectives on identity are important here (Hall, 1996):

1. *Essentialist* perspectives focus on 'who I am,' treating identity as a fixed concept that does not change.

> When English language learners choose to participate or withdraw, their decisions are connected to the teacher's cultural inclusivity in her approach to teaching and learning.

2. *Anti-essentialist* viewpoints focus on 'who I become,' dealing with identity as a shifting notion and keeping options for change open. Identity is a noun, but it acts like a verb (Bauman, 1996); it is a constant becoming (Wenger, 1998).

The anti-essentialist stance allows us to observe ELLs' identity development. ELLs shift their identities as powerful or powerless according to the contexts they are in, demonstrating that their identities are multiple and changing. Identity is not the presentation of 'who I am' but 'who I become' in a social matrix, which is continuously changing in relationship to others (Greene, 1991).

The following example shows that an individual's identity can be detected through speech acts and that identity can be influenced by differences in context (Hall, 1996).

> One of the students in my study (Yoon, 2004), Natasha, introduced herself with "I am Russian" before she presented her writing project to her mainstream peers and parents. However, none of the American students began introductions with "I am American." Natasha mentioned that she would not present herself in the same way when she was in her country, Russia. In other words, she would adjust her presented identity according to whom she was with. The student 'became' Russian in the U.S. context. In short, identity can be explained only in a situated context. When Natasha was with Russians, she probably would not have to represent herself as Russian, just as her peers did not present themselves as American in the U.S. context. Natasha's identity was shaped through her awareness that she was different from others.

Others play an important part as children achieve their cultural and social identity. Natasha's identity development as a powerful or powerless student is dependent, in part, upon her perception of how the others position her. Consider how important this concept is to teachers of ELLs. Teachers can intentionally or unintentionally position students in more-positive or more-negative ways through their teaching approaches.

Teachers may position ELLs without realizing that they may be expanding or limiting the students' opportunities to develop their positive sense of themselves as learners. Theoretically, if teachers position ELLs as powerful and provide them with many opportunities to develop their positive identity, the students could participate more actively in their own learning.

Culturally Relevant Pedagogy (Teaching)

Culturally relevant pedagogy (Ladson-Billings, 1995) provides insights into the specific roles that teachers need to play when working with ELLs. Scholars describe culturally relevant teaching with different terminology such as *culturally congruent* (Mohatt & Erickson, 1981),

Theoretically, if teachers position ELLs as powerful and provide them with many opportunities to develop their positive identity, the students could participate more actively in their own learning.

culturally appropriate (Au & Jordan, 1981), and *culturally compatible* (Jordan, 1985).

However, Ladson-Billings argues that these terms all lead to accommodating ELLs within the mainstream culture. She, therefore, proposes the term *culturally relevant*, which identifies a more-dynamic relationship between home culture and school culture.

Focusing on the patterning of day-to-day activities, culturally relevant pedagogy emphasizes the significance of teachers' expanding roles. It underscores that teaching always goes beyond language. It suggests that teachers should aim to accomplish three main goals:

1. Develop students who can achieve academically.
2. Produce students who can demonstrate cultural competence.
3. Develop students who can both understand and critique the existing social order.

Instead of students accommodating themselves to the dominant culture, teachers should value students' social and cultural identities (Delpit, 1995). And, instead of attributing students' academic failure to their own faults, teachers assume the role of meeting the students' diverse needs to help them be academically successful, culturally competent, and sociopolitically critical.

Culturally relevant pedagogy does not clearly specify what teaching methods are used by effective teachers of students from diverse cultures. It suggests a broader concept of effective teachers as those who position themselves as cultural supporters and position students as cultural resources for improving teaching and learning.

Ladson-Billings (1995) studied effective teachers who incorporated culturally relevant teaching in their classrooms. Some teachers were more strict and some teachers were more casual in teaching methods. In other words, teaching styles varied. However, one common feature was that all the teachers positioned themselves as cultural bridges and respected students' cultures and values. Instead of devaluing individual students' differences, the teachers respected them. They were the teachers who facilitated students' literacy learning and identity construction in meaningful contexts.

In contrast to an assimilation approach, culturally relevant teaching emphasizes meeting students' cultural and social needs by having them sustain their own cultural values while living in mainstream culture. Instead of assimilating to mainstream cultures and losing their own culture and identity, ELLs need to have their cultural and social needs served in the classroom (Ladson-Billings, 1992, 1994). Teaching ELLs goes beyond the realm of language teaching.

Positioning theory is related to culturally relevant pedagogy. Taken together, the two theories suggest that teachers should position them-

> Positioning theory is related to culturally relevant pedagogy. Taken together, the two theories suggest that teachers should position themselves to meet the students' diverse needs and to empower ELLs by positioning them as important.

selves to meet the students' diverse needs and to empower ELLs by positioning them as important.

Practical Suggestions on Working Effectively with ELLs

Based on these theoretical perspectives, I offer suggestions for teachers to help ELLs develop their cultural and social identities and become engaged in language and literacy learning.

Build Understandings of ELLs' Cultural and Social Needs

To promote students' engagement in learning, teachers must understand ELLs' cultural and social needs and respond to their needs in an active manner. Although research focuses on English proficiency as a major determiner of ELLs' classroom participation (e.g., Harklau, 2000; Kanno & Applebaum, 1995), my study suggests the major determiner is culturally relevant teaching in the classroom (Yoon, 2007). In classrooms where ELLs are accepted as cultural social beings, their interaction and participation are promoted.

> As Thanksgiving Day approached, Mrs. Y asked her ELLs if they celebrated this day in their countries before she shared the story *The Thanksgiving Visitor* by Capote (1997). Dae (from Korea) said, "Yes!" in an excited voice and talked about how Korean people eat rice cake called "Songpyun." Mrs. Y's positioning of Dae as an important cultural member of the class community offered him the right to participate in the activity.

But in classrooms where the ELLs are regarded as language learners who simply sit in the classroom with little encouragement for participation, they are disengaged and silent.

> Mr. B wanted his ELLs to view him as "a model of an English speaker." He rarely approached the ELLs and seldom invited them to a class discussion. For instance, when Mr. B brought up American football games for a whole-group discussion, many of his students were highly interactive and excited about the issues. But Natasha and Jun, the two ELLs in his classroom, did not engage in the dialogue and simply sat silently while their peers talked. Neither Mr. B nor their classmates invited the ELLs to the discussion.

Cultural and social aspects shed light on ELLs' language learning. When teachers are involved in a complex system of cultural values and ways of acting in the classroom, they are in a position to help ELLs learn a language — "culture and language are intricately intertwined" (Brown, 1994, p. 25). Thus, in order to facilitate ELLs' active participation in language and literacy learning, teachers should acknowledge their acceptance of these children by viewing them as complex cultural social beings rather than simply as language learners.

In classrooms where ELLs are accepted as cultural social beings, their interaction and participation are promoted.

Children actively negotiate and achieve their multiple identities as they are positioned by others and as they position themselves in different contexts (Greenwood, 1994).

Position Yourself as a Teacher for All Students

The way teachers position themselves in the classroom can be a critical factor in influencing ELLs' participatory patterns. In my study (Yoon, 2008), I found that teachers who position themselves as the teachers for *all* children invite ELLs' active participation by assuming full responsibility for their learning.

> Mrs. Y, who views herself as "a teacher of children," attempted multiple ways of supporting the ELLs' diverse needs without solely depending on the ESL teacher. It was often observed that she was tutoring her ELLs during her lunch time and after school. In this classroom, the ELLs frequently raised their hands to express their opinions.

But teachers who position themselves for regular education students do not invite the students' participation and shift their responsibilities to the ESL teacher to meet the ELLs' cultural and social needs.

> Mr. B, also a regular classroom teacher, talks about his role with ELLs: "I have never seen myself as an ESL teacher. I don't do a lot of special things for my ESL students.... I think the ESL teacher's job is to make their time beneficial." By positioning the ESL teacher as a teacher for ELLs, Mr. B relinquishes his responsibility for teaching ELLs to the ESL teacher.

> Mrs. T, another regular classroom teacher, also does not view her role as meeting ELLs' diverse needs: "I am their English teacher. The ESL teacher has to be more of a generalist. She has to know a little bit of everything, whereas I concentrate on one subject, English."

Teachers with a narrow notion of their roles limit their teaching approaches for ELLs. Their roles often are related to how they view ELLs' learning in the regular classroom. Teachers may hold the precarious belief that if children are just exposed to English, they will learn it (Díaz-Rico & Weed, 2002). This "automaticity" principle (Brown, 1994) is incomplete because it ignores ELLs' complicated language learning processes and their individual differences in those processes. Furthermore, teachers may blame the students when they do not progress in the English-speaking context. By viewing language learning as a simple subconscious process, the automaticity principle also fails to recognize the importance of the teacher's active and diverse role in supporting ELLs' learning. It is vital to form a new concept of teachers' roles to include ELLs' diverse needs and to take full responsibility for their needs.

Build a Culturally Inclusive Classroom

When English language learners choose to participate or withdraw, their decisions are connected to the teacher's cultural inclusivity in her approach to teaching and learning. That is, teachers' approaches are related to ELLs' levels of participation and their positioning of themselves in the classroom. In my study (Yoon, 2008), I found that ELLs feel like uninvited guests and withdraw in regular classrooms when teachers focus only on subject matter or American monoculturalism and do not show any special interest in the students.

> While many of their American peers sat on a rug and exchanged their ideas, the ELLs in these classrooms usually listened at their desks without coming down to the rug. They rarely presented their ideas in class discussions. Sandra, a Bolivian girl in Mrs. T's classroom, usually bent her head down or scribbled something in her notebook, leaning against the back of her chair. Ha, a Korean boy in her classroom, often yawned and closed his eyes during classroom activities.

> Culturally relevant teaching demonstrates that teachers are the most important factor in promoting students' opportunities to learn.

When ELLs feel powerless and invisible, they tend to socially affiliate with other ELLs or students who are perceived by the teacher and students as problematic students. An interesting finding in my study was that non-ELLs followed the teacher's model in interacting with ELLs. The mainstream students interacted with the ELLs in classrooms with teachers who encouraged ELLs to participate in classroom activities.

> The students in Mrs. Y's classroom frequently praised the ELLs' efforts. One day, Dae received 83% on a social studies test. He usually got under 70%. His American partner, who got 98%, encouraged Dae by saying, "Wow, you did a good job." Dae responded to the boy's encouragement with "Thank you." When I asked the boy later to explain his comments, he said, "He is Korean. English is not his language, but he did a wonderful job. It is amazing." The boy understood Dae's difficulties as a non-English speaking person. Instead of positioning Dae as a poor student since he earned a lower grade, he positioned him as a capable student.

However, when teachers did not encourage ELLs' participation in the classroom, the mainstream students did not show any interest in the ELLs and resisted working with them.

> Natasha, a Russian student in Mr. B's classroom, was sitting with two boys and two girls for small-group work. After the group read about famous Egyptian leaders, they were busy writing the important characteristics of the leaders. Natasha could not write a sentence, but nobody seemed to care about her difficulties. When Natasha showed her frustration by saying, "I could not follow you," one of the American girls said bluntly, "You didn't say you didn't understand" as if blaming Natasha for not being able to follow the conversation. Her partner (academically strong and characteristically nice, according to Mr. B) who sat next to her usually went to work with other friends. Unable to find a partner, Natasha usually worked with special education students or the students who did not associate with other mainstream peers.

My findings show that a teacher's active or passive involvement plays a role in the mainstream peers' interactive positioning of the ELLs as acceptable or unacceptable.

Teachers' Approach to English Language Learners Makes a Difference

ELLs not only need effective teaching methods but also teachers who care and are sensitive to their cultural differences and needs. What clearly influences ELLs' engagement in language and literacy learning is not the teacher's specific methods, but the teacher's approach to the students. Student-centered teaching methods have been advocated in

> What clearly influences ELLs' engagement in language and literacy learning is not the teacher's specific methods, but the teacher's approach to the students.

educational fields (Haley, 2004; McCombs & Whisler, 1997), but my studies (Yoon, 2007, 2008) show that this method does not necessarily promote ELLs' active participation when it is implemented under a hidden power mechanism. Culturally relevant teaching demonstrates that teachers are the most important factor in promoting students' opportunities to learn. Teachers who have knowledge of language approaches that support ELLs must also possess and use teaching approaches that invite—rather than distance—the students.

In sum, success is only achievable when ELLs are viewed as "learners" along with all other students who need to be provided meaningful opportunities for learning. It is *teachers* who can assist ELLs to achieve their positive and legitimate positioning as learners in the classroom.

Suggestions for teachers

First, a brief assessment . . .

Take time to think about ELLs in your classroom or school setting.
- Are they engaged?
- Do they think they can act to accomplish their own goals?
- How do they position themselves with you and with their classmates?
- Do they view themselves as able to become a language and literacy learner?

Take time to think about how you position ELLs in your classroom or school setting.
- Do you place them on equal footing with their classmates?
- Do they have your acceptance as learners?
- Are there hidden agendas?

Take time to think about how the non-ELLs in your classroom position the ELLs.
- Do they accept ELLs as learners?
- How do non-ELLs interact with ELLs?
- Is there a 'power' agenda or is there a collaborative learning environment?

Then, a commitment . . .

Learn more about the social and cultural needs of all children in your classroom or school setting, with special attention to ELLs, in order to promote interactions and active participation of all children.

Work to position yourself as a responsive teacher to all children, especially ELLs, building a culturally inclusive classroom environment.

Work to position all children, but especially ELLs, as learners who are capable and valued, and who will be actively involved in their own learning.

References

Adams, J. L., & Harré, R. (2001). Gender positioning: A sixteenth/seventeenth century example. *Journal for the Theory of Social Behaviour, 31*(3), 331–338.

Au, K. H., & Jordan, C. (1981). Teaching reading to Hawaiian children: Finding a culturally appropriate solution. In H. Trueba, G. Guthrie, & K. Au (Eds.), *Culture and the bilingual classroom: Studies in classroom ethnography* (pp. 139–152). Rowley, MA: Newbury.

Bauman, Z. (1996). From pilgrim to tourist – or a short history of identity. In S. Hall & P. du Gay (Eds.), *Questions of cultural identity* (pp. 18–36). London: Sage.

Brown, D. H. (1994). *Teaching by principles: An interactive approach to language pedagogy*. Englewood Cliffs, NJ: Prentice-Hall.

Capote, T (1997). *The Thanksgiving visitor*. New York: Scholastic.

Davies, B., & Harré, R. (1990). Positioning: The discursive production of selves. *Journal for the Theory of Social Behaviour, 20*, 43–63.

Delpit, L. (1995). *Other people's children: Cultural conflict in the classroom*. New York: The New Press.

Díaz-Rico, L. T., & Weed, K. Z. (2002). *The crosscultural, language and academic development handbook: A complete K–12 reference guide* (2nd ed.). Boston: Allyn and Bacon.

Greene, M. (1991). Forward. In C. Witherell & N. Noddings (Eds.), *Stories lives tell: Narrative and dialogue in education* (pp. ix–xi). New York: Teachers College.

Greenwood, J. D. (1994). *Realism, identity, and emotion: Reclaiming social psychology*. London: Sage.

Gutiérrez, K. D., & Orellana, M. F. (2006). The "problem" of English learners: Constructing genres of difference. *Research in the Teaching of English, 40*(4), 502–507.

Haley, M. H. (2004). Learner-centered instruction and the theory of multiple intelligences with second language learners. *Teachers College Record, 106*(1), 163–180.

Hall, S. (1996). Introduction: Who needs identity? In S. Hall & P. du Gay (Eds.), *Questions of cultural identity* (pp. 1–17). London: Sage.

Harklau, L. (2000). From the 'good kids' to the 'worst': Representations of English language learners across educational settings. *TESOL Quarterly, 34*, 35–67.

Harré, R., & Moghaddam, F. (2003). *The self and others: Positioning individuals and groups in personal, political, and cultural contexts*. Westport, CT: Praeger Publishers.

Harré, R., & van Langenhove, L. (Eds.). (1999). *Positioning theory*. Malden, MA: Blackwell Publishers.

Hollway, W. (1984). Gender difference and the production of subjectivity. In Henriques, J., Hollway, W., Urwin, C., Venn, C., & Walkerdine, V., *Changing the subject: Psychology, social regulation and subjectivity* (pp. 227–263). London: Methuen.

Johnston, P. (2004). *Choice words*. Portland, ME: Stenhouse Publishers.

Jordan, C. (1985). Translating culture: From ethnographic information to educational program. *Anthropology and Education Quarterly, 16*, 105–123.

Kanno, Y., & Applebaum, S. D. (1995). ESL students speak up: Their stories of how we are doing. *TESL Canada Journal, 12*, 32–49.

Ladson-Billings, G. (1992). Reading between the lines and beyond the pages: A culturally relevant approach to literacy teaching. *Theory into Practice, 31*(4), 312–320.

Ladson-Billings, G. (1994). *The dreamkeepers: Successful teaching for African American students.* San Francisco: Jossey-Bass.

Ladson-Billings, G. (1995). Toward a theory of culturally relevant pedagogy. *American Educational Research Journal, 32*(3), 465–491.

McCombs, B. L., & Whisler, J. S. (1997). *The learner-centered classroom and school: Strategies for increasing student motivation and achievement.* San Francisco: Jossey-Bass.

Miller, J. (1999). Becoming audible: Social identity and second language use. *Journal of Intercultural Studies, 20*(2), 149–165.

Mohatt, G., & Erickson, F. (1981). Cultural differences in teaching styles in an Odawa school: A sociolingistic approach. In H. Trueba, G. Guthrie, & K. Au (Eds.), *Culture and the bilingual classroom: Studies in classroom ethnography* (pp. 105–119). Rowley, MA: Newbury.

Norton, B. (2000). *Identity and language learning: Gender, ethnicity and educational change.* New York: Longman.

Skinner, E. A., Zimmer-Gembeck, M. J., & Connell, J. P. (1998). Individual differences and the development of perceived control. *Monographs of the Society for Research in Child Development, 63*(2-3, Serial No. 254).

Tan, S. L., & Moghaddam, F. M. (1995). Reflexive positioning and culture. *Journal for the Theory of Social Behaviour, 25*(4), 388–400.

Walsh, C. A. (1991). *Pedagogy and the struggle for voice: Issues of language, power, and schooling for Puerto Ricans.* Toronto: OISE Press.

Wenger, E. (1998). *Communities of practice.* New York: Cambridge University Press.

Yoon, B. (2004). *Uninvited guests: The impact of English and ESL teachers' beliefs, roles, and pedagogies on the identities of English language learners* (Doctoral dissertation, University at Buffalo, 2004). Dissertation Abstracts International, 65, 226.

Yoon, B. (2007). Offering or limiting opportunities: Teachers' roles and approaches to English language learners' participation in literacy activities. *The Reading Teacher, 61*(3), 216–225.

Yoon, B. (2008). Uninvited guests: The influence of teachers' roles and pedagogies on the positioning of English language learners in regular classrooms. *American Educational Research Journal, 45*(2), 495–522.

The responsibility for teaching K–12 English language learners (ELLs) is no longer the exclusive realm of specialist English as a second language (ESL) or bilingual teachers. As the number of K–12 ELLs continues to grow throughout the United States (Capps, Fix, Murray, Ost, Passel, & Herwantoro, 2005), the need for mainstream teachers who are prepared to work effectively with ELLs has also increased (Zehler, Fleischman, Hopstock, Stephenson, Pendzick, & Sapru, 2003). The professional preparation of mainstream teachers for ELLs is a relatively recent phenomenon that has not yet been implemented widely or consistently (Menken & Antunez, 2001). Therefore, a key question for elementary teacher education programs is, "What knowledge and skills must be developed among their teacher candidates in order to be effective with ELLs?"

Although this question may seem uncontroversial, comments from our teacher education colleagues as well as from preservice and inservice teachers reveal the assumption that ESL teaching mirrors the existing knowledge and skill base of good mainstream teachers. In this view, ESL expertise consists primarily of teaching strategies such as accessing students' background knowledge, structuring group work, and providing visual and contextual support in teaching.

Using ESL Teachers' Expertise to Inform Mainstream Teacher Preparation

Candace Harper
Ester de Jong
University of Florida

Elsewhere, we have summarized this perception of ESL as "just good teaching" (Harper & de Jong, 2005). However, little research has been conducted to examine the relationship between ESL and mainstream teaching or between ESL specialist teacher preparation and mainstream teacher preparation for ELLs.

The purpose of this chapter is to articulate the specialized knowledge and skills of ESL teachers with the goal of better preparing mainstream teachers for classrooms with ELLs. To inform this process, we conducted interviews with 12 experienced ESL teachers and asked for their perspectives on what effective ESL teachers know and do that is distinct from what mainstream teachers of (diverse) English-proficient speakers know and do. Following a brief overview of the educational context influencing the inclusion of ELLs in mainstream classrooms, we outline the ESL teachers' responses and discuss their implications for mainstream teacher education, with a particular focus on literacy development.

Educational Context

In addition to the growing ELL student population and the need for specialist ESL and bilingual teachers to meet their language and literacy development needs, a number of trends in general education have converged to promote the mainstream classroom as the best instructional environment for ELLs, regardless of their English proficiency level. Recent federal and state legislation has supported the inclusion of all learners in general education classrooms rather than serving students in separate settings, such as pull-out classes and resource rooms, based on learners' needs for specialized instructional support.

In the field of special education, for instance, the 1975 Education for All Handicapped Children Act, now the Individuals with Disabilities Education Act (IDEA, 1990), followed by the inclusion movement, positioned the "least restrictive environment" of the mainstream classroom as the optimal learning environment (Kavale & Forness, 2000). With these trends came support for the preparation of general educators to teach students with special needs (Paul, Lavely, Cranston-Gingras, & Taylor, 2002; Sapon-Shevin & Zollers, 1999).

More recently, the reauthorization of the Elementary and Secondary Education Act as No Child Left Behind (NCLB) and its requirement for schools to demonstrate annual yearly progress (AYP) for specific subgroups led to greater visibility for ELLs. Whereas ELLs had previously been considered the primary responsibility of ESL or bilingual teachers, NCLB set the expectation that teachers and schools would be accountable for *all* students, including ELLs and students with disabilities. State and local policies following the implementation of NCLB have focused educators' attention on reading, and ELLs' reading achievement has become a key factor in schools' ability to meet AYP targets and avoid punitive sanctions. In addition to NCLB, state and local policies have also encouraged the rapid exit of ELLs from ESL/bilingual

> A key question for elementary teacher education programs is, "What knowledge and skills must be developed among their teacher candidates in order to be effective with ELLs?"

programs, resulting in their full-time placement in mainstream class-rooms (de Jong, 2004; Gándara, 2000; Mora, 2000).

Developments in the field of ESL teaching have also facilitated the preferred placement of ELLs in mainstream classrooms. Current theory and practice in ESL emphasize the academic needs of ELLs in schools, reflecting a shift away from general communication goals toward language teaching approaches that use academic content learning as a vehicle for language development. The most recent P–12 ESL student standards (TESOL, 2006) are directly tied to academic content standards in the core curriculum areas of math, science, social studies, and English language arts. The alignment of language and content learning goals is evident in both (a) *content-based ESL curriculum development* (e.g., Crandall, 1995; Snow & Brinton, 1997; Snow, Met, & Genesee, 1989) and (b) *sheltered content area instruction* (Echevarria, Vogt, & Short, 2007; Short, 2002).

In the first approach, the curriculum of other content areas is used as the vehicle for second language learning. This is in contrast to the more traditional ESL curriculum that treated various aspects of language (such as grammar or pronunciation) as the object of study. In the second approach—sheltered content instruction—content area teachers adapt their instruction according to the linguistic needs of ELLs using a wide range of strategies such as graphic organizers, visuals, and hands-on experiences in order to make learning new concepts more comprehensible. This type of ESL-informed pedagogy is particularly effective for ELLs at the intermediate level of English language proficiency (Krashen & Terrell, 1983). As a result, mainstream classrooms have begun to appear (at least in principle) as the optimal instructional setting for ELLs (Cochran, 2002; Mohan, Leung, & Davison, 2001).

The move toward full inclusion (or *mainstreaming*) has significant implications for general education teacher preparation. A large body of research has found that ELLs are often marginalized or completely overlooked in general education classrooms, either because mainstream teachers do not understand their specific instructional needs or because they are unwilling or unable to make the necessary changes in their teaching practices (Bourne, 2001; Cameron, Moon, & Bygate, 1996; Creese, 2000; Franson, 1999; Harklau, 1994; Harper & Platt, 1998; Reeves, 2004; Sharkey & Layzer, 2000; Walker, Shafer, & Iiams, 2004). Verplaetse (2000), for example, found that secondary teachers directed very few questions to the beginning ELLs in their classrooms and failed to include them in class discussion. ELLs can also be excluded by their native English-speaking peers in group work if the teacher does not know how to structure and monitor group work to accommodate linguistic and cultural differences (Valdés, 2001; Yoon, 2007).

Today, most mainstream teachers are poorly prepared to meet the complex challenges of inclusion. A recent survey of more than 5,000 teachers in California reported that half of the teachers in classrooms

> A large body of research has found that ELLs are often marginalized or completely overlooked in general education classrooms, either because mainstream teachers do not understand their specific instructional needs or because they are unwilling or unable to make the necessary changes in their teaching practices.

with an ELL student population of 25–50% or higher had received little or no professional development in working with ELLs (Gándara, Maxwell-Jolly, & Driscoll, 2005). Even teachers who have had the opportunity to pursue professional development related to ELLs are likely to have attended brief inservice workshops. Often these workshops focus on the similarities of first- and second-language development and on general "effective teaching" strategies, rather than on key differences between teaching ELLs and English-proficient students and the implications for teachers. These workshops typically emphasize general language acquisition processes and encourage teachers' expectations that ELLs will learn English easily as a natural consequence of being immersed in a language-rich environment (Harper & de Jong, 2004). Although such workshops can be useful, they address only the surface of what teachers need to know and be able to do, particularly if they are the primary English language arts teachers for ELLs.

> If effective teaching of ELLs is different from good general education, we must be able to articulate its distinctive nature.

As more and more ELLs find themselves in mainstream classrooms, and as pressures on ELL achievement increase under NCLB, more states are considering or have already included ELL teacher preparation requirements in all teacher education programs (cf., California, Florida, and Texas, among others). In the following sections we explore the knowledge and skills that characterize effective ESL specialist teaching, with the goal of informing mainstream learning environments for ELLs and the preparation of all future teachers for ELLs.

A Study of ESL and Mainstream Teacher Expertise

Few studies have compared the knowledge and skill base of general education and ESL/bilingual teachers with respect to teaching ELLs. Research by Constantino (1994) identified teacher attitudes and teacher roles as key areas of difference between the two groups. Constantino found that the teachers differed in the degree to which each group perceived their own classroom as a context for language development, and they differed in the extent to which they made instructional adaptations for ELLs. The general education teachers did not feel that ELLs' language development was their responsibility; they believed that "they were teaching *content* not language" (p. 43). In contrast, Constantino found that the ESL teachers considered language explicitly when they planned and implemented their lessons, and they made more instructional accommodations for students' linguistic differences, particularly in the area of vocabulary development.

Other studies have also noted the challenge of shifting roles from content teacher to content and language teacher taking responsibility for ELLs and their learning (Mora & Grisham, 2001; Penfield, 1987; Reeves, 2004; Short, 2002). The practice of dividing rather than sharing the responsibility for teaching ELLs between specialist (ESL/bilingual) teachers and general education/subject area teachers has a long history in U.S. schools. This division proved to be relatively straightforward as long as ESL teachers focused on (oral) language development and literacy skills for ELLs. However, now ESL teaching is focused more on academic language development through the content areas (TESOL, 2006). ELLs are increasingly held to grade-level performance expectations and may be placed in intensive reading classes with native English-speaking students whose reading test scores have identified them as "struggling readers" (Callahan, 2006; Harper, Platt, Naranjo, & Boynton, 2007). Therefore, the lines between ESL and the mainstream curriculum and between ESL teachers and general education teachers have become blurred. This shift is not always easy or welcomed by the teachers involved. As one of the social studies teachers in Short's (2002) study admitted, "I believed that was someone else's job" (p. 21).

Although professional standards for ESL specialist teacher education programs have been established by TESOL,[1] the linguistic, cultural, and pedagogical knowledge base needed to prepare general educators for effective teaching of ELLs in mainstream contexts is relatively unexplored (Richards & Farrell, 2005). Relatively few studies have documented the experiences of effective mainstream teachers of ELLs (but see Brisk, Dawson, Hartgering, MacDonald, & Zehr, 2002). If effective teaching of ELLs is different from good general education, we must be able to articulate its distinctive nature.

Methodology

Our study examined the nature of ESL expertise from the perspectives of a dozen ESL specialist teachers. We interviewed 12 experienced ESL teachers who had worked with us in professional development contexts in the past (see Table 1). These teachers were selected on the

Table 1
Background Characteristics of 12 Experienced ESL Teachers

Teacher	Years	Grade Levels	Current Positions
1	7	Secondary	ESL teacher, ESL teacher education faculty
2	15	Secondary and adult	ESL teacher, ESL teacher education faculty
3	12	Secondary	ESL teacher
4	8	Secondary	ESL teacher
5	27	Elementary and secondary	ESL teacher, ESL teacher education faculty
6	18	Elementary, secondary, and adult	ESL teacher, district administrator
7	25	Secondary	ESL curriculum developer
8	5	Secondary	ESL teacher, ESL teacher education faculty
9	25	Elementary and secondary	ESL teacher, program coordinator
10	21	Elementary	General education teacher in inclusion classroom
11	20	Secondary	ESL teacher
12	15	Elementary	ESL teacher

basis of their strong records of experience as ESL teachers in different contexts in the U.S. and internationally. They had served as ESL specialists in their schools or districts and provided ESL preservice and inservice professional development for general education teachers. They all had graduate degrees with specializations in ESL or applied/educational linguistics; they all were White, middle class, and all but one were female. They had between 5 and 27 years of teaching experience, with an average of 16.5 years.

We asked these ESL specialists to describe what (good) ESL teachers should know and be able to do. Because of their extensive experience teaching ELLs and providing ESL inservice training for their mainstream colleagues, they were well prepared to perceive the distinctions between teaching ESL and teaching ELLs in mainstream classrooms. We therefore asked them to explain how the professional knowledge and skills of ESL teachers differ from those of other good teachers.[2] (See Table 2 for the interview protocol used in the study.)

The interviews lasted 35–55 minutes and were conducted by the researchers. Nine of the interviews took place at the teachers' schools or in other convenient locations; three were conducted by telephone. The nine face-to-face interviews were recorded and transcribed; handwritten notes were taken for the three telephone interviews. All interviews were coded for primary components (Spradley, 1980). Both researchers participated in the coding of data, first working independently and then conferring to discuss overlapping categories or discrepancies in the data. To analyze the transcripts and interview notes we borrowed the conceptual categories of knowledge, skills, and dispositions used by the National Council for Accreditation of Teacher Education (NCATE). We also used the theoretical framework we had developed previously (based on an extensive literature review) to help analyze the

---

Table 2
ESL Teacher Interview Questions

1. What do ESL teachers *know* and *do* that *sets them apart* from (good) mainstream teachers?

2. *In addition to* knowledge and skills, what is required of an ESL teacher that might not be expected of a good mainstream teacher?

3. What are the similarities/differences between the knowledge and skills of teachers of *secondary* (versus elementary) ESL students?

4. What makes a good ESL teacher an *excellent* ESL teacher?

5. How do ESL teachers best *acquire/learn* their (specialized) knowledge/skills? (courses, personal/professional experience)

6. What is most important for teachers in mainstream classes to know/do in order to work effectively with ESL learners?

gap between ESL and mainstream teacher practices for ELLs in the domains of language and culture (de Jong & Harper, 2005; Harper & de Jong, 2005).

Findings: What is the Specialized Nature of ESL Teacher Expertise?

The following sections summarize patterns that emerged in the teacher responses regarding the expertise of ESL teachers and their perspectives as to what distinguishes effective ESL teachers from good mainstream teachers. In Table 3 we summarize the main themes related to the core knowledge, essential skills, and key dispositions of ESL teachers as reported by the interviewees. We do not consider these domains to be entirely separate and distinct.

In general, according to these experienced ESL teachers, effective ESL teachers are positively disposed toward linguistic and cultural differences. They

- have a strong conceptual understanding of language and culture,
- consciously apply their knowledge in classroom practice,
- vary their instructional repertoires according to their students' specific linguistic and cultural needs,
- understand the language demands of school, and
- realize that second language acquisition is a long-term process that requires ongoing support and scaffolding.

Table 3
Summary of Responses on the Nature of ESL Teachers' Expertise

Core Knowledge	Essential Skills	Key Dispositions
• awareness of the language skills needed in academic content learning	• ability to explain and teach important language structures to ELLs	• broad world view and interest in different ways of living and learning
• understanding of second language acquisition and recognition of opportunities for second language development	• ability to combine language learning objectives with grade-level instruction	• empathy for ELLs; experience living in other countries, learning other languages, making new friends among people different from themselves; personal experience with culture shock and displacement
• metaknowledge of English language (especially grammar) to inform their teaching	• integration of oral language and literacy skills development for ELLs	• *desire* to teach language and to teach ELLs
• awareness of a range of cultural differences and use of this knowledge to understand ELLs' behaviors in school	• learning about students and their families; connecting with home and community	• viewing the native languages and cultures of their ELL students as assets and resources in the classroom rather than as problems to be resolved

Mainstream and ESL teachers collaboratively discuss effective book choices for ELLs.

In addition to these general understandings, these ESL teachers highlighted specific areas where their practices and those of mainstream teachers diverged most clearly. These have been grouped under two domains: responding to ELLs' linguistic needs, and responding to ELLs' cultural needs.

Responding to ELLs' Linguistic Needs

The ESL teachers perceived that their mainstream teacher colleagues typically do not realize the extended time required for many ELLs to develop high levels of academic language proficiency in English. Mainstream teachers typically believe that English language development will take place quickly and easily if ELLs are provided with sufficient exposure to the second language. They tend to assume that classroom practices such as cooperative learning, process writing, and dramatic role play will provide ELLs with sufficient opportunities to use English. However, these incidental language learning opportunities do not adequately meet the specific linguistic needs of ELLs (Langman, 2003).

For example, one of the ESL teachers we interviewed described a warm-up activity for a process-writing lesson she taught in a mainstream classroom with several ELL students.

I read them . . . *Ira Sleeps Over* and it's about a little boy's first sleepover and I read that as a prewriting activity, writing about a child's own experience. And then after reading it I talk about a childhood experience of my own, and then we start talking about a childhood experience of their own. Well, that worked for my mainstream class. For second language learners it was just reading a story without showing pictures — you know, it was just a lot of language without any... so it was prewriting activities, but it wasn't ideal for a second language learner in that class. (teacher 1)

Although process writing has been recommended for ELLs (e.g., Peregoy & Boyle, 2005) as well as for native speakers of English, teachers must know how to make appropriate adjustments in the process according to ELLs' English proficiency. In the example above, the prewriting activity was not helpful in generating or activating background knowledge for the ELL students because they did not have access to the story through the medium of oral language. Although the teacher's oral reading of the story may have had the intended result with her other (English proficient) students, it was not helpful for the ELLs in her classroom because they could not understand it.

While many ELLs do acquire social/communicative language naturally, they often need much more time and more-explicit scaffolding to access the academic language of school tasks and texts. As a result, mainstream teachers cannot rely solely on students' exposure to English as a primary vehicle for their English language development. Teachers must purposefully structure opportunities for ELLs to hear, see, read, write, and speak English in school. In other words, their teaching practices need to be linguistically "stretched" for ELLs. Commins and Miramontes (2005) describe how teachers of ELLs extend the "picture walk" step in guided reading to facilitate their conceptual and vocabulary development in English. An expert ESL teacher we interviewed illustrates this point, describing her use of the K-W-L chart, a widely recommended prereading strategy in mainstream classrooms.

> Like for example on a K-W-L chart, the teachers will do, "OK, what do you know?" They go over what do you want to know, and go on and establish that background knowledge. But for [ESOL] students you really have to involve them more in the four areas. So for example, you would do something with having a think-write-pair-share so that they have a safer environment to try and orally express to a partner what they know and hear what the other partner knows before they put it out before a larger group. They'll do a little bit more of copying and writing of the K-W-L chart. In terms of taking those ideas then and categorizing them, for [ESOL] students they may not have the vocabulary to categorize, but they may be able to associate and link the words, and then the teacher can direct the categories,

> Teachers must purposefully structure opportunities for ELLs to hear, see, read, write, and speak English in school. In other words, their teaching practices need to be linguistically "stretched" for ELLs.

knowing that they may not have that vocabulary or background knowledge. (teacher 6)

This example shows that ESL teachers actively seek opportunities to structure and reinforce language development. They go beyond using graphic organizers or other comprehension strategies to make reading and learning new concepts more accessible, using them to extend and develop students' oral language and literacy skills in English. Gloria Tang (1992) described the potential of graphic organizers when they are used to scaffold ELLs' writing in addition to supporting reading comprehension and vocabulary development (their more-traditional roles as learning tools for native English speakers).

Other ESL teachers we interviewed also indicated that a key difference between ESL and mainstream teachers is that ESL teachers set instructional goals for ELLs that go beyond comprehension. Rather than compensating for students' limited English proficiency and simply "getting around" the language barrier to facilitate content area learning, ESL teachers strategically target ELLs' oral language and literacy development in English. They plan their instruction around the linguistic and cultural knowledge and skills that students need in order to learn and communicate in their content area classes, making language visible in the process (Diaz-Rico & Weed, 2005).

Responding to ELLs' Cultural Needs

Familiarity with students' cultures and an interest in learning about different cultures were cited as important characteristics of teachers working with ELLs. One ESL teacher commented,

> I think that [ESOL] teachers are more aware of culture and aspects of culture that mainstream teaches aren't aware of, and how it affects the individual child in the classroom. So for example — this comes back to me because of a [teacher education] student who bitterly complained about one of the Korean children she was working with smelling like garlic and just, "Oh, how could they feed that child garlic for breakfast? He comes to school reeking of garlic." Where an [ESOL] teacher would understand that part of their culture is they eat kimchi for breakfast, kimchi has a lot of garlic in it and that's part of their culture and perhaps they can do some sort of sensitizing activity to help other children understand. There's more cross-cultural... I think [ESOL] teachers try to build more cross-cultural relationships than mainstream teachers might. (teacher 2)

As with English language development, a common assumption regarding teaching ELLs is that their culture learning needs will be met adequately through a welcoming learning environment. Although many ELLs do indeed make the cultural adjustment process naturally in this manner, others will need more-explicit instruction and support from

---

Familiarity with students' cultures and an interest in learning about different cultures were cited as important characteristics of teachers working with ELLs.

their teachers and other school staff. ESL teachers often provide opportunities for ELLs to build needed background knowledge by helping them make personal connections with the U.S.-based curriculum. Prior to reading texts, ESL teachers pay significant attention to the prerequisite knowledge required of the reader and they work to develop this context with their ELLs.

> If you're reading a story and you can't be sure that everybody is familiar with something that is common in American culture, you're going to stop and talk about that…you're going to stop and do it because you don't have that assumption…you're starting from a different assumption. (teacher 8)

The ESL teachers we interviewed stressed the affective domain of teaching ELLs, which often includes extending the role of the classroom teacher into that of advocate or caregiver. In addition to monitoring ELLs' language development and academic achievement, many ESL/bilingual teachers reach out beyond the school setting and into the community helping immigrant families negotiate their new world (Igoa, 1995; Olsen, 1997). Understanding ELLs' cultural beliefs and practices, communicating with and advocating for ELLs and their families, and helping them adjust to and succeed in school and in the larger U.S. culture are roles that ESL teachers typically (and willingly) assume. The importance of positive dispositions in teachers' ability to perform these roles successfully should not be underestimated in considering the preparation of mainstream teachers for ELLs.

What Mainstream Teachers Need to Learn

In this study, we elicited insights from experienced ESL teachers to identify key characteristics that distinguish teaching ELLs from teaching diverse but fluent English-speaking students. These teachers affirmed a common foundation of second language acquisition, acculturation, and approaches to second language teaching (Crandall, 2000; Grabe, Stoller, & Tardy, 2000). Mainstream teachers typically are not exposed to ELL-specific preservice or inservice professional development (Menken & Antunez, 2001) and therefore need to develop a basic understanding of this knowledge and skill set in order to work effectively with ELLs.

The teacher interviews helped us to understand specific ways in which ESL specialist teachers approach their teaching that are distinct from those of many mainstream teachers. Attention to the various aspects of ESL teacher expertise in teacher preparation programs may prevent teachers from mistakenly assuming that teaching ELLs requires only minimal modifications to existing classroom practices. The two primary areas that emerged from our ESL teacher data are (a) negotiating the language demands of school, and (b) cultural brokering and advocacy for ELLs in school and beyond.

> Mainstream teachers need to understand the critical role of language as a medium of learning, recognize the specific language demands in their classrooms, and be able to mediate these for ELLs at different levels of English proficiency.

Mainstream teachers need to understand the critical role of language as a medium of learning, recognize the specific language demands in their classrooms, and be able to mediate these for ELLs at different levels of English proficiency (de Jong & Harper, 2005). This includes being able to

- recognize and teach vocabulary words that are likely to be unfamiliar to ELLs (though familiar to their English-proficient students) in addition to those words that will be new or difficult for all students in their classroom;
- recognize complex sentence and discourse structures;
- simplify the language of texts that students must read in order to learn;
- monitor their own use of language and adjust their questioning techniques for beginning- and intermediate-level ELLs without resorting to asking only lower-order questions (de Jong & Derrick-Mescua, 2003); and
- consciously plan and scaffold language learning opportunities for ELLs, applying an understanding of the role of student interaction and teacher feedback in the process of second language acquisition.

Teacher candidates must receive multiple opportunities to analyze classroom talk and texts from a second language learning perspective. This will require teacher candidates to

- acquire a foundation in educational linguistics (Wong Fillmore & Snow, 2002), including an awareness of cross-linguistic differences;
- understand that writing systems vary across languages and that the linguistic "cueing systems" used in reading English, such as word formation, sentence structure, and discourse patterns are not universal across languages;
- know how to adapt phonics instruction developed for native English speakers according to oral and written differences between English and students' home languages; and
- provide rich opportunities for ELLs to build the English vocabulary and oral language foundation that phonics instruction assumes.

Also, because many ELLs arrive in U.S. schools with literacy skills and reading strategies already developed in their home languages, teachers can accelerate their English literacy development by building on these skills and strategies, such as developing cognate awareness.

Mainstream teachers must also move beyond the idea that they play only a passive role in providing a welcoming environment for ELLs.

> Mainstream teachers must be able (and willing) to take on active roles as facilitators of cross-cultural communication and help both majority and minority language speakers negotiate linguistic and cultural diversity in the classroom and beyond.

They must be able (and willing) to take on active roles as facilitators of cross-cultural communication and help both majority and minority language speakers negotiate linguistic and cultural diversity in the classroom and beyond. Ladson-Billings' (1995) culturally relevant pedagogy provides a framework for building on students' diversity in concrete ways. Platt and Troudi (1997) document the case of Mary, a young Grebo-speaking student from Liberia, whose mainstream classroom teacher believed that her own cultural sensitivity, her welcoming classroom environment, and Mary's cultural adjustment would lead to eventual success in the mainstream classroom. Instead, Mary's social integration and skillful coping behaviors masked her real academic language and literacy needs. Her academic development stalled, placing her at serious risk of failing in school over the long term.

Mainstream teachers must be able to identify cross-cultural issues that may affect the school experience of ELLs (Cooper, Denner, & Lopez, 1999). They must invite their students' diverse world views and knowledge into their classrooms as an integral and meaningful part of the curriculum (Moll, Amanti, Neff, & González, 1992; Yoon, 2007). One former ELL student recalled an incident in her fifth-grade classroom in which a caring and experienced teacher attempted to include her in a mainstream social studies class discussion on environmental issues.

> I knew I was put on the spot for being from a pro-whaling country. I knew my parents, neither of whom from traditionally whale-consuming areas of Japan, had to eat whale meat as part of the government school lunch program in the 1950s because Japan was too poor to feed children with other sources of protein. I also knew that some in Japan ate whale meat, as others ate insects, because that was part of their regional culture. However, not having the command of the English language to state that logically,…I tuned myself out for the rest of class discussion. [The teacher] did not bring up the pro-whaling side of the argument either, not even mentioning how the Alaska Natives have whaled for centuries, and my classmates energetically talked about protecting the precious sea mammal. On that day, I learned the unspoken message that my culture was not appreciated, nor were any other nonmainstream cultures for that matter. (Y. Fujino, personal communication, Oct. 14, 2004)

Applying this body of linguistic and cultural knowledge and skill to teaching ELLs requires a shift in attitudes and roles for mainstream teachers. As ELLs are increasingly placed in classrooms with little or no direct ESL instruction and support, mainstream teachers must take responsibility for the linguistic, cultural, and academic development of their ELLs. They must be able to integrate language and content instruction to meet ELLs' dual language and content learning needs (de Jong & Harper, 2007; Meyer, 2000), ideally in collaboration with ESL teachers.

Teacher education programs should prepare mainstream teachers to collaborate with reading, ESL, and other specialist educators in the shared responsibility for the school success of ELLs.

Teacher education programs should prepare mainstream teachers to collaborate with reading, ESL, and other specialist educators in the shared responsibility for the school success of ELLs which Tsui (2003) refers to as "distributed expertise." In order to develop this kind of collaborative commitment, ELLs' needs must be included visibly, systematically, and comprehensively in course work and in field placements for future teachers and other educational personnel such as school counselors, school psychologists, and school administrators (Brisk, 2007). In order to truly include ELLs in their mainstream classrooms, teacher candidates must be provided with a wide range of opportunities to work with linguistically and culturally diverse students, including field experiences and structured assignments that promote self-reflection and inquiry into the assumptions and values that guide their teaching practices (Gay, 2002; Hadaway, 1993).

> Specific knowledge, skills, and dispositions related to ELLs must be infused into general teacher education in systematic and visible ways.

Conclusion

There is little disagreement about the need for general educators to be better prepared to work with ELLs. We have argued that ESL teacher education programs must ensure that teacher preparation takes into account the expertise of ESL teachers so that mainstream classroom teachers can provide effective learning environments for ELLs as well as for fluent English speakers. Specific knowledge, skills, and dispositions related to ELLs must be infused into general teacher education in systematic and visible ways. Without this explicit preparation for ELLs, mainstream teachers may be forced to rely on a static, generic list of "just good teaching" strategies and fail to recognize or create opportunities to develop ELLs' language and literacy, or to connect the curriculum meaningfully to their students' lives. Rather, in order to provide effective instruction for ELLs, teachers need to be able to make instructional decisions that are grounded in a common pedagogical foundation between teaching ELLs and teaching fluent English speakers and that draw from a distinct body of ESL teacher expertise.

Endnotes

[1] The ESL teacher education standards developed in 2002 for TESOL/NCATE accreditation of initial ESL teacher preparation programs are currently under revision (TESOL, in press).

[2] Although bilingual education is a viable instructional model for ELLs, ESL programs are more common throughout Florida, and these teachers' experience and expertise lie in the area of ESL instruction. Therefore, the interview data are biased toward ESL rather than bilingual issues.

References

Bourne, J. (2001). Doing what comes naturally: How the discourses and routines of teachers' practice constrain opportunities for bilingual support in UK primary schools. *Language and Education, 15(4)*, 250–268.

Brisk, M. E. (Ed.). (2007). *Culturally responsive teacher education: Language, curriculum, & community.* Mahwah, NJ: Lawrence Erlbaum.

Brisk, M. E., Dawson, M., Hartgering, M., MacDonald, E., & Zehr, L. (2002). Teaching bilingual students in mainstream classrooms. In Z. Beykont (Ed.), *The power of culture. Teaching across language difference.* Cambridge, MA: Harvard Publishing Group.

Callahan, R. M. (2006) The intersection of accountability and language: Can reading intervention replace English language development? *Bilingual Research Journal 30(1)*, 1–20.

Cameron, L., Moon, J., & Bygate, M. (1996). Language development of bilingual pupils in the mainstream: How do pupils and teachers use language? *Language and Education, 10(4)*, 221–236.

Capps, R., Fix, M., Murray, J., Ost, J., Passel, J. S., & Herwantoro, S. (2005). *The new demography of America's schools: Immigration and the No Child Left Behind Act.* Washington, DC: Urban Institute.

Cochran, E. P. (Ed.). (2002). *Mainstreaming.* Alexandria, VA: TESOL.

Commins, N. L., & Miramontes, O. B. (2005). *Linguistic diversity and teaching.* Mahwah, NJ: Lawrence Erlbaum.

Constantino, R. (1994, Spring). A study concerning instruction of ESL students comparing all-English classroom teacher knowledge and English as a second language teacher knowledge. *Journal of Educational Issues of Language Minority Students, 13*, 37–57.

Cooper, C. R., Denner, J., & Lopez, E. M. (1999). Cultural brokers: Helping Latino children on pathways toward success. *The Future of Children, 9*(2), 51–57.

Crandall, J. A. (2000). Language teacher education. *Annual Review of Applied Linguistics, 20*, 34–55.

Crandall, J. A. (Ed.). (1995). *ESL through content-area instruction.* Washington, DC: Center for Applied Linguistics.

Creese, A. (2000). The role of the language specialist in disciplinary teaching: In search of a subject? *Journal of Multilingual and Multicultural Development, 21*(6), 451–470.

de Jong, E. J. (2004). After exit: Academic achievement patterns of former English language learners. *Education Policy Analysis Archives, 12*(50). Retrieved October 5, 2008 from http://epaa.asu.edu/epaa/v12n50/

de Jong, E. J., & Derrick-Mescua, M. (2003). Refining preservice teachers' questions for second language learners: Higher order thinking for all levels of language proficiency. *Sunshine State TESOL Journal, 2*(2), 29–37.

de Jong, E. J., & Harper, C. A. (2005). Preparing mainstream teachers for English language learners: Is being a good teacher good enough? *Teacher Education Quarterly, 32*(2), 101–124.

de Jong, E. J., & Harper, C. A. (2007). ESL is good teaching 'plus:' Preparing standard curriculum teachers for all learners. In M. E. Brisk (Ed.), *Language, Culture, and Community in Teacher Education* (pp. 127–148). Mahwah, NJ: Lawrence Erlbaum.

Diaz-Rico, L. T., & Weed, K. Z. (2005). *The cross-cultural, language, and academic development handbook: A complete K–12 reference guide* (3rd ed.). Needham Heights, MA: Allyn and Bacon.

Echevarria, J., Vogt, M. E., & Short, D. J. (2007). *Making content comprehensible for English learners: The SIOP Model* (3rd ed.). Boston: Allyn and Bacon.

Franson, C. (1999). Mainstreaming learners of English as an additional language: The class teacher's perspective. *Language, Culture, and Curriculum, 12*(1), 59–71.

Gándara, P. (2000). In the aftermath of the storm: English learners in the post-227 era. *Bilingual Research Journal, 24*(1 & 2), 1–14.

Gándara, P., Maxwell-Jolly, J., & Driscoll, A. (2005, April). *Listening to teachers of English language learners: A survey of California teachers' challenges, experiences, and professional development needs.* The Center for the Future of Teaching and Learning.
Retrieved October 5, 2008, from http://www.cftl.org/publications_latest.php

Gay, G. (2002). Preparing for culturally responsive teaching. *Journal of Teacher Education, 53*(2) 106–116.

Grabe, W., Stoller, F. L., & Tardy, C. (2000). Disciplinary knowledge as a foundation for teacher preparation. In J. K. Hall, & W. G. Eggington (Eds.), *The sociopolitics of English language teaching* (pp. 178–194). Clevedon, UK: Multilingual Matters.

Hadaway, N. (1993). Encountering linguistic diversity through letters: Preparing preservice teachers for second language learners. *Equity & Excellence in Education, 26*(3), 25–30.

Harklau, L. (1994). ESL versus mainstream classes: Contrasting L2 learning environments. *TESOL Quarterly, 28*(2), 241–272.

Harper, C. A., & de Jong, E. J. (2004). Misconceptions about teaching ELLs. *Journal of Adolescent and Adult Literacy, 48*(2), 152–162.

Harper, C. A., & de Jong, E. J. (2005). Working with ELLs: What is the difference? In A. Huerta-Macias (Ed.), *Working with English language learners: Perspectives and practice* (pp. 55–68). Dubuque, IA: Kendall Hunt.

Harper, C. A., & Platt, E. J. (1998). Full inclusion for secondary ESOL students: Some concerns from Florida. *TESOL Journal, 7*(5), 30–36.

Harper, C. A., Platt, E. J., Naranjo, C. J., & Boynton, S. S. (2007). Marching in unison: Florida ESL teachers and No Child Left Behind. *TESOL Quarterly, 41*(3), 642–651.

Igoa, C. (1995). *The inner world of the immigrant child.* Mahwah, NJ: Lawrence Erlbaum.

Kavale, K. A., & Forness, S. R. (2000). History, rhetoric, and reality: Analysis of the inclusion debate. *Remedial and Special Education, 21*(5), 279–296.

Krashen, S. D., & Terrell, S. D. (1983). *The natural approach: Language acquisition in the classroom.* New York: Pergamon Press.

Ladson-Billings, G. (1995). Toward a theory of culturally relevant pedagogy. *American Educational Research Journal, 32*(3), 465–491.

Langman, J. (2003). The effects of ESL-trained content area teachers: Reducing middle-school students to incidental English language learners. *Prospect: The Journal of the Adult Migrant Education Program, 18*(1), 14–26.

Menken, K., & Antunez, B. (2001). *An overview of the preparation and certification of teachers working with limited English proficient (LEP) students.* Washington, DC: National Clearinghouse for Bilingual Education.

Meyer, Lois M. (2000). Barriers to meaningful instruction for English learners. *Theory into Practice, 39*(4), 228–236.

Mohan, B., Leung, C., & Davison, C. (Eds.). (2001). *English as a second language in the mainstream: Teaching, learning and identity.* White Plains, NY: Longman.

Moll, L. C., Amanti, C., Neff, D., & González, N. (1992). Funds of knowledge for teaching: A qualitative approach to connect households and classrooms. *Theory Into Practice, 31*(2), 132–141.

Mora, J. K. (2000). Staying the course in times of change. Preparing teachers for language minority education. *Journal of Teacher Education, 51*(5), 345–357.

Mora, J. K., & Grisham, D. L. (2001). ¡What deliches tortillas! Preparing teachers for literacy instruction in linguistically diverse classrooms. *Teacher Education Quarterly, 28*(4), 51–70.

Olsen, L. (1997). *Made in America. Immigrant students in our public schools.* New York: The New Press.

Paul, J. L., Lavely, C. D., Cranston-Gingras, A., & Taylor, E. L. (Eds.). (2002). *Rethinking professional issues in special education.* Westport, CT: Ablex.

Penfield, J. (1987). ESL: The regular classroom teacher's perspective. *TESOL Quarterly, 21* (4), 21–39.

Peregoy, S. F., & Boyle, O. F. (2005). *Reading, writing, and learning in ESL: A resource book for K–8 teachers* (4th ed.). New York: Longman.

Platt, E., & Troudi, S. (1997). Mary and her teachers: A Grebo-speaking child's place in the mainstream classroom. *Modern Language Journal, 81*(1), 28–49.

Reeves, J. (2004). "Like everybody else:" Equalizing educational opportunity for English language learners, *TESOL Quarterly, 38*(1), 43–66.

Richards, J. C., & Farrell, T. S. C. (2005). *Professional development for language teachers: Strategies for teacher learning.* Cambridge, UK: Cambridge University Press.

Sapon-Shevin, M., & Zollers, N. J. (1999). Multicultural and disability agendas in teacher education: Preparing teachers for diversity. *International Journal of Leadership in Education, 2*(3), 165–190.

Sharkey, J., & Layzer, C. (2000). Whose definition of success? Identifying factors that affect English language learners' access to academic success and resources. *TESOL Quarterly, 34*(2), 352–368.

Short, D. J. (2002). Language learning in sheltered social studies classes. *TESOL Journal, 11*(1), 18–24.

Snow, M. A., & Brinton, D. M. (1997). *The content-based classroom: Perspectives on integrating language and content.* White Plains, NY: Longman.

Snow, M. A., Met, M., & Genesee, F. (1989). A conceptual framework for the integration of language and content in second/foreign language instruction. *TESOL Quarterly, 23*(2), 207–217.

Spradley, J. (1980). *Participant observation.* New York: Holt, Rinehart, & Winston.

Tang, G. (1992). Teaching content knowledge and ESOL in multicultural classrooms. *TESOL Journal, 2*(2), 8–12.

TESOL (in press). *Draft Revised TESOL/NCATE standards for P–12 ESL teacher education programs (March 2008)*. Alexandria, VA: Author. Retrieved October 5, 2008, from http://www.tesol.org/s_tesol/sec_document. asp?CID=219&DID=10698

TESOL (2006). *Pre-K–12 English language proficiency standards.* Alexandria, VA: Author.

Tsui, A. B. M. (2003). *Understanding expertise in teaching: Case studies of ESL teachers.* Cambridge, UK: Cambridge University Press.

Valdés, G. (2001). *Learning and not-learning English. Latino students in American schools.* New York: Teachers College Press.

Verplaetse, L. S. (2000). How content teachers allocate turns to limited English proficient students. *Journal of Education, 182*(3), 19-35.

Walker, A., Shafer, J., & Iiams, M. (2004). "Not in my classroom:" Teacher attitudes towards English language learners in the mainstream classroom. *NABE Journal of Research and Practice, 2*(1), 130–160.

Wong Fillmore, L., & Snow, C. E. (2002). What teachers need to know about language. In C. T. Adger, C. E. Snow, & D. Christian, (Eds.), *What teachers need to know about language* (pp. 7–53). Washington, DC: Center for Applied Linguistics.

Yoon, B. (2007). Offering or limiting opportunities: Teachers' roles and approaches to English–language learners' participation in literacy activities. *The Reading Teacher, 61*(3), 216–225.

Zehler, A. M., Fleischman, H. L., Hopstock, P. J., Stephenson, T. G., Pendzick, M. L., & Sapru, S. (2003). *Descriptive study of services to LEP students and LEP students with disabilities.* (Volume 1 Research Report). Retrieved October 5, 2008, from http://www.ncela.gwu.edu/resabout/research/descriptivestudy-files/index.htm

Adriana was a first-grade English language learner (ELL) in Reading Recovery. Look at the changes in her written messages across her lessons. What do you observe about changes in her literacy behaviors across 15 weeks of lessons?

Lesson 3:   She like me.

Lesson 4:   Saturday my birthday.

Lesson 20: Did you taked your baby from school?

Lesson 21: I go to San Antonio tomorrow.

Lesson 50: First we went to the mall and then we rented a movie named *Christmas Story*.

Lesson 51: Are you going to see me on Wednesday and Thursday?

Adriana's increasingly more complex and structurally accurate stories exemplify the acceleration in writing that an ELL can accomplish in a short amount of time. Concurrent with improved writing, Adriana's instructional text level went from a 2 to a 17 by the end of her 15-week lesson series. At midyear she had clearly reached the average level of the first-grade classroom; she completed the school year in a 'high-middle' reading group.

English Language Learners: Lessons Learned from Reading Recovery

Cynthia Rodríguez-Eagle
Texas Woman's University

My experience with Adriana and several other ELL students in Reading Recovery has led me to new understandings about effective literacy practices for ELLs. Each student provides a new opportunity for me to refine my teaching interactions based on each individual's strengths and weaknesses, with a particular emphasis on English language learning. Furthermore, my role as trainer of teacher leaders for Reading Recovery and Descubriendo la Lectura (Reading Recovery in Spanish) allows me to work extensively with adult learners to learn more about teaching decisions that support ELLs.

Following years of experience teaching in elementary bilingual and English as a second language (ESL) classrooms, my work with ELLs in Reading Recovery and ongoing study with Reading Recovery colleagues has led me to identify key lessons, or understandings, that seem critical for the literacy success of all ELL students.

> My work with ELLs in Reading Recovery and ongoing study with Reading Recovery colleagues has led me to identify key lessons, or understandings, that seem critical for the literacy success of all ELL students.

Lessons Learned
- Native-language instruction makes literacy learning easier.
- Close analysis of initial assessments is critical to early acceleration.
- Careful book selections and book introductions make a difference.
- Expertly guided conversations are critical to developing language.
- The reciprocity between reading and writing helps to accelerate a child's learning.
- High teacher expectations are essential for ELLs.

In this chapter, I address each of these lessons that I have learned. Excerpts of my conversations with Reading Recovery teacher leaders and teachers are included throughout the chapter. These colleagues shared experiences and understandings they have developed from their ELL students. I also share several examples from ELLs in Reading Recovery.

As you read, consider your own role in working with ELLs: How can the lessons I have learned through my work with ELLs in Reading Recovery apply to your work in individual, small-group, or classroom settings?

Native-Language Instruction Makes Literacy Learning Easier

Many different languages are spoken by students in our schools. It would be impossible to provide native-language instruction for all ELLs. However, as a former bilingual teacher and a Descubriendo la Lectura trainer, I feel it is important to share what I have learned through my experience with native-language instruction and the subsequent outcomes for these students.

There is extensive research to support native-language instruction for an extended period of time to allow students the opportunity to have comprehensible instruction before they transition into mainstream monolingual English classrooms (Cummins, 1999; Guadarrama, 1999; Krashen, 1996; Ramirez, Pasta, Yuen, Billings, & Ramey, 1991; Thomas & Collier, 2002). "Reading in one's native language facilitates reading in a second language…. [And] children's achievement in a second language depends on their mastery of their native language" (Gandara et al., 2000, p. 43). The majority of my own work with native-language instruction is with Descubriendo la Lectura (DLL).

DLL is the reconstruction of Reading Recovery for students receiving classroom literacy instruction in Spanish. Bilingual educators from Tucson, Arizona, initiated DLL in 1988. Since that time, DLL has expanded to sites in California, Colorado, Illinois, Massachusetts, New York, Texas, and Washington.

My dissertation research focused on the subsequent literacy gains of students who received DLL lessons in first grade (Rodriguez, 2006). Scores on the third- and fourth-grade Texas Assessment of Knowledge and Skills (TAKS) state exam for former DLL students were gathered and analyzed to respond to several research questions.

One of the analyses focused on the interaction between DLL outcomes and the language of administration on the state assessment. Of all the students who successfully completed DLL in Grade 1 and subsequently took the TAKS test in Grades 3 and 4 in Spanish, 85.5% had a passing rate. Students who transitioned out of bilingual classrooms earlier and subsequently took the TAKS test in English had a 53.1% passing rate. These data provide evidence that extended native-language instruction makes a difference.

A solid foundation in the students' native language best prepares them for learning in English. In DLL, teachers are working with the lowest literacy achievers in first-grade bilingual classrooms. These students have the dual challenge of catching up to the average literacy level in their classrooms and learning a new language in order to transfer to all-English instruction. It is unfortunate (but understandable) that each child in our schools cannot have the benefit of native-language instruction.

> A solid foundation in the students' native language best prepares them for learning in English.

Close Analysis of Initial Assessments is Critical to Early Acceleration

In Reading Recovery, this lesson has been demonstrated repeatedly. Teachers from a Reading Recovery training class shared the following:

> One thing that we (the class) came to understand was how important it was to really analyze the assessment results and use them to prepare for our first lessons. I saw how helpful that analysis was for my two ELL students. I felt more prepared to lead conversations, compose stories, and choose books, adjusting my level of support based on what their strengths were.

> I'm just amazed at how I'm able to pick up patterns in what they do in reading and writing just by looking across their Observation Survey tasks.

These teachers-in-training gained important insights about the power of the in-depth analysis of initial assessments. It is an understanding that becomes more salient once teachers work with several rounds of Reading Recovery students. Using the Observation Survey results as data, a teacher is able to summarize specific strategic behaviors students are using in reading and writing. Areas of literacy strengths and weaknesses emerge, and individual lessons are planned accordingly. For students whose level of language proficiency is unknown, the Record of Oral Language (Clay, Gill, Glynn, McNaughton, & Salmon, 1983, 2007) can be used.

In this section, I describe these two assessment tools and explain how they help to support early acceleration.

The Observation Survey

Student selection in Reading Recovery is based on results of *An Observation Survey of Early Literacy Achievement* (Clay, 2002, 2006). The Observation Survey adheres to characteristics of good measurement instruments — namely, a standard task, a standard way of administering the task, ways of knowing about reliability of observations, and a real-world task that establishes validity of the observation. United States stanines are available.

The Observation Survey is comprised of six literacy tasks with established validity and reliability (Clay, 2002, 2006):

- Letter Identification
  to identify known letters and preferred mode of identification
- Word Test
  to determine whether the child is building reading vocabulary
- Concepts About Print
  to find out what the child has learned about the way spoken language is put into print
- Writing Vocabulary
  to find out whether the child is building a writing vocabulary
- Hearing and Recording Sounds in Words
  to assess phonemic awareness by responses to sound-letter associations
- Text Reading
  to determine appropriate level of text difficulty and to record, using a running record, what the child does when reading continuous text

After a student is selected for the intervention, the teacher must carefully prepare for lessons to begin. Information about a child's knowledge of letters, words, and text can be learned by summarizing the student's results on each of the tasks from the Observation Survey. For ELLs, it is important to take a second look at each of the tasks, asking questions such as these:

> Using the Observation Survey results as data, a teacher is able to summarize specific strategic behaviors students are using in reading and writing.

- How did s/he identify letters? (by name, sound, or word? in which language?)
- Does the writing reflect literacy understandings in the child's first language?
- If there was minimal conversation, was s/he able to understand the tasks?

Adriana's home language was Spanish. By first grade, she had been in mainstream English classrooms for 3 years. (She had participated in a Head Start program since age 3.) It was clear that Adriana communicated more comfortably in Spanish, but she understood and spoke English fairly well. Although I had observed her to be a social child among her peers, she was often quiet and reserved in her classroom. During the initial testing, she responded to me with one-word answers (in English), or not at all.

She did understand all the tasks and seemed to try her best on each one. Table 1 shows Adriana's fall scores on each of the survey tasks, followed by a brief description of what I learned about her strengths and weaknesses in reading and writing.

Table 1
Fall Observation Survey Results for Adriana

Task	Score	Stanine
Letter Identification	6 of 54 letters	1
Word Test	0 of 20 words	1
Concepts About Print	9 of 20 concepts	1
Writing Vocabulary	2 words	1
Hearing and Recording Sounds in Words	0 of 37 sounds	1
Text Reading	Instructional Text Level: 1	

Summary of Adriana's strategic activity in reading
Adriana is aware that print carries the message and understands directional movement, including return sweep. She consistently uses meaning. Structural and visual information are used less. She seems to have a good memory for simple, patterned text, especially those composed of her oral language.

Summary of Adriana's strategic activity in writing
Adriana wrote two words (*Adriana*, *mom*) that were correct in every detail. She wrote two words in Spanish in response to English prompts of *dog* and *red*. The words were written correctly in Spanish. She can locate her known words in text.

Record of Oral Language

Because Adriana was initially hesitant to converse with me, it was difficult to hypothesize her level of language proficiency. I used the Record of Oral Language (Clay et al., 1983, 2007) to help me gather this information. The Record of Oral Language (ROL) is an assessment instrument that helps teachers learn about a child's control over language, providing information about how the child handles varying grammatical structures. Reading Recovery teachers express the value of using the ROL with their ELL students:

> My teachers regularly use the ROL with their ELLs. We can learn more about what they understand structure-wise in English. So we can hold them accountable for structures we know they control, and plan opportunities to work more with new ones. (teacher leader)

> In Reading Recovery, we always talk about really 'knowing' the child. We try to gather all the information we can to work right at the 'cutting edge' of the student's learning. Using the ROL just helps us know more, to be more prepared to work with our ELL students. I just think it's imperative to use it for students whose first language is not English. (teacher)

Administration of the ROL is not time consuming. The teacher says a sentence to the child who then attempts to repeat it. The exact response is recorded immediately to analyze following the administration. The sentences use different grammatical structures and become more difficult as the assessment continues. See Table 2 for a sampling of the types of sentences included in the assessment.

Questions to Guide Book Selection for ELL Children

Does the book
- have a story based on the child's personal knowledge or experience?

- use language structures that match the child's level of oral proficiency, becoming more complex over time?

- use language structures that the child has had the opportunity to write?

- support strategic literacy development?

- have sufficient text on which the child can engage in problem solving?

- have sufficient text on which the child can practice fluent reading?

- represent ethnic, cultural, and language diversity in a way that values all persons?

Will the book
- help establish new competencies?

- be interesting/enjoyable to the child?

- ensure a successful experience for the child?

Adapted from Anderson (2004) and Clay (2005b)

Table 2
Sampling of Record of Oral Language Sentence Types

Sentence Type	Example
Type A: noun phrase, followed by some form of the verb 'to be' and another simple statement (no object)	My sister's face is dirty.
Type B: noun or noun phrase, followed by a verb phrase, followed by a noun phrase which is a direct object	My aunt and uncle want to build a new house.
Type E: noun phrase, followed by a verb, followed by a noun clause	My mother knows what time we need to leave for the party.
Type G: noun phrase, followed by a verb or verb phrase, followed by an object, followed by some additional construction (e.g., adverb or adverbial phrase)	My brother usually leaves his bicycle outside at night.

Before my first lesson with Adriana, I was able to form a hypothesis about her understandings (and misunderstandings) in reading and writing. The ROL also gave me an idea about her level of language proficiency. My hypothesis would be revised and modified as I had more opportunities to work with Adriana. However, initially it provided me with a starting point that was much more on target than if I had only noted the scores of the assessment to help with student selection.

Careful Book Selections and Book Introductions Make a Difference

Selecting a New Book

> Each year I facilitate at least two sessions where we (the Reading Recovery teachers) spend time discussing text selection. We have to consider the meaning of the story and its structure. And we have to ask, 'Does this support what the child knows in reading?' (teacher leader)

Books selected for every child, but especially for ELLs, should be well within his control. The child should be able to use what he knows or can get to with the teacher's help. Although one or two things may require new learning, the child has the opportunity to practice behaviors and strategies that are emerging (Clay, 2005b). For ELLs, a good book selection includes familiar concepts, structures that have been practiced, and a minimum of new and unknown words. (See the questions to guide book selection on the previous page.)

While the majority of responses to the questions should be 'yes,' there may be exceptions. The book introduction is the teacher's opportunity to confirm what the child may know about the book as well as uncover any new learning that needs to take place in order to ensure a successful first reading.

Book Introductions

> I have to spend a little more time planning book introductions for my ELL students. I want to make sure I am considering what they are bringing to the table meaning- and structure-wise. Then I think about what I need to bring to their attention so the book is manageable. (teacher)

When planning book introductions for individual students, consider the questions at right.

Early in the lesson series, it is expected that book introductions will be more supportive and will be led by the teacher. Later in lessons, the child is able to contribute more to the orientation to the book before reading. At that point, the teacher is more the facilitator of the conversation, making sure to emphasize the meaning of the story and any other structural issues that might be difficult.

Mrs. Long worked with Alexander, an ELL student whose first language was Russian. Below is one of her book introductions early in the

Questions to Guide Book Introductions for ELL Children

- Is the child familiar with the concepts in the story?

- Are there unknown words that I need to bring to the child's attention?

- Are there words that are partially known that I want the child to practice? (Partially known words may include words the child is not consistently reading or writing—but has been able to at times.)

- Are there new structures that I will demonstrate and have the child repeat?

- Is the layout/format of the story familiar?

- What links can I make to help the child make connections to the story?

lesson series. Alexander was going to read *The Photo Book* (Randell, 2007), Level 3. The book is about pictures in a photo album and focuses on whose photos are in the book (e.g., Mom, James, Teddy Bear).

Orientation to *The Photo Book*

T: Do you have photos of your family at home?

A: Like pictures?

T: Yes, pictures. In this book they are called photos. You say that.

A: photos

T: Do you have those photos in a book?

A: Some of them.

T: Well, in this story we are looking at a family's photo book. The whole family is in the photo book. Look. Mom is in the book. You say that.

A: Mom is in the book.

T: Write *here* (a known word in writing vocabulary)
(child writes *here*)

T: Show me that word on this page, and this page? Good job! Look, even Teddy Bear is in the book. Where does it say Teddy Bear?
(child points to the words)

T: That's funny—Teddy Bear is in the book, too! Now you read it.

During Alexander's last week in Reading Recovery lessons, the teacher introduced him to *And I Mean It, Stanley* (Bosall, 1974), Level 17. The book is about a boy who is working hard to make things he says he doesn't want Stanley to see.

Orientation to *And I Mean It, Stanley*

T: This book is called 'And I Mean it, Stanley.' The boy in the story is working hard to make things he says he doesn't want Stanley to see. Let's look at it.

A: Where is Stanley?

T: I don't know. Let's look and see.

A: He's talking by himself! There is no one there! He's making lots of stuff.

T: Yes, he says he's making a "truly, great thing." Where does it say that?
(child points)

T: He does say he wants to play all "by myself." So, you're right. It does look like he wants to be alone.

T: I wonder if he really doesn't want Stanley to play with him.

A: I don't think so. I think he's just pretending.

> An emphasis must be placed on the power of genuine conversation between the teacher and student in facilitating English language development.

T: You are really using those pictures to help you!

A: OH! Stanley's his dog! He's playing with his dog!

T: You read it and see!

Note that in the later introduction, Mrs. Long continued to prompt Alexander to use meaning, structure, and visual information as he read. However, she was allowing him to lead the conversation and make his own observations about the text as well.

Expertly Guided Conversations Are Critical to Developing Language

> Honestly, what frustrates me sometimes is just not knowing how to get my ELL students to talk to me. Getting a story can be like pulling teeth and a lot of times I feel like I end up generating the story for them!   (teacher)

This forthright observation came from an experienced Reading Recovery teacher who has recently seen an increase in the ELL population at her campus. Her sentiment is shared by many other teachers who have not had previous experience teaching English language learners. An emphasis must be placed on the power of genuine conversation between the teacher and student in facilitating English language development. "To foster oral language development, create opportunities for them to talk, and then talk with them (not at them)" (Clay, 1991, p. 69).

One of the components of the Reading Recovery lesson is the conversation that leads the child to compose and write a message. Each day, the teacher facilitates a conversation with the student. Together, they generate a story that the child will write with the support of the teacher.

For ELL students, this short period of time in the Reading Recovery lesson is a critical tool for developing language. The genuine exchange, expertly guided by the teacher, provides an opportunity for the student to practice English through natural conversation. It makes sense that young students learning English would be hesitant to contribute extensively to the conversation, especially early in the lesson series. This is a challenge for teachers who are accustomed to curtailing students' stories because they have so much to share. Although it is not always easy, it is *critical* to elicit conversation from ELL students.

See the following conversation between Mrs. Flores and Robert, an ELL student, about a book that Robert has just read. It is a nice example of a teacher working hard to guide the conversation and elicit more talk from Robert.

T: Why is *Baby Bear* your favorite story?

R: Because — he's cute.

T: Oh, so you like small bears?

R: Yeah.

> To foster oral language development, create opportunities for them to talk, and then talk with them (not at them).
>
> — Marie Clay

T: Do you like stuffed teddy bears?

R: Yeah.

T: Do you have some?

R: Yes.

T: Well, I used to have a lot of stuffed animals. But puppies were my favorite. I had one who I named J-Bird. I took him everywhere!

R: At my house I have two dogs. But they're real.

T: You do? I love playing outside with my dogs! What do you do with yours?

R: We all play outside and inside and they sleep with me.

T: Let's write that!

The conversation began slowly but ultimately produced a much more-complex story than we might have predicted at the beginning. The closed-ended questions at the beginning of the conversation did not require anything more than a one-word answer. Mrs. Flores then took a different direction by sharing briefly her own experience. Robert responded with more conversation than he had to any of the questioning. When the topic shifted from Baby Bear to stuffed animals to real dogs, Mrs. Flores followed along naturally. After Robert produced a clear descriptive statement, Mrs. Flores jumped on it and asked him to write it.

The excerpt above is one glimpse of an interaction between Mrs. Flores and Robert. Robert had the benefit of many more conversations with Mrs. Flores during reading and writing events. Even brief exchanges can make a significant difference in developing language for ELLs. This comment from a Reading Recovery teacher reveals the importance of conversations to the ELLs with whom she works.

> I feel bad admitting that I did not think I should have Grace as a first-round student. I thought she needed more time in the classroom to learn English. But I ended up learning more from her than any of my other students. After just a few weeks working with me every day, her English got so much better!

Reading Recovery teachers are able to see language develop quickly and naturally when they engage ELL students in conversation and work hard to encourage—and value—their contributions.

Errors that Signal Language Learning

> I know I'm not supposed to change the child's story. But it's one of my biggest struggles. If the story is structurally wrong—grammatically inaccurate—it still doesn't make sense to me why I would have them write it. (teacher)

> Reading Recovery teachers are able to see language develop quickly and naturally when they engage ELL students in conversation and work hard to encourage—and value—their contributions.

This is another common challenge for Reading Recovery teachers. Without a clear understanding of language learning, it is difficult for teachers to be comfortable allowing students to write grammatically incorrect sentences. It is important to know that many errors are developmental and will eventually be replaced by conventional forms without specific intervention (Peregoy & Boyle, 2005). "Our efforts should never make him reluctant to offer up his ungrammatical but expressive attempts to construct sentences. As we talk with a child he revises and refines his language, experimenting making funny errors but gaining all the while in control over the expressiveness and the complexity of the language" (Clay, 1991, p. 69).

The Reciprocity Between Reading and Writing Helps to Accelerate a Child's Learning

> The two activities of reading and writing are similar in many ways. It is useful to assume that working effectively in one activity will help with working in the other. I assume that they affect each other reciprocally, and that oral language is a further rich resource for serving both those activities. (Clay, 2005a, p. 2)

Planning individual lessons daily requires the teacher to reflect on what new learning the child is acquiring, both in reading and writing. New understandings that emerge in writing may not have emerged yet in reading, or vice versa.

For example, Adriana consistently monitored her work when writing. She independently reread what she wrote and thought about what word was next in the story. If she made an error, she self-corrected it or appealed for help to correct it. In reading, however, she did not reread and rarely self-corrected or appealed for help. I had to repeatedly bring this behavior to Adriana's attention, mostly through praising it during writing. "Wow! You reread your story and fixed it all by yourself! That helps you when you're reading books, too!" Sometimes simply making the reading-writing connection for the child is enough to help him understand how the knowledge transfers. For other students, the connection is not made as easily.

> I felt like a broken record telling James "if you can write it, you can read it" but after week 13 or so, it seemed to click for him. All of a sudden, he wasn't stopping at known words and his reading fluency improved by leaps and bounds. (teacher)

> For me, once I saw how closely reading and writing are connected, that's when I really saw the payoff with my lessons. For my ELL students, it provides more links they can use to help them to understand the new language. (teacher)

Planning individual lessons daily requires the teacher to reflect on what new learning the child is acquiring, both in reading and writing.

Following are some examples of processes common to both reading and writing activities:

- Controlling serial order
- Problem solving with more than one kind of information
- Drawing on stored information and acting on it
- Using visual information
- Using phonological information
- Using the meaning of what was composed
- Using the vocabulary and structure of what was composed
- Searching, checking, and correcting
- Categorizing, using rules, and estimating probabilities of occurrence

(Clay, 2001, p. 32)

In Table 3 you can see samples of Robert's stories across his 17-week lesson series and compare them to excerpts from the instructional texts he was reading at the same points in time. As you look at the table, think about questions you may ask yourself about the match between the messages a child writes and the texts he is reading at a given point in time.

Table 3
Samples of Texts Robert is Reading and Writing at Three Points in Time

Time	Text He is Reading	Message He is Writing
Early Lessons	I am eating. I am drinking.	I like color blue best.
	I like to read in the van. I like to read in the car.	I taked him with me.
	Look at me. I am a mouse. Look at me. I am a cat.	I love mom.
Midpoint of Lessons	On Pet Day, Bingo went to school with Sam and Mom. They saw a little boy with a black cat.	The red one is my favorite. I putting the lids on the boxes.
	Six crabs sat on a rock. A dog took one. Three crabs sat on a rock. A fish took one.	Yesterday we go to the movies. It's my birthday.
Late Lessons	The leaves have blown away. They will grow back in spring. The pond has no ducks. Where have the ducks gone?	Titch has a big brother like me. I played video games on Saturday. Sunday it was John's party.
	In the spring, the tree was covered with pink blossoms. Bees came to sip the nectar.	My baby sister walks now.

Consider the following:

- Does the level of structural complexity match?
- Are there "echoes across my lesson?" In other words, does my emphasis and prompting during reading match with what I'm prompting for during writing?
- Has the student produced a variety of sentence types?
- Am I providing a variety of books (genres, structures, concepts, fiction/nonfiction)?

Exercises such as the one shown in Table 3 can assist us in taking a closer look at the reciprocity between reading and writing. Doing such an analysis midway through a child's lessons might facilitate teaching shifts. For example, based on the results of the comparison, a teacher might hold the child more accountable for more-complex stories — in reading or in writing.

High Teacher Expectations Are Essential for English Language Learners

It would seem unnecessary to talk with teachers about maintaining high expectations for their students. I cannot imagine a teacher who does not want each student to reach the highest potential possible. However, I discovered that this concept may be more difficult for teachers of ELLs, as revealed in conversations with teacher leaders and teachers.

Teacher Leader Comments
About Teachers' Expectations of English Language Learners

Actually, I think it's more sympathy than anything else. I've seen my teachers just want to help too much, more than they would with native English-speaking students.

I've noticed that some assumptions come up when teachers are talking about their ELL students. They'll say things like, 'We're still on text level 4 at week 11 — but that's okay because he has limited language.' They aren't introducing the harder texts, not producing complex stories because the teacher is not expecting them to.

My teachers often say their ELL students have 'limited or low language.' Then I observe their lessons and the child is a chatterbox! Granted, the structures might not all be 100% right, but they are getting their messages across! It doesn't seem like the conversations with these students are as rich as they could be if the teachers kept high expectations for what they (the students) could contribute to the conversations.

Teacher Comments About Expectations of English Language Learners

I actually do feel it's a lot of pressure for young students to learn English, especially when they are struggling with reading and

> Exercises such as the one shown in Table 3 can assist us in taking a closer look at the reciprocity between reading and writing. Doing such an analysis midway through a child's lessons might facilitate teaching shifts.

writing! Now I'm learning how I can teach my lessons in ways that help him — without it being overwhelming for him. I'm working on expecting them to be as successful as my other Reading Recovery students.

It's not that I didn't believe my ELL students could be successful. I knew they could do it. I just wasn't sure if I could be the one to teach them how to do it! I do think there are certain methods we need to use with our ELL students that we don't necessarily have to with others. I'm still trying to feel more confident with my ELLs. So I guess I need to maintain high expectations for myself!

It does seem like common sense to maintain high expectations for all our students. However, sometimes we need to reflect on our perceptions and understandings about different groups to ensure that all students are reaching their highest potential.

Engaging in daily conversations that lead to increasingly more-complex stories is a powerful tool that supports language development for ELLs.

Table 4
Adriana's Observation Survey Scores Across the School Year

Task	Week 1 RR Entry	Week 15 RR Exit	End of Year
Letter Identification	6 / 54	54 / 54	54 / 54
Word Test	0 / 20	16 / 20	19 / 20
Concepts About Print	9 / 24	17 / 24	20 / 24
Writing Vocabulary	2	65	69
Hearing and Recording Sounds in Words	0 / 37	30 / 37	35/ 37
Text Reading (instructional level)	Level 1	Level 17	Level 24

Note: If there are maximum scores on the task, that number follows the slashmark. For example, 6 / 54 indicates that Adriana had a score of 6 out of a possible score of 54.

Conclusion

Let's revisit Adriana, the student I discussed at the beginning of this chapter. Look at Table 4 for her scores at three points across the year — beginning, middle, and end of the school year.

Adriana started the year as one of the four lowest students in all of the first-grade classrooms at her school. After 15 weeks of individualized instruction and her classroom literacy program, she had exceeded the average reading level in her class. Her literacy gains continued for the remainder of the school year, as is evidenced by her end-of-year results. It is because of students like Adriana that I continue to pursue new understandings of effective literacy practices for ELLs.

In this chapter, I shared some of the lessons I have learned based on my experiences with ELL students and interactions with teachers of ELLs in Reading Recovery. My understandings are tentative and constantly evolving — my lessons are expanded and modified daily as I learn from the children.

The following quote from a Reading Recovery teacher nicely summarizes the challenges and the rewards of her work with ELL students:

> The fact is that it is more work for me to get those higher outcomes from my ELL students. It can get tiring, reviewing books, considering structures, our conversations—everything—all that thinking for ONE student. But those are the ones I feel more rewarded by when they do start picking it up. My work with them really makes a difference in how they succeed in school. The extra work is worth it!

References

Anderson, N. (2004). *Booklist field testing procedures.* [Technical Report]. Columbus, OH: Reading Recovery Council of North America.

Clay, M. M. (1991). *Becoming literate: The construction of inner control.* Portsmouth, NH: Heinemann

Clay, M. M. (2001). *Change over time in children's literacy development.* Portsmouth, NH: Heinemann.

Clay, M. M. (2002, 2006). *An observation survey of early literacy achievement.* (2nd ed., rev. 2nd ed.). Portsmouth, NH: Heinemann.

Clay, M. M. (2005a). *Literacy lessons designed for individuals part one: Why? when? and how?* Portsmouth, NH: Heinemann.

Clay, M. M. (2005b). *Literacy lessons designed for individuals part two: Teaching procedures.* Portsmouth, NH: Heinemann.

Clay, M. M., Gill, M., Glynn, T., McNaughton, T., & Salmon, K. (1983). *Record of oral language: Biks and gutches.* (2007, Rev. ed.). Portsmouth, NH: Heinemann.

Cummins, J. (1999). Alternative paradigms in bilingual education research: Does theory have a place? *Educational Research, 28(7),* 26–41.

Gándara, P., Maxwell-Jolly, J., García, E., Asato, J., Gutiérrez, K., Stritkus, T., & Curry, J. (2000). *The initial impact of Proposition 227 on the instruction of English learners.* Davis, CA: University of California Linguistic Minority Research Center.

Guadarrama, I. (1999). The empowering role of service learning in the preparation of teachers. In C. R. O'Grady (Ed.). *Integrating service learning and multicultural education in colleges and universities.* Philadelphia, PA: Lawrence Erlbaum Associates.

Krashen, S. (1996). Principles of English as a foreign language. *English Teachers Journal, 49,* 11–19.

Peregoy, S. F., & Boyle, O. F. (2005). *Reading, writing and learning in ESL: A resource book for K–12 teachers* (4th ed.). Boston: Pearson Education, Allyn and Bacon.

Ramirez, J. D., Pasta, D. J., Yuen, S., Billings, D. K., & Ramey, D. R. (1991). *Final report: Longitudinal study of structural immersion strategy, early-exit, and late-exit transitional bilingual education programs for language-minority children.* Aguirre International (Report to the U.S. Department of Education). San Mateo, CA.

Rodríguez, C. (2006). *An examination of TAKS outcomes of former Descubriendo la Lectura students.* Unpublished doctoral dissertation. Texas Woman's University, Denton, TX.

Thomas, W. P., & Collier, V. P. (2002). *A national study of school effectiveness for language minority students' long term academic achievement.* Santa Cruz, CA: University of California, Center for Research on Education, Diversity, and Excellence.

Children's Books Cited

Bonsall, C. (1974). *And I mean it, Stanley.* Harper Collins Publishers, Inc.

Randell, B. (2007). *The photo book.* Rigby.

English language learners (ELLs) are often viewed as a literacy challenge for schools. Yet, we have compelling evidence that these children *can* 'catch up' to their peers and continue to move forward with good classroom instruction. In this chapter, after showing evidence of the success of Reading Recovery with ELLs, I will share some of the underlying principles of Reading Recovery that may contribute to that success. Those principles should help us think about effective teaching practices for ELLs.

Early Intervention with English Language Learners: The Impact of Reading Recovery

In a recent large national study, my colleagues and I examined the effectiveness of Reading Recovery as an intervention for first-grade ELLs (Kelly, Gómez-Bellengé, Chen, & Schulz, 2008). We knew it was effective for native English speakers (D'Agostino & Murphy, 2004; Pinnell, Lyons, DeFord, Bryk, & Seltzer, 1994, Schwartz, 2005; Shanahan & Barr, 1995). We also had evidence of its effectiveness for ELLs (Ashdown & Simic, 2000; Hobsbaum, 1995; Neal & Kelly, 1999). Our goal was to extend those research efforts to take a closer look at the influence of language proficiency on reading acquisition of ELL children.

English Language Learners in Primary Classrooms: Literacy Assessment and Instruction

Patricia R. Kelly
San Diego State University

We found that Reading Recovery was effective in accelerating the progress of ELL children to reach average levels of performance, just as it has been for native-speaking Reading Recovery children. Overall, 69% of the ELLs who had a complete intervention successfully reached grade-level proficiency in reading. The percentages of children who successfully completed Reading Recovery were higher for children with higher fall oral English proficiency levels (Levels 4 & 5), but even children with a very low fall oral proficiency level (Level 1) had a 60% discontinuing rate (meeting grade-level expectations).

Grade 1 spring reading scores of ELLs after Reading Recovery were comparable to their English-speaking peers. Their average text reading level at the end of the year was 18.33, a level indicative of beginning second-grade performance. ELL children demonstrated excellent phonemic awareness as well. Furthermore, the length of ELL children's interventions was on average only four sessions more than native English speakers in Reading Recovery. Although there were some small differences across language proficiency groups in year-end scores, the effect size of the fall oral English proficiency level was small. In other words, ELL children had a wide range of fall oral English proficiency levels, yet they reached grade-level expectations after Reading Recovery.

Interventions with this high success rate are not common. In fact, traditionally, ". . . schools have not been successful in their attempts to help lower achieving students 'catch up' to their peers. Unfortunately, most children who get off to a slow start in reading remain behind in reading" (Hiebert & Taylor, 1994, p. 4). Yet Reading Recovery has demonstrated that the lowest literacy achievers *can* catch up. Success rates for ELLs are comparable to those of native English speakers.

Many factors contribute to achievement gains made by ELLs (and native English-speaking children) who are selected for Reading Recovery as the lowest readers in their first-grade classrooms. The theoretical foundations and the essential design of Reading Recovery with expert one-to-one teaching contribute to the success of the intervention. In Table 1a and 1b, I briefly describe some Reading Recovery principles; consider how each principle would influence teachers in ways that benefit ELLs. Take a moment to review these principles on pages 61 and 62.

Did you associate these principles with English language learners — or in fact with *all* learners? Could you use these principles to assess your current thinking about your work with ELLs? Take some time with colleagues to discuss the impact of each principle on your teaching of ELLs.

Educators have found that effective English as a second language (ESL) literacy instruction incorporates much of what is found in Reading Recovery instruction:

- Activation and use of prior knowledge
- Purposeful language tasks
- Use of scaffolding

> We found that Reading Recovery was effective in accelerating the progress of ELL children to reach average levels of performance, just as it has been for native-speaking Reading Recovery children.

Table 1a
Underlying Principles of Reading Recovery That Support English Language Learners

Principles	Explanation
A complex constructivist theory of literacy learning (Clay, 2001)	Reading Recovery is a complex constructivist model of literacy learning based on studies of successful learners (Clay, 2001) and informed by theories of language acquisition, literacy, and learning. Instruction in Reading Recovery is different from instruction found in many interventions that target a single component, usually instruction on decoding words (Hiebert & Taylor, 2000). In Reading Recovery, the learner is viewed as active and constructive. The term *strategic activity* refers to what goes on when the brain picks up information, works on it, makes a decision, and evaluates the response. At first, the child constructs very simple action systems that become more complex. As a child temporarily assembles more complicated systems, he or she finds new ways to solve problems (Clay, 2001).
Informed by theories of language acquisition	The role of oral language is fundamental to the task of learning to read. "The very foundation of literacy learning lies in the language the child has already constructed" (Clay 1998, p. 2). A child's acquisition of reading and writing abilities links to both his ability to learn and expand his oral language and his knowledge of the structure of language. "If we harness the established power of children's oral language to literacy learning from the beginning, so that literacy knowledge and oral language processing power move forward together, linked and patterned from the start, that will surely be more powerful" (Clay, 2001, p. 95). Reading Recovery teachers use the language competencies of the children they teach and help them make links between what they already know about language with the new activity of reading. Genuine conversations within lessons build language foundations for reading and writing.
Guided by an expert teacher's skillful and flexible instruction	The teacher's skillful interactions with the young reader underlie the success of Reading Recovery. Lessons are specifically designed for individual children by specially trained teachers who observe closely the behaviors of the child and adjust their teaching based on the new learning that has occurred (Clay, 2005b; Clay & Cazden, 1990). Accelerated literacy learning so that a child can catch up to his peers and reach grade-level performance is the expected outcome of Reading Recovery (Clay, 2005a; Klenk & Kibby, 2000). This outcome is based on high expectations, expert teaching, and a commitment to bring each child's achievement up to expected class performance.
High expectations within an environment for risk taking and learning	Strong relationships that form between Reading Recovery teachers and children create an environment for risk taking and learning (Kelly et al., 2008; Yerington, (2004).
Assessment that guides teaching decisions	Reading Recovery teachers use systematic observation to inform their teaching. *An Observation Survey of Early Literacy Achievement* (Clay, 2002, 2006) is designed to record how children work on literacy tasks and guides teachers to modify their teaching accordingly. Running records of text reading can provide a clear account of a child's literacy processing for teachers to use. Daily observation records allow teachers to document change over time in a child's progress in learning to read and write.

Table 1b
Underlying Principles of Reading Recovery That Support English Language Learners

Principles	Explanation
Building on the learners' existing knowledge	Reading Recovery teachers incorporate students' experiences during lessons, increasing motivation to learn (Kelly et al., 2008). Teachers begin with what the learner already knows—value it—and build on it. Children bring their own personal resources into their lessons (e.g., their oral language and their knowledge of everyday life). Teachers hold children accountable for using what they know and waste no time teaching what the child already controls.
Development of student independence/autonomy	For an intervention to be successful and have staying power, it has to "produce learners who do more than accumulate item knowledge and specific skills. It must ensure that readers and writers become independent processors of new information" (Clay, 2001, pp. 219–220) so that they can go beyond the known to new learning. As the child is provided increasingly more-complex text, he is actively engaged in finding more ways to work on texts and expand his system of strategies for problem solving.
	An ultimate goal of all teaching during Reading Recovery is for the child to take control and work independently to write and read texts that gradually increase in difficulty. It involves the development of autonomy (Moll, 1988) on the part of the child. Reading Recovery instruction leads to the beginning of a self-extending system (Clay, 2001, 2005a). As children develop this self-extending system, they continue to learn more about reading each time they read, independent of instruction.
Reading and writing connected texts	Because both reading and writing enrich the child's understanding of language, language is both a resource to and a beneficiary of learning to read and write. Furthermore, beginning reading and writing are understood as reciprocal processes (Clay, 2001, 2005a).
	Reading and writing connected texts are at the heart of each Reading Recovery lesson, and the lesson design provides both structure and flexibility to meet the unique needs of each child.
Emphasis on *individual* learners who take different routes to literacy learning	Reading Recovery teachers recognize great differences between children who are having literacy difficulty; therefore, they incorporate differentiated instruction and provide learners with opportunities to develop reading, writing, and oral language in many ways (Clay, 2001). Individualized expert instruction and scaffolding of students' literacy attempts also promote student risk-taking and discovery (Boyle & Peregoy, 1998) and successful reading (Graves & Fitzgerald, 2003; Truscott & Watts-Taffe, 2003). Marie Clay recognized the need to "accommodate diversity" and recognize that children take different paths to literacy learning. (Clay, 1998).
Emphasis on the *prevention* of literacy difficulties	As soon as literacy difficulties are detected, a plan for preventing failure is necessary. Reading Recovery teachers recognize that literacy difficulties arise for many reasons and a preventive intervention must address the various factors that may affect a particular child. Early intervention and prevention of difficulties will have positive outcomes for children and for schools.

- Focus on comprehension
- Explicit communication
- Emphasis on active construction of meaning
- Differentiated reading materials
- Cognitive strategy instruction
  (Truscott & Watts-Taffe, 2003)

In short, successful teaching of ELLs calls for teachers who have a strong theoretical understanding of effective teaching and learning and who provide flexible instruction that is customized to meet each learner's individual academic needs (Kelly et al., 2008).

Success for English Language Learners in Primary Classrooms

Let me first cite the experiences that led me to the suggestions in this section: (a) my Reading Recovery teaching; (b) my experiences working with primary teachers in a large inner-city elementary school with almost 80% of students identified as ELL, speaking 39 different languages (Frey & Kelly, 2002; Kelly, Frey, & Begley, 2003); and (c) my study of the literature on ELLs. These experiences led me to three crucial understandings: the importance of classroom environment, careful observational assessment, and teaching practices that work with ELLs.

My experiences in the inner-city classrooms resulted from a long-term professional development offering that I provided for primary teachers in the school. The professional development sessions drew heavily from Marie Clay's theory of early literacy acquisition as well as the work of others influenced by Clay (i.e., Fountas, Pinnell, etc.). Professional development sessions spanned almost 12 months and topics included

- literacy theory,
- assessment of reading and writing skills to inform instruction,
- selection of appropriate texts for beginning readers,
- guided reading,
- writing development,
- interactive writing,
- using sound-symbol relationships in learning to read and write,
- the role of fluency, and
- organizing for instruction.

In addition to professional development sessions, in-class modeling and coaching were provided for 2 additional years.

In particular, I learned from Kerri, a kindergarten teacher in this inner-city school. Her work with a large number of ELLs provided an opportunity for us to collaborate and learn more about successful teaching and learning for these children. I will share many of her insights in the following sections.

> Successful teaching of ELLs calls for teachers who have a strong theoretical understanding of effective teaching and learning and who provide flexible instruction that is customized to meet each learner's individual academic needs.

Supportive Environments for Learning

All children benefit when they feel safe, secure, and that they 'belong' in the school environment. This is doubly true for children who enter our classrooms speaking a language other than English. Not only are their surroundings new, but ELL children may understand few, if any, of the words they are hearing. By assigning a 'personal buddy' to each newcomer, and if possible one who speaks the child's language, teachers reduce the child's anxiety levels (Peregoy & Boyle, 2005). The buddy helps the child navigate the classroom and the school. Daily routines also help newcomers become assimilated to the new environment. After a few days, they are able to predict reasonably well what will happen next. This gives them some sense of stability and security.

A sense of belonging is further developed in classrooms where teachers pay close attention to structures that make children feel welcome and that promote social interactions among children by assigning children to 'home groups' or by using cooperative learning (Peregoy & Boyle, 2005; Slavin & Chung, 2003). Also, by carefully placing students who speak little or no English toward the middle or front of the classroom, teachers can more closely observe them and the ELLs can easily see everything that is going on around them (Peregoy & Boyle).

Nieto (1996) writes about *mutual accommodation*: "accepting and building on students' language and culture as legitimate expressions of intelligence and as the basis for the academic success" (p. 336). It is important for teachers to learn as much as possible about the language and culture of the students they teach. This allows them to select appropriate materials, make connections for students, and better understand the attempts made by children as they learn to read and write. For example, some phonemes in English are not present in the native languages of the newcomer students, so it may be more difficult for them to learn some sounds, letters, and/or words. When the teacher is aware of differences between languages, she can scaffold the learning situation in supportive ways.

A climate of acceptance for all children, regardless of their background, language level, or reading ability is essential (Cappellini, 2005). In Reading Recovery, teachers notice and praise students' partially right attempts in both reading and writing and they accept children's language, even when it is not "grammatically correct." Classroom teachers can learn to notice, praise, and accept the language and attempts made by their students as well.

High teacher expectations also play a role in student learning. Reading Recovery teachers hold high expectations that their students will learn how to read and write. They teach purposefully and target instruction specifically to each child's strengths. We all know about the detrimental effects of low expectations (Nieto, 1996) and the importance of high expectations for children to learn to speak and read (Cappellini, 2005; MacGillivray, Rueda, & Martinez, 2004). Effective teachers of ELL

> Effective teachers of ELL children hold high expectations for their students and help their students attain high levels of literacy and language.

children hold high expectations for their students and help their students attain high levels of literacy and language.

The learning environment in Kerri's kindergarten classroom

Kerri identified high expectations as one of the most-essential elements of her instructional decision making. Her students come to school from linguistically and culturally diverse, low socioeconomic working class families. She holds high expectations for every child, every day. From the first day of school, Kerri models, teaches, and explains the whys and hows of every aspect of school, from how children should manage their environment to how to develop as thinkers and learners. Routines are developed; Kerri teaches and children practice what is expected, and she reteaches when necessary. Then, she holds children accountable for everything they can do — from getting themselves to school, to acting appropriately in school, to working with others, to achieving to their highest abilities. All of this is done with a warm smile and a soft touch!

Embedded Assessment that Guides Teaching

While there is much emphasis on standardized testing of ELLs, classroom-based assessments (CBAs) embedded in daily routines provide teachers with the ongoing information about students' strengths and needs which are most useful in guiding instruction (Barone & Xu, 2008).

Assessments used in Reading Recovery

Reading Recovery teachers use several assessments to gather information about students' reading, writing, and language behaviors. They observe each child's responses to real tasks of reading and writing.

- Using *An Observation Survey of Early Literacy Achievement* (Clay, 2002, 2006), initial information is collected about the child's concepts about print, letter identification, word identification, words the child can write independently, phonemic awareness, and ability to read leveled texts. Throughout the administration of the tasks, the teacher also pays attention to the child's communication skills and language.

- If the teacher wants to know more about a child's control of syntax, she might use another informal assessment such as the Record of Oral Language (Clay, Gill, Glynn, McNaughton, & Salmon, 1983, 2007) or record her assessment sessions and take notes about the language children use during their interactions with her.

- As she works with students, the Reading Recovery teacher uses daily observation records of lessons and running records to gather day-to-day shifts in students' language, literacy behaviors, and understandings.

Assessment tools used by Reading Recovery teachers can also be used by classroom teachers to gather valuable information about their students.

> Classroom-based assessments embedded in daily routines provide teachers with the ongoing information about students' strengths and needs which are most useful in guiding instruction.

Kelly

Assessment tools used by Reading Recovery teachers can also be used by classroom teachers to gather valuable information about their students.

Additional measures to assess language and literacy supplement these tools and are suggested below.

Assessment of language

Regular classroom activities provide many opportunities for teachers to record children's language development.

Examples:

- Teachers may take notes of language production during "show and tell time," during small-group interactions, or at recess on the playground.
- Teachers may choose to record children telling the story in a wordless picture book (Peregoy & Boyle, 2005). Each child might have an individual tape and across several months, various books could be used. This ongoing collection of recordings provides a record of ELLs' language development over time.

- Informal anecdotal records also may be used to collect various types of information or samples of students' language during any time of the day. For example, if children are working in small groups around a mathematics or science lesson, the teacher can move around the room observing interactions and jotting down language she hears from targeted students.

Peregoy and Boyle (2005, p. 144) provide a structured observational instrument that teachers can use to assess students' oral proficiency: Student Oral Language Observation Matrix (SOLOM) from California State Department of Education. It examines five traits based on teacher observations: comprehension, fluency, vocabulary, pronunciation, and grammar. Four phases of English language proficiency are provided as well:

- Phase I, non-English proficient
- Phases II and III, limited English proficient
- Phase IV, fully English proficient

SOLOM data, if collected periodically, form a developmental picture of oral language progress over time and help teachers make appropriate instructional decisions (Peregoy & Boyle, 2005).

Assessment of literacy acquisition of young children

An Observation Survey of Early Literacy Achievement (Clay, 2002, 2006) is frequently used by kindergarten and first-grade teachers to assess children's literacy development. Initially, kindergarten teachers may administer Letter Identification and Concepts About Print tasks from the survey to each child to determine current understandings or confusions about letters and print concepts, and modify instruction accordingly.

When students are beginning to read, running records can be taken on a regular basis so that teachers can analyze reading behaviors and plan instruction. Near the end of the kindergarten year, Hearing and Recording Sounds in Words may also be used to assess phonemic awareness and emerging sound-symbol correspondences. Kindergarten teachers often record information in a summary format and pass along student profiles so that first-grade teachers have background information and a starting point for further assessments.

First-grade teachers often use the Text Reading measure (running record) along with Writing Vocabulary and Ohio Word List from Clay's Observation Survey or district word lists to assess students' developing literacy skills. Teachers might include all the assessments available in the Observation Survey along with district assessments to inform their instruction if they have children who do not seem to be making progress or children new to the school.

> Running records can be taken on a regular basis so that teachers can analyze reading behaviors and plan instruction.

Kerri's use of classroom-based assessments in kindergarten

Kerri incorporates a variety of assessments into her kindergarten program. A few are shared here.

1. Each ELL in Kerri's room is evaluated at the beginning of the year using the California English Language Development Test (California State Department of Education, 2006). Kerri does not get the results of this state-mandated test immediately, so she uses an informal assessment, Express Placement Assessment for Systematic ELD (Dutro, 2008), to capture language development.

2. From the first day of school, Kerri collects literacy information on every child:

   • Can they write their first name?

   • Can they name letters and do they know letter sounds? Using upper- and lowercase letters on index cards and out of order, she invites her students one at a time to name the letters and tell the sound each makes.

   • What do they know about writing? She invites each child to produce an independent writing sample in a journal. These samples usually consist of a picture or a picture with letter-like marks (see Figure 1) or random letters or attempts at words. Some children with considerable letter knowledge may write letters of the alphabet with their pictures (see Figure 2).

3. In examining student writing samples, Kerri discovers each child's rudimentary understanding about print.

   • She notices which children can write their names independently, which children attempt to write their names, and which children will not even try to write their names.

   • For those who have written their name or made an attempt to write it, she notices if they use upper- and lowercase letters.

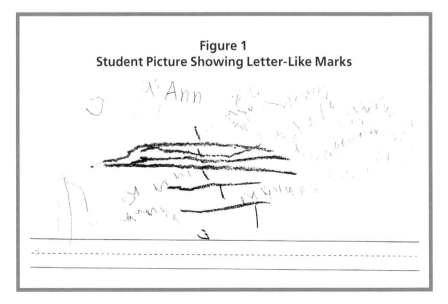

Figure 1
Student Picture Showing Letter-Like Marks

Figure 2
Student Picture with Letters of the Alphabet

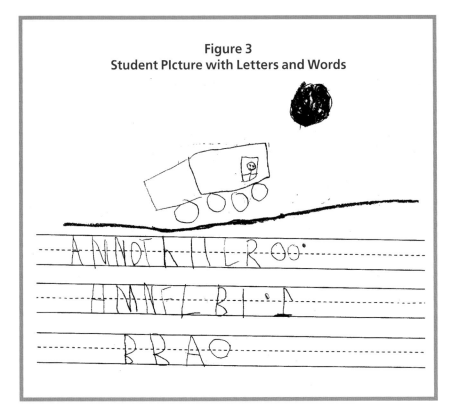

- She also checks to see if they have an understanding of left-to-right directionality and whether they use it consistently in writing.
- Kerri observes the ways in which children form letters.
- She observes each child's use of spacing. At the beginning of the year, most of the kindergarten children in Kerri's school do not actually write words or understand spacing between letters or words; however, some do understand that letters make up words (see Figure 3).

Figure 3
Student Picture with Letters and Words

> Only through close observation of behaviors and how those behaviors change over time can Kerri design her teaching to meet the needs of her learners. Assessment and teaching are linked at all times.

4. By combining evidence from writing samples and letter and sound identification tasks, Kerri has information about each student that informs her decisions about literacy instruction.

5. Kerri keeps track of students' progress through a literacy assessment notebook that she creates with sections for each student that she can easily access during and following instruction. She charts their progress, adds additional assessments, and repeats assessments as necessary throughout the year. In this way she has ongoing information about each student's current understandings.

6. At about the 4-week point, Kerri assesses each child individually using a little book to find out what book handling skills and concepts about print they are beginning to grasp including
   • front and back of book,
   • where to start reading,
   • directionality,
   • one-to-one matching of voice with print, and
   • the difference between a letter and a word.

This assessment informs Kerri about which children are taking on book handling skills and concepts about print through class instruction via shared reading, reading-aloud, and interactive writing. It also helps her to decide which children need extra support to learn these essential reading and writing behaviors.

7. During the second month of school, informal phonemic awareness tasks are administered as appropriate to provide information regarding students' levels of phonemic awareness. These include blending, rhyming, and segmenting tasks.

8. Another major type of ongoing assessment used by Kerri is focused observation of writing. Small groups of students are assembled during independent writing so that Kerri can closely observe what things they can do independently, what things are coming under control, and what things are well beyond their current control. Kerri documents her observations over time and collects student samples which illustrate developing understandings about writing. The results from all of these assessments provide the input Kerri needs to organize or reorganize students into small groups for focused instruction.

9. In November, Kerri integrates guided reading into her daily literacy schedule. At the beginning of a guided reading lesson, Kerri systematically takes a running record of one child reading the new book from the previous day, while the other students in the group are rereading books they read on previous days. Over 2 weeks, she collects a running record on every student. She analyzes the running records to assess students'

literacy behaviors and evidence of strategic processing. If there are some students not making expected progress, she takes extra running records to inform her instruction with those children and she initiates extra instruction.

Using overall accuracy scores and evidence of processing from running records, Kerri monitors each child's group placement. If someone is not able to read texts selected for the group at an instructional reading level (90–95% accuracy) for a couple of days based on running records, she places that child in a group that is reading more-appropriate level books, or if necessary, she provides individualized instruction until the child is ready to work in a group setting again. When students in a group consistently demonstrate that they are able to read books specifically selected for them at an independent reading level (95% and above), Kerri selects new books at a higher level. This very gradual shift to harder texts works well.

10. Kerri continues to use running records to gather information about the reading behaviors and use of strategies by her students. She uses this information to determine where to direct students' attention during instruction. Initially, she may focus on one-to-one matching or using picture cues to help problem solve new words. As students become more accomplished in these areas, she may direct their attention to specific high-frequency words, the first letter of a word, or some other aspect of print. While some groups of children are progressively ready for more-complex texts, others may take longer to master one-to-one matching, learn a few sight words, or incorporate initial letters to help them read.

Because each child brings different understandings to literacy learning, instructional decisions and sequences vary according to the needs of class members. Only through close observation of behaviors and how those behaviors change over time can Kerri design her teaching to meet the needs of her learners. Assessment and teaching are linked at all times.

Literacy Instruction: Guided Reading as an Example

Current research indicates that as ELL children learn to read and write, they develop their oral language proficiency.

Fortunately, the research indicates a bidirectional support for oral language and reading and writing proficiency. As students increase their oral language proficiency they simultaneously increase reading and writing proficiency. Conversely, as they increase their reading and writing proficiency, there is similar increase in oral language proficiency (Barone & Xu, 2008, p. 108).

In basing reading and writing instruction upon a complex model of early literacy, teachers pay attention to much more than letters, sounds,

> As students increase their oral language proficiency they simultaneously increase reading and writing proficiency.

and their relationships to words. The beginning reader will need to learn much about operating on print in both reading and writing. Classroom instruction will include a wide array of opportunities for literacy learning. I advocate an integrated approach to literacy instruction with many opportunities across the day to learn reading, writing, and language. Elements of literacy instruction for young children will include the following:

- Reading interesting books aloud
- Shared reading
- Directed listening-thinking activities
- Guided reading
- Readers' theater
- Independent reading
- Partner reading
- Language experience activities
- Story mapping
- Interactive writing
- Fluency development
- Response to literature
- Independent writing
- Structured writing
- Letter work
- Writing workshop
- Word work
- Spelling activities

> Classroom instruction will include a wide array of opportunities for literacy learning.

Reading Recovery lessons provide demonstrations of scaffolding children's learning during text reading. The remainder of this section examines how guided reading instruction provides the learning environment and supportive teaching that results in positive gains for ELLs in classroom settings.

The term *guided reading* has been described by educators in a variety of ways. My definition coincides with that of Fountas and Pinnell (1996, p. 22), "The teacher works with a small group who have similar reading processes. The teacher selects and introduces new books and supports children reading the whole text to themselves, making teaching points during and after the reading." Guided reading instruction is complex with several factors affecting its successful implementation in the classroom. (See Fountas & Pinnell, 1996, for a complete description of guided reading.) After addressing these factors, I will provide an example from Kerri's classroom.

Grouping students for guided reading

In order to group children appropriately for guided reading, the teacher has to know how to determine each student's instructional reading level and how to observe students as they work on texts. Teachers can use information from running records to place children in small groups according to their current reading levels and processing abilities.

Working with small groups allows teachers to observe reading behaviors closely and assist children as necessary, differentiating instruction according to each child's strengths. Grouping that is tentative and flexible allows teachers to move children who are reading well into more-challenging texts, while those who need more assistance in learning are provided with appropriate texts and additional instruction. According to MacGillivray, Rueda, and Martinez (2004), "Educators need to figure out what children know, and to use those strengths to move them forward" (p. 150). Guided reading provides the forum for the kind of differentiated and responsive instruction that supports language and literacy development of ELLs.

Selecting appropriate texts

Having many sets of texts at various reading levels allows teachers to select the best new book to advance students' reading and language. In kindergarten and first grade, this will mean having sets of books from the very simplest books (e.g., one sentence per page) to print-rich texts that increase gradually in difficulty, providing new opportunities for children to develop problem-solving strategies and use more-complicated meanings and language. This will also mean having both narrative books with interesting stories and expository texts that provide content-rich information. Whenever possible, teachers should select books with which their students identify.

Choosing the right book requires careful consideration by the teacher, especially for the ELLs.

Careful attention to text meaning is also essential.

Choosing the right book requires careful consideration by the teacher, especially for the ELLs. Teachers are often deceived by books that have one or two words (e.g., the ball, the bat, the bases) per page. While these types of books seem to be very simple, they actually may be harder for ELLs. If children do not know the names of the items, they are unable to read the book. In Reading Recovery, we have found that initially using books with natural language and with language patterns that our students can control is especially supportive of ELLs' literacy and language development. "While the child is trying to work out what reading is, and how he should work at it, natural language texts draw on his oral language competencies and allow him to build bridges across more literary texts" (Clay, 1991a, p. 191). Natural language texts have simple sentences rather than phrases or individual words. The language structure helps to scaffold children's reading because it is similar to the language they use or hear (e.g., I am in the truck.).

> Because most teachers are fluent users of English, they often underestimate the impact that text structure has on the processing system of the beginning ELL reader.

Because most teachers are fluent users of English, they often underestimate the impact that text structure has on the processing system of the beginning ELL reader. Therefore, when selecting books for use in guided reading with ELLs, teachers need to carefully evaluate the structure of the text to determine how well it matches the language structures controlled by children in the group and what structures might need rehearsal prior to reading. By reading the books aloud, teachers can hear language that may be too challenging for ELL students or that may need to be rehearsed. Over time, as students gradually acquire more language, teachers will select texts that contain more-diverse structures in order to develop more-complex language among their ELL students.

Careful attention to text meaning is also essential. How many new concepts are introduced? Too many new things may place too many demands on the fragile processing systems of ELLs. Teachers also need to consider how helpful the text itself is in fostering comprehension. Does the book have a story to tell or is it just a series of pages with a repetitive pattern? An advantage of many little books available today is that they represent a variety of cultures and topics, and they have real stories to tell with interesting plots, realistic characters, and events with which children identify. These types of story structures boost young readers' ability to construct meaning while reading (Kelly, 2001). Also, by selecting books with familiar characters and plots that are interesting and replicate real occurrences in children's lives, teachers help children make connections from one book to another and with their own lives.

Providing rich book introductions

One of the most important and least understood aspects of guided reading is the introduction that the teacher provides prior to children's reading. Teachers need to be very familiar with their little books so they can supply appropriate book introductions, thus providing the scaffolding which enables children to read novel texts on their own. According to Clay (1991b), "if we want children to learn to read new texts independently, we can facilitate this by providing a rich introduction to the story instead of reading the whole story to them in advance.... A good introduction makes the new text more accessible to the reader" (pp. 264-265).

Some argue that providing an extensive introduction gives the children "too much." I think differently: Proficient readers are so facile in decoding print and so familiar with English structures that they focus most of their attention on getting the meaning of the text as they read. On the other hand, beginning readers are just learning how to deal with the print. If they know nothing about the meaning and the language of the text, then they are trying to figure out three information sources at the same time:

- visual information, including letters and sounds;
- structure, which may be different from the language they hear and use; and
- meaning at the word, sentence, and story levels.

This puts a great deal of stress on the beginning reader's ability to process information and makes for very slow and often unsuccessful word-by-word reading. With a carefully planned book introduction—which includes helping children understand the meaning of the story, new words and concepts, and the novel structures they will encounter—children can more easily work out the visual information they are seeing often for the first time.

Prior to reading a new book, Reading Recovery teachers engage the child in a discussion about the book and provide a rich story introduction to prepare the child for reading. We have found an adaptation of this practice to be very successful during guided reading with ELLs (Kelly, Frey, & Begley, 2003).

- Teachers introduce the story to be read by giving an overview of the meaning of the story.
- They then engage the children in a conversation about what is happening in the story. Children use the pictures to gain meaning from page to page and they talk about what is happening in the pictures. This conversation provides an excellent forum for language production and development.
- As part of the conversation about the story, teachers introduce new concepts and vocabulary.
- They also have children repeat novel structures which will be encountered in the book.

This front-loading helps ELLs become familiar with new concepts, text meaning, and English structures, and fosters their ability to problem solve as they read new texts. Furthermore, this enhances their ability to read with phrasing and fluency, further increasing comprehension.

> One of the most important and least understood aspects of guided reading is the introduction that the teacher provides prior to children's reading.

Even when ELL children are reading books at higher levels, teachers should continue to provide the kind of introductions and conversations that prepare children for the meaning, language, and visual demands of new texts. It is especially supportive if children hear and repeat key structures that are likely to be new to them (Kelly & Neal, 1998). The first reading of the new book should be successful and not hard. Effective book introductions ensure easy and successful processing.

Scaffolding reading as children read the new book independently

After a guided reading group of early readers has been introduced to the story, they each read the entire book quietly as their teacher listens in on their reading, one at a time. Just as in Reading Recovery lessons, if teacher support is needed for a child to problem solve an unknown word, she is able to prompt the child to use information he is ignoring. Teachers use prompts to support the development of reading behaviors such as self-monitoring, detecting and correcting errors, searching for and using sources of information, and phrased and fluent reading. For example,

- If the child is learning to control early reading behaviors and fails to match voice with print, the teacher might say, "Did you run out of words?"
- To support self-monitoring after a hesitation or a stop, she might say, "What did you notice?" Or, she might draw attention to information not noticed by the child. "Check it. Does it look right and sound right to you?"
- To foster self-correction, she might say, "You're nearly right. Try that again."

Fountas & Pinnell (1996, p. 161)

These types of prompts focus the child's attention on the print and require some additional work on their part. This helps the child to notice something new and to work out the word for himself, empowering further problem solving in the future. The goal is for children to begin to ask themselves these kinds of questions. The teacher gradually reduces her level of support as the child takes on more problem solving on his own (Fountas & Pinnell, 1996).

Prompting the child to figure out new words is much more effective in developing problem-solving strategies than simply telling the child the unknown words. (At times, however, the teacher will provide a new word when she knows that it is unlikely that the child will be able to figure it out, even with prompting.)

> These problem-solving opportunities, surrounded by a backdrop of successful reading, are what enables [*sic*] young readers to build a reading process. It is the quality of assistance given by the teacher that directs the child's attention to efficient, effective ways of learning how to solve problems for themselves. (Fountas & Pinnell, 1996, p. 162)

Prompting the child to figure out new words is much more effective in developing problem-solving strategies than simply telling the child the unknown words.

Teachers provide prompts quickly to the child who is faltering as he reads in order to bolster his ability to figure something out. Scaffolding students' reading is central to successful instruction of ELLs: "You provide enough scaffolding that students will succeed with the reading they are asked to do, but not so much that they do not have to work to achieve that success" (Graves & Fitzgerald, 2003, p.121).

Furthermore, teachers may let some things go (when they do not affect meaning) and come back after the book is finished to draw a student's or the group's attention to something useful for future problem solving.

Encouraging expressive output following the reading

Children also learn from sharing their responses to the text they have just read. Conversations following the reading of the same text provide language support for ELLs. The following quote by Marie Clay is representative of the notion of opportunities for expressive output following the reading of a book.

> The child's encounter with text may be brought to a new level of understanding if he follows the reading with some kind of expressive output — not comprehension questions or workbook exercises but something which calls upon the child to show he understands what was read like recasting some aspect of the story in art, or construction, or acting or re-telling. (Clay, 1991a, p. 335)

Guided reading in Kerri's kindergarten class

In a recent visit to Kerri's kindergarten classroom during week 20 of school, I observed a guided reading lesson. Children who were not in the guided reading group were doing a variety of literacy activities at centers as assigned on a classroom chart. Some children were using computers with programs to reinforce literacy skills such as phonemic awareness, phonics, or sight words; some were reading big books together; some were making words with magnetic letters; others were reading books from their book boxes.

By this time of the year, all children had developed early reading behaviors such as one-to-one matching, directionality, return sweep, etc., and all reading groups were reading little books that contained narrative stories ranging from Level 3 to Level 9. Levels were determined by the kindergarten teachers in this school and were similar to Reading Recovery levels or to the levels assigned by the publisher of many of the books they used, such as Rigby PM and PM Plus. Groups ranged in size from three to six children. Children in the largest group were making very good progress, while the children who needed more support were in groups of three so that more attention could be directed to individual children.

The lesson described below focused on a group of six children who were reading at Level 9, a level indicative of early first-grade performance. Interestingly, the children in this group represented a mixture of lan-

Teachers provide prompts quickly to the child who is faltering as he reads in order to bolster his ability to figure something out. Scaffolding students' reading is central to successful instruction of ELLs.

When a child slows or stops, the teacher provides help so that the child can problem solve the word.

guage proficiencies identified in the fall, reflecting the research results about fall oral English proficiency levels that were described at the beginning of this chapter (Kelly et al., 2008). Fall oral English proficiencies in this group varied: one was 'beginning,' three 'early emergent,' and two 'emergent.' None of these children had been designated as fully proficient in the fall and one had been at the lowest level of proficiency, yet all were successfully reading Level 9 books.

Before beginning the guided reading lesson, Kerri took a running record on one of the students as the others reread familiar books. Children paired up and took their reading boxes to the rug for this activity. When Kerri finished taking the running record, she invited the group back to the U-shaped reading table where she began the guided reading lesson.

Selecting the book
Kerri selected the story, *Bingo Goes to School* (Smith, 2001). This group previously read stories about the dog, Bingo, and his owner, Sam (Samantha), so she knew they would be familiar with the characters in the book.

Introducing the book

Pointing at the cover of the book, Kerri began, "Guess what? Sam wants to bring Bingo to school on Pet Day this Saturday."

She invited the children to look through the pictures and talk about what was happening in the story. The children engaged in an animated conversation about the story based on pictures and their previous experience reading about Bingo. Kerri interjected some of the ideas children would not get from the pictures as well as language she wanted them to hear or repeat.

- "Sam's mom said she could take Bingo to school, so Sam said, 'You will have to be a good dog'."
  (Kerri invited the children to repeat Sam's words so that the language would be familiar to them.)

- Kerri went on, "Now Sam's teaching Bingo how to walk. 'Walk with me, Bingo.'"
  (Again, she invited the children to repeat the language, which had a novel placement of the word *walk*.)

- Kerri continued, "Look at the dogs on page 11. What are they doing?"
  (Children indicated that the dogs were running away.)
  "Yes, they are running away. And, they are being *naughty*. Have you heard that word before?"
  (Children had heard the word and they said that it meant 'being bad.')

- As they looked at the picture of Bingo noticing a cat nearby in a kennel, Kerri said, "Sam's saying, 'Stay with me'."
  (As they looked at the last page showing Bingo with a *Best Dog* ribbon, a child commented, "Bingo got a ribbon for being the best dog.")

Before children began to read the book on their own, Kerri talked with them about what they should do if they got stuck on a word. She, with input from the children, generated several ways to problem solve tricky words, such as thinking about what is happening in the story and listening to their voices to see if what they are saying makes sense.

Supporting the first reading of the book

Each child read the story independently as Kerri watched and listened. When a child slowed or stopped, she provided help so that the child could problem solve the word.

- When one student had trouble with the word *again*, Kerri pointed to the affix *a*, covered the rest of the word with her finger, then she pronounced *a* as she removed her finger. He immediately said *again*.

- When a child said *looked* for *looking*, Kerri said, "You almost got that word. Reread the sentence and check the ending." This resulted in a correction.

> Before children began to read the book on their own, Kerri talked with them about what they should do if they got stuck on a word.

- The new word *saw* provided difficulty for some children. Because they had no way to get to it, Kerri told them the word.
- The word *black* which described the cat was hard for a child. Kerri prompted him to "Check the picture and check the word." This resulted in a correct response.

In addition to the scaffolding Kerri provided, I observed children employing useful strategic moves while reading this new book including

- rereading to help themselves establish meaning and problem solve a new word,
- running their finger under a word to help themselves read it (e.g. *jumped*),
- checking the pictures as they turned the page to help establish meaning, and
- self-correcting words independently.

Supporting after the first reading
As children finished the book, Kerri engaged them in a lively discussion about how Bingo won the ribbon. They noted that he was a much better dog than he had been in an earlier story. Then she took them to the page where some had trouble with the word *saw*. She provided each child with the necessary magnetic letters for constructing the word *saw*. Children then practiced building and saying *saw*.

This guided reading lesson took approximately 15 minutes; however, when working with children who need more support, the lessons may go longer. If necessary, Kerri keeps a child with her after the group has finished in order to reteach something that is still tentative in his early behaviors, to reinforce an emerging strategic behavior, or to foster fluent reading.

The guided reading format in Kerri's class allowed for both literacy and language development. Conversations before the reading provided opportunities for children to construct language and for Kerri to furnish comprehensible input about new concepts (Krashen, 1981) and a framework for the overall meaning of the text upon which children could draw as they negotiated the print. Deliberate attention to language structures allowed children to hear and use novel language so that it was familiar when encountered in print. Teacher prompting and interactions with students during reading enabled children to learn how to problem solve new words. Because of the careful attention to getting children ready for reading and the scaffolding provided during reading, children read the new book successfully, fostering the development of reading skills and positive attitudes about learning to read. Conversations after the reading allowed for further language production by these ELL children and a reinforcement of the idea that reading is a meaning-making endeavor.

> Because of the careful attention to getting children ready for reading and the scaffolding provided during reading, children read the new book successfully, fostering the development of reading skills and positive attitudes about learning to read.

Writing as Integral to Beginning Reading

While this chapter does not specifically describe writing instruction, it is important to note that beginning reading and writing are two sides of the same literacy coin. They should both be taught from the start because each enhances learning in the other and both enhance language learning. Two of the most beneficial instructional practices for ELL children in kindergarten and first grade are *interactive writing* (Button, Johnson, & Furgerson, 1996: McCarrier, Pinnell, & Fountas, 2000) and *independent writing*.

Interactive writing is a collaborative endeavor in which the teacher and children coconstruct a message and share the pen in writing it down. McCarrier, Pinnell, and Fountas (2000) dedicate an entire book to describing this process. Interactive writing introduces children to the writing process and scaffolds their learning.

Independent writing is valuable because it allows children to practice what they are learning about writing by composing and constructing their own messages.

Kerri uses both interactive writing and independent writing to foster literacy and language development in her kindergarten classroom. At the beginning of the year, she and her students cowrite big books and other messages using interactive writing as the vehicle. Each day, children then return to their tables and write independent messages. Later in the year as children become more self-sufficient in their writing, Kerri integrates a writing workshop approach, as well. Here, children talk with friends about what they are going to write, then they write. Conversations are central to both interactive writing and Kerri's writing workshop. Children rehearse what they are going to write, further enhancing language development with writing development.

Discussion

Significant numbers of ELLs are entering primary classrooms every year. While in an ideal setting all children would be taught first to read and write using their primary language, practically speaking this is impossible. Nevertheless, quality instruction can result in successful learning even for children in very early levels of English acquisition. This was evident in the large national Reading Recovery study described at the beginning of this chapter. It was also evident in Kerri's kindergarten classroom, as well as the other primary classrooms in her school (Kelly, Frey, & Begley, 2003).

In this chapter, parallels between Reading Recovery teaching and classroom instruction were drawn. In both settings, teachers need to hold high expectations for their students, adhere to a complex constructivist view of literacy development, scaffold students' learning through skillful interactions, and differentiate instruction based on what their students know. These teachers will make a significant difference in the literacy achievement of children regardless of levels of English language

> While this chapter does not specifically describe writing instruction, it is important to note that beginning reading and writing are two sides of the same literacy coin.

proficiency. With skillful teaching, ELLs are successful in Reading Recovery and in classrooms.

It seems appropriate to close with a quote from Marie Clay, whose literacy work has influenced both classrooms and interventions.

> Children who come to school speaking any language will have a preparation for literacy learning that is to be valued, whatever that prior language is. Research is clear that most children can add a second language at this age with relative ease, and although it does not happen overnight, it does not take them long. We need to see them as competent children who speak and problem-solve well in their first culture and who are lucky to be learning a second language while they are young and active language learners. It is surprising how rapid their progress can be. (Clay, 2005a, p. 6)

With skillful teaching, ELLs are successful in Reading Recovery and in classrooms.

Acknowledgements

The author wishes to thank Kerri Keough and her kindergarten students who always welcomed me into their classroom. I also wish to thank Kerri's colleagues in the kindergarten cohort who invited me into their classrooms many times. I learned so much from observing both how they implemented effective assessment and literacy instruction with their young students and how they worked together as a team to improve literacy instruction in their school.

References

Ashdown, J., & Simic, O. (2000). Is early literacy intervention effective for English language learners? Evidence from Reading Recovery. *Literacy Teaching and Learning: An International Journal of Early Reading and Writing, 5*(1), 27–42.

Barone, D. M., & Xu, S. H. (2008.). *Literacy instruction for English language learners pre-K–2.* New York: Guilford Press.

Boyle, O., & Peregoy, S. (1998). Literacy scaffold strategies for first- and second-language readers and writers. In M. Opitz (Ed.), *Literacy instruction for culturally and linguistically diverse students* (pp. 150–157). Newark, DE: International Reading Association.

Button, K., Johnson, M., & Furgerson, P. (1996). Interactive writing in a primary classroom. *The Reading Teacher, 49*(6), 429–438.

California Department of Education (2006). California English Language Development Test (CELDT). Monterey, CA: CTB/McGraw-Hill.

Cappellini, M. (2005). *Balancing reading and language learning.* Portland, ME: Stenhouse Publishers and Newark, DE: International Reading Association.

Clay, M. M. (1991a). *Becoming literate: The construction of inner control.* Portsmouth, NH: Heinemann.

Clay, M. M. (1991b). Introducing a storybook to young readers. *The Reading Teacher, 45*(4), 264–273.

Clay, M. M. (1998). *By different paths to common outcomes.* York, ME: Stenhouse.

Clay, M. M. (2001). *Change over time in children's literacy development.* Portsmouth, NH: Heinemann.

Clay, M. M. (2002, 2006). *An observation survey of early literacy achievement.* (2nd ed., rev. 2nd ed.). Portsmouth, NH: Heinemann.

Clay, M. M. (2005a). *Literacy lessons designed for individuals part one: Why? when? and how?* Portsmouth, NH: Heinemann.

Clay, M. M. (2005b). *Literacy lessons designed for individuals part two: Teaching procedures.* Portsmouth, NH: Heinemann.

Clay, M. M., & Cazden, C. B. (1990). A Vygotskian interpretation of Reading Recovery. In L. C. Moll (Ed.), *Vygotsky and education* (pp. 206–222). Cambridge, UK: Cambridge University Press.

Clay, M. M., Gill, M., Glynn, T., McNaughton, T., & Salmon, K. (1983). *A record of oral language: Biks and gutches.* (2007, Rev. ed.). Portsmouth, NH: Heinemann.

D'Agostino, J. V., & Murphy, J. A. (2004). A meta-analysis of Reading Recovery in United States schools. *Educational Evaluation and Policy Analysis, 26*(1), 23–38.

Dutro, M. (2008). *A focused approach to systematic ELD instruction* (2nd ed.). San Marcos, CA: E. L. Achieve.

Frey, N., & Kelly, P. R. (2002). The effects of staff development, modeling and coaching of interactive writing on instructional repertoires of K–1 teachers in a professional development school. In D. L. Schallert, C. M Fairbanks, J. Worthy, B. Maloch, & J. V. Hoffman (Eds.), *Fifty-first yearbook of the National Reading Conference* (pp. 176–185). Oak Creek, WI: National Reading Conference.

Fountas, I. C., & Pinnell, G. S. (1996). *Guided reading: Good first teaching.* Portsmouth, NH: Heinemann.

Graves, M. F., & Fitzgerald, J. (2003). Scaffolding reading experiences for multilingual classrooms. In G. Garcia (Ed.), *English learners: Reaching the highest level of English literacy* (pp. 96–122). Newark, DE: International Reading Association.

Hiebert, E. H., & Taylor, B. M. (1994.) *Getting reading right from the start: Effective early literacy interventions.* Boston: Allyn and Bacon.

Hiebert, E. H., & Taylor, B. M. (2000). Beginning reading instruction: Research on early interventions. In M. L. Kamil, P. B. Mosenthal, P. D. Pearson, & R. Barr (Eds.), *Handbook of reading research, volume 3* (pp. 455–482). Mahwah, NJ: Erlbaum.

Hobsbaum, A. (1995). Reading Recovery in England. *Literacy, Teaching and Learning: An International Journal of Early Literacy, 1*(1), 21–39.

Kelly, P. R. (2001). Working with English language learners: The case of Danya. *The Journal of Reading Recovery, 1*(1), 1–11.

Kelly, P. R., Frey, N., & Begley, M. (2003, December). *The effects of ongoing professional development on student achievement in kindergarten.* Paper presented at the 53rd Annual National Reading Conference, Scottsdale, AZ.

Kelly, P. R., Gómez-Bellengé, F. X., Chen, J., & Schulz, M. M. (2008). Learner outcomes for English language learner low readers in an early intervention. *TESOL Quarterly, 42*(2), 135–160.

Kelly, P. R., & Neal, J. C. (1998). Keeping the processing easy at higher levels of text reading. *The Running Record 11*(1), 1–4, 8–10.

Klenk, L., & Kibby, M. W. (2000). Re-mediating reading difficulties: Appraising the past, reconciling the present, constructing the future. In R. Barr, M. L. Kamil, P. B. Mosenthal, & P. D. Pearson (Eds.), *Handbook of reading research volume 3* (pp. 667–690). Mahwey, NJ: Lawrence Erlbaum.

Krashen, S. (1981). Bilingual education and second language acquisition theory. In California State Department of Education, Office of Bilingual Education, *Schooling and language minority students: A theoretical framework* (pp. 51–79). Los Angeles: Evaluation, Dissemination and Assessment Center, California State University, Los Angeles.

MacGillivray, L., Rueda, R., & Martinez, A. M. (2004). Listening to inner-city teachers of English language learners: Differentiating literacy instruction. In F. B. Boyd, & C. H. Brock (Eds.), *Multicultural and multilingual literacy and language* (pp. 144–160). New York: Guilford Press.

McCarrier, A., Pinnell, G. S., & Fountas, I. C. (2000). *Interactive writing: How language and literacy come together, K–2.* Portsmouth, NH: Heinemann.

Moll, L. C. (1988). Some key issues in teaching Latino students. *Language Arts, 65*(5), 465–472.

Neal, J. C., & Kelly, P. R. (1999). The success of Reading Recovery for English language learners and Descubriendo la Lectura for bilingual students in California. *Literacy Teaching and Learning: An International Journal of Early Reading and Writing 4*(2), 81–108.

Nieto, S. (1996.) *Affirming diversity: The sociopolitical context of multicultural education* (2nd ed.). White Plains, NY: Longman.

Peregoy, S. F., & Boyle, O. F. (2005). *Reading, writing and learning in ESL: A resource book for K–12 teachers* (4th ed.). Boston: Pearson Education, Allyn and Bacon.

Pinnell, G. S., Lyons, C. A., DeFord, D. E., Bryk, A., & Seltzer, M. (1994). Comparing instructional models for the literacy instruction of high risk first graders. *Reading Research Quarterly, 29*(1), 8–39.

Schwartz, R. M. (2005). Literacy learning of at-risk first-grade students in the Reading Recovery early intervention. *Journal of Educational Psychology, 97*(2), 275–267.

Shanahan, T., & Barr, R. (1995). A synthesis of research on Reading Recovery. *Reading Research Quarterly, 30*(4), 958–996.

Slavin, R. E., & Cheung, A. (2003.) *Effective reading programs for English language learners: A best-evidence synthesis.* (Report No. 66.) Baltimore, MD: Johns Hopkins University, Center for Research on the Education of Students Placed at Risk.

Truscott, D. M., & Watts-Taffe, S. (2003). English as a second language, literacy development in mainstream classrooms: Application of a model for effective practice. In A. I. Willis, G. E. Garcia, R. B. Barrera, & V. J. Harris (Eds.), *Multicultural issues in literacy research and practice* (pp. 185–202). Mahwah, NJ: Lawrence Erlbaum Associates.

Yerington, L. (2004). Language interactions between Reading Recovery teachers and their English language learners. (Doctoral dissertation, University of San Diego, 2004). *Dissertation Abstracts International, 65/05,* 1635.

Children's Books Cited

Smith, A. (2001). *Bingo goes to school.* Rigby PM Plus.

Increasing numbers of English learners in our classrooms give testament to the burgeoning diversity of our society. This diversity is to be embraced by acknowledging that, as with other children, English learners bring twin strengths with them at the start of their schooling:

1. They have negotiated the world meaningfully for years before getting to us.
2. They have acquired language and learned how to learn language (albeit a different one than the language of instruction they will receive in school).

Clay (1991a) described these two early systems of learning as *self-extending*; that is, each represents a network of competencies that extends itself through application to new challenges. Through the self-extending system of making sense of the world, children develop a cognitive framework that is ever expanding as new experiences are encountered and interpreted. Similarly, through the self-extending system of learning language, children develop a growing mastery over the sounds and symbols of their specific language through interaction with their oral communities. So it is that, when young learners come into the classroom, they possess already two powerful systems of learning to harness the challenges of learning to read and write (Clay, 1991a).

Teaching for Comprehension and Language Development of English Learners: Insights from Reading Recovery

Judith Chibante Neal
California State University, Fresno

When instruction is grounded in a perspective that all learners bring two major sources of strength to new learning tasks, a remarkable thing—*accelerated progress*—can happen for those whose early knowledge and achievement lag behind that of their peers.

When instruction is grounded in a perspective that all learners bring two major sources of strength to new learning tasks, a remarkable thing—*accelerated progress*—can happen for those whose early knowledge and achievement lag behind that of their peers. Only an approach with the goal of accelerating the current rate of learning will enable low achievers to 'catch up' to others in their age cohort. The remarkable occurrence of accelerated progress happens regularly in Reading Recovery, a one-to-one early literacy intervention intended for the most-vulnerable of young readers in Grade 1.

Among the population of children served in the U.S. over the past 24 years, English learners comprise a distinct and ever-increasing subgroup whose progress has been carefully monitored. Others in this volume have cited studies establishing the success of English learners in Reading Recovery. Those studies have documented that, given language-rich interactions in meaningful contexts of reading continuous text and constructing stories, English learners served in Reading Recovery can achieve the same rate of accelerated progress in learning to read and write as their English-only counterparts — and they can achieve at the same levels as well (Ashdown & Simic, 2000; Hobsbaum, 1995; Neal & Kelly, 1999. See Neal, 2001, for a synthesis of research studies).

The purpose of this chapter is to consider specific ways teachers can support English learners in confronting several challenges involved in learning both a new language, and in learning how to read and write. These 'lessons' about what works for English learners come from Reading Recovery on the strength of its proven effectiveness with this subgroup of learners. In this way, Reading Recovery represents a research-based source of instructional exemplars for what works successfully for English learners.

Although Reading Recovery is delivered as one-to-one instruction, key insights can be applied to classroom instruction. Three 'best practices' for early reading and writing classroom instruction are *guided reading*, *interactive writing*, and *reading aloud*. In this chapter, I begin by providing a brief overview of each of these practices as important teaching frameworks for achieving the differentiated instruction of English learners required for their full participation in classroom learning activities. Next, I discuss four common reading challenges for English learners: (a) unknown concepts (b) unfamiliar vocabulary (c) abstract ideas, and (d) restricted access to the structure of English as a source of information for "knowing how it goes." I conclude the chapter with a summary of the teaching implications embedded in the discussion of the four challenge areas for English learners, as well as with closing observations and suggestions.

Differentiating Instruction Through Classroom 'Best Practices'

A trio of proven teaching frameworks for early reading and writing instruction hold special promise for the instruction of English learners. Each practice is grounded in theory that emphasizes learner-centered interactions and active teacher decision making. Using the learning needs of pupils as the starting point for planning and teaching (rather than delivering 'canned' curriculum) is the essence of Reading Recovery. Similarly, the best classroom practices of guided reading, interactive writing, and reading aloud represent frameworks within which the same learner-centered emphases are preserved. These practices include

- the major approach in the field of early literacy for the direct, mediated teaching of reading (guided reading);
- a writing context that capitalizes on the reciprocity between reading and writing (interactive writing); and
- one of the most-potent means by which to develop the language, motivation, interest, and listening comprehension of young readers (reading aloud).

Each of these frameworks has been explicated in numerous books and articles, so I only review each briefly here as instructional contexts within which the teaching suggestions in the discussions that follow may be put into practice.

Guided Reading

As the 'gold standard' for teaching children to read, guided reading (Anderson, Wilkinson, & Mason, 1991; Dymock, 1998; Fountas & Pinnell, 1996; Morrow, 2001) consists of deliberately planned instruction around books that are arranged along a gradient of text difficulty. Teachers mediate the varying and increasing demands of reading increasingly difficult text to assure that children are learning more-complex strategies for success at each next-higher level. They accomplish this through scaffolded interactions with young readers, beginning with a carefully prepared orientation to each new book, prompting and coaching children's reading as they read it for themselves, and following up with specific lessons using the text-just-read (and children's behaviors while reading it) as reference points.

Guided reading enables developing readers to gradually access, problem solve, and master increasingly complex text, thereby fueling their overall reading achievement. Guided reading is carried out with small groups of students with similar learning strengths and levels of reading achievement. (See Kelly, this volume, for an in-depth explanation and discussion of the power and significance of the new book orientation in guided reading lessons.)

Interactive Writing

Interactive writing (Button, Johnson, & Furgerson, 1996; Drucker, 2003; Hall, 2000; McCarrier, Fountas & Pinnell, 1999) represents a dynamic interaction between teacher and children used for myriad purposes in primary classrooms. This coconstruction of written-to-be-read text is the next progression from *language experience* (Stauffer, 1970;

> Using the learning needs of pupils as the starting point for planning and teaching is the essence of Reading Recovery. Similarly, the best classroom practices of guided reading, interactive writing, and reading aloud represent frameworks within which the same learner-centered emphases are preserved.

Tompkins, 2006) toward readers' own writing efforts; it involves support from the teacher in supplying everything needed to write what is not yet controlled by children — either as individuals or as a group. Literally any conceivable writing product is appropriate for interactive writing: original stories, summaries of or other responses to stories read, reports about the classroom events of the day, letters to authors, planning ideas and lists of tasks for trips or parties — these are just a few of the possibilities.

As ideas are composed through negotiated conversation between teacher and children, transcription takes place on large chart paper which provides a common reference point for the process of building up and creating new text; the cocreated text is reread together, perhaps several times, then later is made available in the classroom for children to return to for rereading. In this way, interactive writing deliberately illustrates the connections between language (composing ideas), writing (transcription of ideas), and reading. Interactive writing may be done with the whole class; however, to maximize the involvement of individual children in contributing to the group process, its effectiveness is enhanced when used with smaller groups of learners.

Reading Aloud

A third instructional approach with great promise for English learners is reading aloud (Elley, 1991; Fox, 2001; Snow, 1998), especially when conducted in active and deliberate interaction with learner-listeners

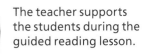

The teacher supports the students during the guided reading lesson.

(Barrentine, 1996; Fisher, Flood, Lapp, & Frey, 2004). Teachers select rich stories to share with children by reading them aloud; children listen and have the opportunity to hear vocabulary and language constructions beyond their own control to lead up to what they will be able to read and understand for themselves one day. In this way, listening comprehension leads reading comprehension, and in the process of building aural input, children

- learn how to focus their attention,
- develop motivation and interest in reading, and
- witness modeling of expression, phrasing, and meaning-making from text by an expert language user.

It is very nearly impossible to overstate the benefits of reading aloud daily in classrooms. Especially for English learners, this practice holds dynamic potential as another rich experience with the language they are learning, in a context of total teacher support.

Four Common Literacy Challenges for English Learners

The three teaching frameworks—guided reading, interactive writing, and reading aloud—are woven into the discussions that follow relative to four major challenges that English learners confront as learners in our classrooms. We now turn to the nature of those challenges in order to understand more about how concepts, vocabulary, abstract ideas, and language structures contribute to learning how to read (and extending the ability to read) by English learners as they expand their system for learning language in their own language to the task of learning English, and learning how to learn in English.

The Challenge of Unknown Concepts

In order to capitalize on a child's self-extending system of meaning-making as a strength for learning, Reading Recovery lessons are *meaning-centered*. Reading Recovery teachers believe in the dignity of children to seek and make sense of any activity in which they are engaged, including learning to read. To believe that young children learning to read and write do not share the common human need to make meaning in each endeavor they undertake is to deny them an essential avenue of cognitive responding at a crucial time in their development. Only adults enamored of a sophisticated analysis of reading mechanics would propose we denigrate children with a code-only early emphasis for their reading instruction.

Meaning-centered instruction is especially relevant and necessary for English learners as they learn how to read. Because the structure of the language of instruction (English) is not available to them as a resource, and they have not yet learned the letters, common words, and sounds of English, meaning becomes the primary resource to draw upon in their early experiences in learning to read in their second language. Consider what you would find useful, given the task of learning Persian (an unusual orthography compared to English). The structure (how it

> Meaning-centered instruction is especially relevant and necessary for English learners as they learn how to read.

sounds) is unfamiliar and letters and words remain mysteries — but if you know the story you are about to read is about a family that survives a devastating flood, you can begin your task of 'reading' with meaning as an overall framework for your first faltering attempts.

To a great extent, the ability to make meaning of text arises directly from an understanding of the concepts represented. English learners who come to us from another culture are likely to encounter many new concepts in what we put before them to read. If I come from Puerto Rico, I don't have a concept of snow—what a snowy day means, that it's a form of precipitation from the sky—nor can I relate to the glorious beauty of a first dusting of snow on pine trees. In contrast, the experience of the indigenous people of the far north includes living in snow of so many different forms and conditions, their language includes 14 distinct words for what we call just *snow*. Even students from other English-speaking countries will have varying levels of interestingly developed concepts. In New Zealand, for example, the concept of a 'waving sheep'—the potentially treacherous outcome for sheep caught in an unseasonal downpour—makes perfect sense as the title of an emergent-level story (Randell, 1995). Yet the term would challenge readers from other English-speaking countries.

Culture also mediates the range of concepts that are expressed in a language. An Asian-American academic colleague remarked that if she really needs her husband to help her around the house, she asks him using English, because Korean doesn't express as well the concept of men acting in equal roles to women.

Because of the central role that conceptual knowledge plays in comprehension for English learners, teachers must become sensitive to and diligent in gauging how the concepts of material to be introduced match children's experiential background. A basic question to ask in selecting a story for guided reading is, "What central concept(s) would children need to have in place in order to understand the ideas which collectively represent its meaning?"

Javier came to school in the earliest stages of learning English. He was virtually silent throughout the administration of the Observation Survey (Clay, 2002), except for saying the letter names for *X* and *O* on Letter Identification and attempting to complete the introduced sentence patterns to 'read' *A Bird Can Fly* (Scott, Foresman and Company, 1979) and *Hats* (Scott, Foresman and Company, 1979). For an early lesson with him in the fall (and close to Halloween), I chose the book, *The Scarecrow* (Bacon, 1988) to introduce — only to discover that the concept of a manmade, big-as-life dummy stuffed with straw and hung on a pole intended to scare crows away from a valuable field crop (a concept known well enough to children who live on farms) was not at all in his realm of experience.

Because I dared not ignore his unfamiliarity with the central concept on which the meaning of the whole story turned, I spent additional time

> A basic question to ask in selecting a story for guided reading is, "What central concept(s) would children need to have in place in order to understand the ideas which collectively represent its meaning?"

in explaining—through words and studying the pictures—the importance of scaring away crows if the farmer wanted his crop to grow, and how a scarecrow helped to do that. (I discovered, too, that the concept of a scarecrow is not a simple one, as it includes hypothetical cause and effect just to explain why one is used on a farm!) After the lesson, as we walked back to Javier's classroom, we passed an open door; there at the front of the room was a crudely made scarecrow propped against a bale of hay that the teacher's husband had donated to her classroom mélange from his farm. Javier looked into the room, grinned a huge smile of recognition, and said, "Oh. . . scarecrow!" He had learned both a new concept and its label (a new vocabulary word) which were immediately accessible to him as new knowledge.

The example of Javier illustrates that texts with unknown concepts can be used with English learners. First, in order to scaffold students' comprehension, the teacher seeks to determine if new concepts are represented in texts she selects for children to read by adopting a self-questioning approach to story selection.

- What central concept(s) would children need to have in place, in order to understand the ideas which collectively represent its meaning?

- Is this a familiar concept for children?

- How central is a thorough understanding of this concept to children's accessing the meaning of the whole story?

And because instruction occurs in real contexts, a next appropriate question would be:

- How much time and energy do I have available for 'front-loading' in order to scaffold learners' understanding of that meaning?

Of necessity, the teacher thinks both about how much is likely to be unknown, and about whether she has the available time and resources to build the necessary background knowledge for full comprehension.

Very possibly, if she has the option to choose from several stories on an appropriate level for children, selecting a story with fewer or no unknown concepts might be the most-prudent choice for the amount of instructional time available while still accomplishing the goals for that lesson. On another day, the time and advance effort to build preknowledge about the new concepts is well worth the up-front investment of time. The hallmark of differentiating instruction effectively for English learners is active teacher decision making in light of students' strengths and needs.

When the teacher determines that a key concept in a text to be read for guided reading is likely to be new to a group of young learners, the chief planning task is how to develop their understanding of it, a

> The hallmark of differentiating instruction effectively for English learners is active teacher decision making in light of students' strengths and needs.

process known as *concept development.* How are new concepts learned? Not surprisingly, much scholarly thought is given to concept development in several bodies of literature, including literacy (Langer, 1967; Nagy, 1988; Nagy & Scott, 2000), educational psychology (Ausubel, 1978; Case, 1993; Guthrie et al., 1998; Tennyson & Park, 1980), and child development (Freeberg & Payne, 1967; Shonkoff & Phillips, 2000).

Developing new concepts for young learners, however, does not need to be esoteric in practice. Think of children who come into your classroom who you immediately realize are concept-rich: What do they have in common? What enables them to bring immediate meaning to stories about camping? going to the zoo? visiting another country? being tucked in bed? getting lost in a crowd? To a great extent, the range and depth of concepts that children bring with them to school is equal to the variety and quality of life experiences they have had (Piaget, 1999; Piaget & Inhelder, 1972; Piattelli-Palmarini, Piaget, & Chomsky, 1980).

> In thinking about developing new concepts, teachers start with the idea of experience: How can I create or stage or simulate an experience as close to the real thing as possible?

Direct experience is what teaches us about basic concepts (*hot* and *cold*, for example) as well as more-complex concepts such as *security*, *acceptance*, and *taking risks.* Experience is the foundational step of the time-proven *language experience approach* (Dixon & Nessel, 1983; Dorr, 2006; Stahl, Dougherty, & McKenna, 2006; Stahl & Miller, 1989; Stauffer, 1970) to beginning reading instruction. Through a group experience (for example, a walk in the park, planting a tree on the playground, baking cookies), children are provided a common and immediate reference point for composing a story that is recorded by the teacher and becomes reading material that children are able to read.

In thinking about developing new concepts, then, teachers start with the idea of experience: How can I create or stage or simulate an experience as close to the real thing as possible? In the real world of busy classrooms, however, real and direct experience to build every new concept children may encounter simply isn't feasible. Yet, understanding the potency of experience as fundamental to concept development helps to create an appreciation for how central experiential learning is for young children in general, and English learners in particular.

Contriving, staging, or otherwise arranging for a real, direct experience may be the most-potent teaching approach for developing a new concept, but other approaches can be used in the service of concept development as well (Dale, 1969; Roe, Stoodt-Hill, & Burns, 2003). Real direct experience along with these other approaches are represented as a commonly accepted continuum of instructional options (Ely & Plomp, 1996; Haines, 2005; Seels, 1997; Weston & Cranton, 1986) that can be used separately or in combination to foster the development of new concepts.

This continuum of concept development approaches is illustrated as a pyramid in Figure 1. If a direct experience isn't feasible or possible, teachers can use simulation, trips, hands-on objects (realia) or exhibits, demonstration and/or modeling, visual images (pictures, video), recordings/audio productions, or verbal symbols (words) to help students learn a new concept. Clara, a 30-year veteran of providing rich reading instruction to the first-grade children in a small rural community, taught the concept of *photosynthesis*—how leaves start out green and later dry up and become brown—through a leaf-gathering outing to the school playground in the fall in order to develop children's conceptual understanding of a complex process in nature. On the continuum of concept-building activities, the school yard outing represented a visit and use of realia to help build children's conceptual knowledge about photosynthesis. (I was observing in Clara's classroom on the day of this science lesson and witnessed firsthand its effectiveness, as first-grade children filed out for lunch talking about what they had learned, using their new word *photosynthesis* with a true sense of empowerment!)

The use of verbal symbols at the tip of the concept pyramid is probably the most-commonly used teaching approach: explaining key ideas of the concept, holding a discussion about it, or talking about the ideas inherent in a concept. In the example of Javier, I used verbal explanation and discussion of the story illustrations to develop the concept of a scarecrow; had I known a real scarecrow was nearby in a classroom, I could have elected to have Javier examine it 'in person' (which also could have served as an excellent language production opportunity for him.)

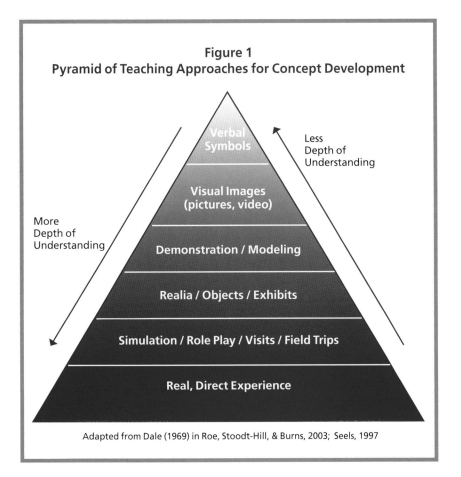

Figure 1
Pyramid of Teaching Approaches for Concept Development

Adapted from Dale (1969) in Roe, Stoodt-Hill, & Burns, 2003; Seels, 1997

For the purpose of my lesson with him that day, though, verbal symbols (explanation) appeared to be effective as indicated by his immediate response when he later saw a scarecrow in the neighboring classroom.

The pyramid continuum serves as a reminder that a variety of approaches are possible for developing new concepts, depending on the importance of the concept in the material to be read and the depth to which students will need to understand it. For Javier, my use of verbal symbols (at the opposite end of the pyramid from real, direct experience) was an appropriate choice, since he needed just a level of understanding to comprehend the story in our lesson for that day. But, given a fundamental concept such as *natural resource*—a thorough understanding of which helps explain a great deal of history and the causes of a great many wars—a combination of realia, an exhibit of precious metals, and a field trip to a mine probably would be both appropriate and feasible in terms of payoff in students' deep level of conceptual understanding.

Attending to the challenge of unknown concepts for English learners means placing comprehension front and center in our teaching. When meaning serves as the anchor for their efforts, English learners are more able to marshal the two self-extending systems: (a) making meaning, and (b) using their ability to learn language as background strengths for learning to read and write in a second language.

The Challenge of Unfamiliar Vocabulary

Although similar to the challenge of unknown concepts, unfamiliar vocabulary does not necessarily mean the concept it denotes is unknown. As highlighted above, conceptual development is greatly influenced by the nature and extent of children's experiences. An English learner may be acquainted with a concept from experience, say going to the mall, but he may not have access to the English word or term (*shopping*) as its label. I was reminded of this when using the little book, *Wake Up, Mom!* (Cowley, 1987). The central concept is about the first meal of the day, *breakfast*: Little Harry wants his breakfast, the pigs want their breakfast, the dogs . . . etc. In selecting the story, I determined that the concept was known, but when I introduced it I discovered that the children did not understand *breakfast* as the oral label for that meal, clearly evident from their quizzical looks when I asked them what they called the first meal of the day.

Unfamiliar vocabulary is a different and less-complex teaching issue than teaching to develop an unknown concept. The task of the teacher of English learners is to distinguish between which new words represent unknown concepts (which is the issue of developing new concepts as discussed above), and which new words are unfamiliar labels for concepts which children already know. To illustrate the difference between identifying central concepts and determining which vocabulary might be unfamiliar, Table 1 provides examples of underlying concepts vs. unknown vocabulary for several popular children's book titles.

> The pyramid continuum serves as a reminder that a variety of approaches are possible for developing new concepts, depending on the importance of the concept in the material to be read and the depth to which students will need to understand it.

Table 1
Concepts and Vocabulary in Selected Trade Book Titles

Title	Level RR	GR	Underlying Concept(s)	Possible Unfamiliar Vocabulary
Cat on the Mat	2	B	a small rug is not a very large space	*mat*, animal names (i.e., *goat*, *elephant*)

Example meaning-centered overview statement: "The cat is sitting on a mat. Then other animals want to sit on it, too. Let's see what the cat does to scare away the other animals."

Title	Level RR	GR	Underlying Concept(s)	Possible Unfamiliar Vocabulary
The Chick and the Duckling	6	D	copying another's actions; learning from our mistakes	*worm*, *swim*, *caught*

Example meaning-centered overview statement: "This story is about a little chick. He wants to do everything the duckling does. Let's see how he gets into some trouble!"

Title	Level RR	GR	Underlying Concept(s)	Possible Unfamiliar Vocabulary
Just Like Daddy	9	F	mimicking a parent; an outing to go fishing	*yawned*, *lake*, *hook*

Example meaning-centered overview statement: "The little bear in this story likes to do everything his father does. One day he goes fishing with his mommy and daddy. Let's see what the little bear does — just like daddy."

Title	Level RR	GR	Underlying Concept(s)	Possible Unfamiliar Vocabulary
We are Best Friends	14	H	losing a best friend; making a new friend	*freckles*, *boring*, *glasses*, *share*, *hatch*

Example meaning-centered overview statement: "Robert's best friend is Peter, but then Peter moves away. Robert is very sad that Peter can't be his best friend any more. Then Robert meets a new kid at school. Let's see if Robert gets a new friend."

Title	Level RR	GR	Underlying Concept(s)	Possible Unfamiliar Vocabulary
Leo the Late Bloomer	16	I	growing up (maturing) more slowly than others	*bloomer*, *sloppy*, *signs*, *patience*, *instead*, *budded*

Example meaning-centered overview statement: "Leo's father was worried because Leo couldn't do a lot of things. But Leo's mother wasn't worried. She said, 'Leo is just a late bloomer.' She thought he was like a flower that blooms after a while. Let's see if Leo bloomed — and how his mother and father could tell."

Title	Level RR	GR	Underlying Concept(s)	Possible Unfamiliar Vocabulary
Sam Who Never Forgets	18	K	being responsible to the needs of others	*zookeeper*, *wagon*, *lovely*, *splendid*, *deliciously*, *bellows*, *golden*, *awfully*, *long-legged*

Example meaning-centered overview statement: "Sam takes care of the animals. He always feeds them on time. One day the elephant thinks Sam has forgotten to feed him. Let's see what happens!"

Title	Level RR	GR	Underlying Concept(s)	Possible Unfamiliar Vocabulary
Happy Birthday Moon	20	L	what an echo is (words or sounds that come back to you)	*chat*, *paddled*, *hiked*, *mountains*, *echoed*, *excited*, *replied*, *moment*, *dumped*, *branches*, *doorstep*, *piggy bank*

Example meaning-centered overview statement: "In this story Bear goes to the mountains to talk to the moon. And guess what? He thinks the moon is talking back to him — but it's only an echo! Let's see what he says to the moon."

RR = Reading Recovery Level; GR = Guided Reading Level

For each title, the table also includes an example of a prepared overview statement centered on the major concept(s) of the story. When written down during the planning process for guided reading, overview statements serve to remind the teacher to start with meaning beginning with her very first words about the story to be read. Directing children's attention immediately to meaning, before going on to other aspects of teaching, keeps the message in front of young learners that reading is always about comprehension of ideas.

Teaching new labels—vocabulary—for known concepts is accomplished in myriad ways. One straightforward method is directing children's attention to story illustrations while labeling the objects, actions, and other details in them. This procedure works easily and effectively into the new book orientation of guided reading, during which you will want to use the same exact words (including verb tense) that students will read in the text. If the teacher or other children in the classroom know the equivalent of the new English word in an English learner's first language, providing it as a reference point creates an immediate link to its meaning (for example, providing the Spanish word *perro* for *dog*). Similar-meaning words in different languages are known as *cognates* and can be a rich source for English vocabulary development when teachers (or others) have some knowledge of children's home languages.

Other vocabulary-building ideas are linking the word to what children know of the background concept, eliciting other children's experience with or use of the word, and using the word in context. In reading aloud, teachers can stop at the unfamiliar word and give or elicit a quick explanation of it — or, alternatively, leave it to children's understanding from the context and return to it later for further discussion (a useful technique for sustaining the flow of meaning with minimal interruptions).

Interactive writing represents a mediated context within which new vocabulary can become the focus of attention and learning. During the joint story-construction of interactive writing, teachers can encourage children to use any new vocabulary that was focused on recently in lessons, for example, asking children, "What's another word we could use for *walk*?" or "What new word did we think about during guided reading today that we could use here?" Because interactive writing results in text that children later will reread several times, English learners continue to benefit from the activity through multiple follow-up opportunities to both hear and see new but increasingly familiar English vocabulary.

The Challenge of Abstract Ideas

Encountering abstract ideas is a third challenge for English learners. When evaluating a story for suitability for English learners, Reading Recovery teachers consider more than if the words are known, as discussed above. In early books especially, meaning is mostly conveyed through the illustrations, since the necessary words to fully explain

> Directing children's attention immediately to meaning, before going on to other aspects of teaching, keeps the message in front of young learners that reading is always about comprehension of ideas.

the story line would be unreadable for beginning readers. So a careful perusal of a text during the selection process includes determining

- the extent to which unknown concepts underlie the actual words to be read,

- which of those words represent unfamiliar vocabulary, and

- to what extent the words refer to abstract ideas.

I use the term *abstract ideas* to mean anytime the meaning of the story is not supported, or is minimally supported, through the illustrations that accompany it. This level of analysis is not about critiquing the adequacy of picture support for the meaning of the story; rather, it involves thinking about how concretely accessible the meaning of the story is through the interplay of words and pictures. In the story, *The Smile* (Cowley, 1987), the underlying concept is about the power of smiling at others (concept analysis). The text follows:

Page 2   Baby gave the smile to Mom.

Page 3   Mom gave the smile to Dad.

Page 4   Dad gave the smile to the gas pump man.

Page 5   The gas pump man gave the smile to the mail carrier.

Page 6   The mail carrier gave the smile to the teacher.

Page 7   The teacher gave the smile to the children.

Page 8   And they kept it all day!

Unfamiliar vocabulary for children in this example may include the terms *gas pump man* and *mail carrier* (vocabulary analysis). Notice, though, the use of *gave* to denote that one person smiled at someone else, which caused that person, in turn, to smile at others. Children may know *gave* as an oral label, but its use in this story is unusual and subtle. Ordinarily, *gave* means handing something over (Mother *gave* the keys to me) which may be directly observed, or perhaps speaking to a group (The principal *gave* us a pep talk*)*. In this example, though, *gave* means the action that occurs when one person smiles, another sees it and so he smiles, and so on; *gave* is used as the sole word that conveys a cumulative cause-and-effect action among story characters by the very subtle interpersonal action of smiling. (Notice that the text could have read, "Baby *smiled* at Mom," etc. — but Joy Cowley didn't write it that way!) To preview a story to be introduced in guided reading with an eye to how directly accessible the ideas are, is to engage in the third level of analysis of considering the nature and extent of abstract ideas embedded within the story.

Words that refer to spatial relationships, the function of most prepositions in English structure, are abstract to the extent that their meaning is illustrated (or not) in pictures. English learners beginning to read can be easily confused by words such as *around, over, behind, under,*

> To preview a story to be introduced in guided reading with an eye to how directly accessible the ideas are, is to consider the nature and extent of abstract ideas embedded within the story.

and *by* which are abstract in that they do not refer to an object that can be pointed at, or an action that can be observed; they literally refer to the relationship of position between characters and objects (and space can't be seen!). The word *over* in *Dan, the Flying Man* (Cowley, 1990) is clearly illustrated in the pictures that show Dan physically flying over a bridge, mountains, flowers, and seas. But in other stories, like *Rosie's Walk* (Hutchins, 1986) and *My Bike* (Martin, 1993) illustrations will need to be carefully examined to 'see' the meanings of words like *through*, *across*, and *past*.

An important point to make here is the need to distinguish between the challenge of abstract ideas for English learners and the major comprehension task that *inferring implied ideas* represents for all children. Teaching how to infer ideas not directly stated is important for all readers starting with their very first book experiences. The inferencing process is at work when children look carefully at illustrations and draw meaning from them to supplement the words of the text (which limitedly convey story meaning). In more-advanced texts, the ability to infer ideas across longer stories and multiple episodes, that is, making intertextual inferences, represents an increasing processing demand for all early readers as they move on to becoming accomplished, fluent readers (see Neal & Kelly, 1998). Helping English learners better interpret and understand abstract ideas may need to go beyond the strong teaching we already do for all learners related to inferential reading demands.

The Challenge of Restricted Access to English Structure

Because English learners do not yet control a working knowledge of English, they have not developed an 'ear' for a range of English language structures to use as a resource in beginning to read. They are unable to anticipate what is likely to come next on the basis of language cues — an important source of information that greatly aids beginning learners who already speak the language they are learning to read. For children to anticipate a certain structure based on familiarity with the unique structural elements of the language they are reading represents a type of *feed-forward mechanism* for the young reader, that is, having a way to "... anticipate the shape of the act yet to occur" (Clay, 1991a, p. 137). They know 'how it goes.'

This is more than understanding or having been exposed to a 'turn of phrase' or to literary constructions such as, "Once upon a time," which children who have been read to easily come to recognize and can anticipate from reading just the first word, "*Once* . . ." Language structure as a source of information means being able to anticipate that the phrase, "Mom is going . . ." is likely to be followed with a preposition, determiner article, and noun (and perhaps a descriptor in front of the noun): ". . . to the store," or alternatively, ". . . to the grocery store."

English learners do not have the benefit of language familiarity as the basis for anticipation. Clay (1982) observed, "... the young child's guesses at points of uncertainty in his reading tend to be dominated by his control over the syntax of his language" (p. 35).

> Helping English learners better interpret and understand abstract ideas may need to go beyond the strong teaching we already do for all learners related to inferential reading demands.

ELL teachers must carefully select books that will be challenging, yet enjoyable, for the students.

The understanding that familiarity with the structures of language greatly influences early successful reading both in terms of increasing word knowledge and developing fluency, is perhaps the single-most important insight for teachers of beginning readers in general, and English learners in particular. Even though English learners have learned a language—the language of their family and culture (the second self-extending system they enter school with)—in our classrooms they are confronted with the task of learning to read in English, and the powerful source of information represented by knowing 'how it goes' is eliminated for them as a resource in their learning-to-read efforts.

Teachers who appreciate language as a dynamic anticipatory source of information for reading ask this question when choosing new texts for guided reading: "What is (are) the kind(s) of English language constructions that characterize(s) the text?" Thinking about the English constructions that English learners will have to navigate as they read puts the teacher on alert for the possible mismatch between what English learners control in their own current use of English structures and the written structures of the text-to-be-read. A general guideline here is that the texts used with English learners who are in the earliest stages of learning English ought to reflect the oral language structures of English that are first learned in verbal interactions with others.

The oral structures of a language represent the first entre into the language by new speakers; these are the structures referred to in language acquisition theory as *basic interpersonal competency skills*, or BICS (Cummins, 1980). In Clay's (1991a) words:

> For the non-reader his own language patterns should be a guide to the type of text he should try to read until the reading process is well-established. Meantime his oral control over language can receive attention so that it develops not from his reading but in book sharing and in conversation. (p. 90)

What this signifies is the need to match, as much as possible, the structures of the texts that English learners read to their current control of English structures in their own language use. In discussing the range of possible early reading texts to use with children, Clay (1991a) refers to *natural language texts* to describe stories that reflect mostly early oral language constructions.

> Natural language texts can be regarded as transitional texts, used when the child is just beginning to relate what he knows about oral language and print to the written texts he is trying to read. While the child is trying to work out what reading is, and how he should work at it, natural language texts draw on his oral language competencies and allow him to build bridges across to more literary text. (p. 191)

Selecting text similar to English learners' early control of English is not a difficult task; consider the first types of language constructions children use in English: "I can. . . ," "I see. . . ," "I am. . . ," "The ___ is/are. . . ," etc. What characterizes children's early language use are simple sentences (many of which are egocentric, as is appropriate to their development) with few words. As language control expands, sentences become longer with prepositional phrases (e.g., "on a log" and "under the stairs"), compound subjects and/or predicates (e.g., "The man and the woman and the child had a picnic"), and eventually evolving to complex constructions with dependent clauses in several different places (e.g., using an introductory clause, "When mother comes home, we'll all help fix dinner.").

In considering texts for guided reading, to think about the type of structure(s) that characterizes a book is to preview it with yet one more lens. Consider the differences in the text structures for these selected early texts, all placed at Reading Recovery Level 4 (/=line breaks, RW=Running Words):

> Texts used with English learners who are in the earliest stages of learning English ought to reflect the oral language structures of English that are first learned in verbal interactions with others.

Example 1: *Mouse* (Cowley, 1983)

    Page 2   Out of the hole,/creep, creep.

    Page 3   Through the grass,/creep, creep.

    Page 4   Up the step,/creep, creep.

    Page 5   Under the door,/creep, creep.

    Page 6   Across the floor,/creep, creep

    Page 7   Into the cupboard,/creep, creep

    Page 8   Up to the cheese,/creep, creep./Nibble, nibble, nibble.
    (RW 40)

Example 2: *I Love Music* (Klein, 1994)

    Page 1   I like to sing.

    Page 2   I like to dance.

    Page 3   I like to/sing and dance.

    Page 4   I like to clap.

    Page 5   I like to tap.

    Page 6   I like to clap and tap.

    Page 7   I like to/sing and dance/and clap and tap.

    Page 8   I love music.
    (RW 41)

Example 3: *Hot Dogs* (Randell, 1996)

    Page 2   "Mom is asleep/and I am hungry,"/said Tom.

                  "Sh-sh-sh!" said Dad.

    Page 4   "The hot dogs are in here,"/said Tom.

    Page 6   "Here are the matches,"/said Tom.

                  "Thank you, Tom," said Dad.

    Page 8   "Look at the fire!"/said Tom.

    Page 10   "Here you are, Tom,"/said Dad. "Here is a hot dog/for you to cook."

    Page 12   "The hot dogs are cooking," said Tom. "I am hungry."

    Page 14   "Here comes Mom,"/said Tom.

                 "Here is a hot dog for you,"/said Dad.

    Page 16   "Thank you," said Mom./"I am hungry, too."
    (RW 84)

In considering texts for guided reading, to think about the type of structure(s) that characterizes a book is to preview it with yet one more lens.

Noticeable differences among the structures of these texts are easily identified once you become accustomed to looking for varying types of constructions. A guiding question for thinking about structurally matching text structures to English learners is, "Which of these texts reflect the language most like the constructions my English learners now control for themselves?" Since a usual progression of learning English doesn't start with using isolated prepositional phrases, Example 1 represents 'tricky' structures for English learners to read. In addition, the literary device of repeating a word (*creep*) for effect (movement, in this case), and the first word of each page beginning with a different and probably unfamiliar word, represent further complications for English learners.

Example 2, on the other hand, reflects the type of oral language constructions that are first learned in English: "I like to. . .". In addition, these high-frequency words, which are commonly learned early, are the first words on each page, enabling beginning readers to gain immediate entre to the print on each page and creating, in effect, a feed-forward mechanism that enables some fluency right from the start.

Interestingly, of the three examples, Example 3 could be the best choice for English learners because it combines oral language structures ("Here you are. . .," "Mom is asleep") with the literary convention of using dialogue tags to identify speakers among the characters. The combination of structures gives readers the ability to use oral constructions as well as learn something new about how dialogue is represented in print. Example 3 also provides for the repetition of names on each page, avoiding having to use pronouns, which would impose yet another reasoning load on early readers.

Providing text, at least in the earliest stages of learning to read, to which English learners can bring a sense of anticipation based upon the naïve structures they themselves control teaches them how to draw upon language as an information source in reading. In essence, this matching of text structure to English learners' current control of English language constructions is enabling them to access text in the same ways as their English-only counterparts.

Some other structural issues to consider when previewing text selections include

- incomplete sentences on a page (as in Example 1, above);
- a one-sentence story that is spread out over 8 or 16 pages of text (for example, *Rosie's Walk* (Hutchins, 1986);
- oral constructions that rely on the language context of the passage for meaning (for example, replies between characters such as, "Me, too" or "Too bad"); and
- literary constructions found predominantly only in written text ("Up in a tree/what do I see?" Cowley, 1986).

> A guiding question for thinking about structurally matching text structures to English learners is, "Which of these texts reflect the language most like the constructions my English learners now control for themselves?"

Any tricky structure issue in new texts for English learners will need to be highlighted during the new book orientation of guided reading. Teachers can use the structure as part of discussing story illustrations, and/or have children rehearse the structure several times. This kind of preparation for reading the story provides for some familiarity with 'what's coming' as an advance scaffold for English learners' efforts to accomplish a successful first reading.

Reading aloud experiences represent an important avenue for language development that will enhance access to English constructions. As English learners listen to stories and other literature (for example, poetry) with more-complex or literary structures beyond their own control of English, they are developing an ear for a greater range of structures and building additional language 'background' for expanding their access to English constructions when reading:

> … When a story is read to children, the shape of the story is created, the characters emerge, and the style of discourse and the literary turn of phrase are "heard." As a consequence, prediction and anticipation become easier at a second hearing. When the language of books is read aloud, this introduces new language forms to the ear making them a little easier to listen to the next time. . . (Clay, 1991b, p. 264)

Reading aloud is an integral aspect of promoting English learners' abilities to access increasingly complex English language structures when reading.

Reading aloud is an integral aspect of promoting English learners' abilities to access increasingly complex English language structures when reading. It needs to be considered an indispensable language arts activity in which to engage English learners on a daily basis.

Summary and Closing Observations

The major theme of this chapter has been teaching from a meaning-based perspective. Everything English language learners, as well as other children, need to learn in order to read and write can be taught through meaning-centered instruction. Reading Recovery teaching is grounded in meaning-making, and more than two decades of research provide evidence that a pedagogical perspective grounded in teaching for comprehension—meaning—is powerful and effective for all subgroups of learners who Reading Recovery serves, including English learners.

A secondary, underlying theme of the chapter is the centrality of teacher decision making in selecting texts and planning how to introduce and use those texts with English learners. Careful selection and planned, advance preparation, including reading new stories carefully for the specific challenges they represent for English learners, is sound pedagogy for creating vital learning opportunities from which they can benefit.

In brief summary, teachers of young English learners who are learning to read and write do well to consider these guidelines:

1. Identify the central concept (or concepts) of material to be introduced and consider to what extent it may be unknown to English learners. To develop new concepts, consider the depth of understanding children need to have for story comprehension. Select concept activities from among many options available on a continuum, keeping in mind that real, direct experience is the most powerful way to create new conceptual understandings.

2. Having identified the underlying concept(s) of a new story, check for specific vocabulary words that will be unfamiliar to English learners, keeping in mind that children may be acquainted with an underlying concept but may not have the English oral label for it or for the words in the story that tell about the concept. Previewing and teaching new vocabulary is a different task than developing new concepts; choose from several informal ways to build the meanings of new words.

3. When analyzing new material, gauge the extent to which ideas are directly accessible or abstract; of particular mischief are stories that are built around references to spatial concepts.

> Everything English language learners, as well as other children, need to learn in order to read and write can be taught through meaning-centered instruction.

4. Consider the types of structures that make up the text as an integral step in previewing and preparing new material to teach. English learners have less access to English structure—less knowledge of language as the basis for anticipating the possible flow of the text—than other young readers. Matching early texts to English learners' own language development enables them to learn how to use language as a source of information and anticipation in reading. Meanwhile, attend to expanding and enlarging their current level of language development through daily reading aloud to provide greater familiarity with English constructions. A background of hearing and responding to more-complex and literary structures will serve as a valuable resource for English learners as they extend their reading achievement to higher levels of text.

Working with English learners with the perspective that they come into our classrooms with two self-extending systems in place—making sense of the world and knowing how to learn language—creates a unique context for teaching not unlike that of Reading Recovery. When we build upon meaning-making and 'languaging,' our teaching of English learners becomes an affirmation of these strengths, even as we seek specific ways to foster greater levels of comprehension and extend their knowledge and use of English in order to better teach them how to read and write in their second language.

> Matching early texts to English learners' own language development enables them to learn how to use language as a source of information and anticipation in reading.

References

Anderson, R. C., Wilkinson, I. A. G., & Mason, J. M. (1991). A microanalysis of the small-group, guided reading lesson: Effects of an emphasis on global story meaning. *Reading Research Quarterly 26*(4), 417–441.

Ashdown, J., & Simic, O. (2000). Is early literacy intervention effective for English language learners? Evidence from Reading Recovery. *Literacy Teaching and Learning: An International Journal of Early Reading and Writing, 5*(1), 27–42.

Ausubel, D. P. (1978). *Educational psychology: A cognitive view* (2nd ed.). New York: Holt Rinehart and Winston.

Barrentine, S. J. (1996). Engaging with reading through interactive read-alouds. *The Reading Teacher, 50*(1), 36–43.

Button, K., Johnson, M. J., & Furgerson, P. (1996). Interactive writing in a primary classroom. *The Reading Teacher, 69*, 446–454.

Case, R. (1993). Theories of learning and theories of development. *Educational Psychologist, 28*(3), 219–233.

Clay, M. M. (1982). *Observing young readers*. Portsmouth, NH: Heinemann.

Clay, M. M. (1991a). *Becoming literate: The construction of inner control*. Portsmouth, NH: Heinemann.

Clay, M. M. (1991b). Introducing a new storybook to young readers. *The Reading Teacher, 45*(4), 264–253.

Clay, M. M. (2002). *An observation survey of early literacy achievement* (2nd ed.). Portsmouth, NH: Heinemann.

Cummins, J. (1980). The cross-lingual dimensions of language proficiency: Implications for bilingual education and the optimal age issue. *TESOL Quarterly, 14*(2), 175–187.

Dale, E. (1969). *Audiovisual methods in teaching.* New York: Holt, Rinehart and Winston, Inc.

Dixon, C. N., & Nessel, D. D. (1983). *Language experience approach to reading (and writing): Language-experience reading for second language learners.* Hayward, CA: Alemany Press.

Dorr, R. E. (2006). Something old is new again: Revisiting language experience. *The Reading Teacher, 60*(2), 138–146.

Drucker, M. J. (2003). What reading teachers should know about ESL learners. *The Reading Teacher, 57*(1), 22–29.

Dymock, S. J. (1998). A comparison study of the effects of text structure training, reading practice, and guided reading on comprehension. *Forty-seventh yearbook of the National Reading Conference* (pp. 90–102*).* Chicago: National Reading Conference.

Ely, D. P., & Plomp, T. (1996). *Classic writings on instructional technology.* Portsmouth, NH: Libraries Unlimited.

Elley, W. (1991). Acquiring literacy in a second language: The effect of book-based programs. *Language Learning, 41*(3), 375–411.

Fisher, D., Flood, J., Lapp, D., & Frey, N. (2004). Interactive read-alouds: Is there a common set of implementation practices? *The Reading Teacher, 58*(1), 8–17.

Fountas, I., & Pinnell, G. S. (1996). *Guided reading: Good first teaching for all children.* Portsmouth, NH: Heinemann.

Fox, M. (2001). *Reading magic: Why reading aloud to our children will change their lives forever.* San Diego, CA: Harcourt, Inc.

Freeberg, N. E., & Payne, D. T. (1967). Parental influence on cognitive development in early childhood: A review. *Child Development, 38*(1), 65–87.

Guthrie, J. T., Meter, P. V., Hancock, G. R., Alao, S., Anderson, E., & McCann, A. (1998). Does concept-oriented reading instruction increase strategy use and conceptual learning from text? *Journal of Educational Psychology, 90*(2), 261–278.

Haines, B. (2005). Cognitive-affective learning bibliography. *Journal of Cognitive Affective Learning, 2*(1), 21–49.

Hall, N. (2000). Interactive writing with young children. *Childhood Education, 76,* 358–364.

Hobsbaum, A. (1995). Reading Recovery in England. *Literacy, Teaching and Learning: An International Journal of Early Literacy, 1*(2), 21–39.

Langer, J. H. (1967). Vocabulary and concept development. *Journal of Reading, 10,* Not available.

McCarrier, A., Fountas, I., & Pinnell, G. S. (1999). *Interactive writing: How language and literacy come together, K–2.* Portsmouth, NH: Heinemann.

Morrow, L. M. (2001). Literacy development in the early years: Helping children read and write. In J. Many (Ed.), *Handbook of instructional practices for literacy teacher-educators*. Hillsdale, NJ: Lawrence Erlbaum Associates.

Nagy, W. E. (1988). *Teaching vocabulary to improve reading comprehension*. Newark, DE: International Reading Association.

Nagy, W. E., & Scott, J. A. (2000). Vocabulary processes. In M. L. Kamil, P. Mosenthal, P. D. Pearson, & R. Barr (Eds.), *Handbook of reading research volume 3* (pp. 269–284). Mahwah NJ: Erlbaum.

Neal, J. C. (2001). What success do English language learners have in Reading Recovery? *The Journal of Reading Recovery, 1*(1), 40–41.

Neal, J. C., & Kelly, P. R. (1998). Keeping the processing easy at higher levels of text reading. *The Running Record, 11*(1), 1–4, 8–10.

Neal, J. C., & Kelly, P. R. (1999). The success of Reading Recovery for English language learners and Descubriendo la Lectura for bilingual students in California. *Literacy Teaching and Learning: An International Journal of Early Reading and Writing, 4*(2), 81–108.

Piaget, J. (1999). *The construction of reality in the child*. New York: Routledge.

Piaget, J., & Inhelder, B. (1972). *The psychology of the child* (H. Weaver, Trans.). New York: Basic Books.

Piattelli-Palmarini, M., Piaget, J., & Chomsky, N. (1980). *Language and learning: The debate between Jean Piaget and Noam Chomsky*. New York: Routledge.

Roe, B. D., Stoodt-Hill, B. D., & Burns, P. C. (2003). *Secondary school literacy instruction: The content areas* (8th ed.). Boston: Houghton Mifflin.

Seels, B. (1997, February). *The relationship of media and ISD theory: The unrealized promise of Dales' cone of experience*. Proceedings of selected research and development presentations at the 1997 National Convention of the Association for Educational Communications and Technology, Albuquerque, NM. (ERIC Document Reproduction Service No. ED409869).

Shonkoff, J. P., & Phillips, D. (2000). *From neurons to neighborhoods: The science of early childhood development*. Washington, DC: National Academy of Sciences, U.S. Department of Education.

Snow, C. E. (1998). *Preventing reading difficulties in young children*. Washington, DC: National Academy of Sciences, U.S. Department of Education.

Stahl, K. A., Dougherty, E., & McKenna, M. C. (2006). *Reading research at work: Foundations of effective practice*. New York: Guilford Press.

Stahl, S. A., & Miller, P. D. (1989). Whole language and language experience approaches for beginning reading: A quantitative research synthesis. *Review of Educational Research, 59*(1), 87–116.

Stauffer, R. G. (1970). *The language-experience approach to the teaching of reading*. New York: Harper & Row Publishers, Inc.

Tennyson, R. D., & Park, O. C. (1980). The teaching of concepts: A review of instructional design research literature. *Review of Educational Research, 50*(1), 55–70.

Tompkins, G. E. (2006). *Literacy for the 21st century: A balanced approach* (4th ed.). Upper Saddle River, NJ: Pearson/Allyn & Bacon.

Weston, C., & Cranton, P. A. (1986). Selecting instructional strategies. *The Journal of Higher Education, 57*(3), 259–288.

Children's Books Cited

Asch, F. (1999). *Happy birthday, moon.* New York: Simon & Schuster.

Asch, F. (1981). *Just like daddy.* New York: Simon & Schuster.

Bacon, R. (1988). *The Scarecrow.* Ill. I. Rowe. Auckland, NZ: Shortland Publications Limited.

Brandenburg, A. (1982). *We are best friends.* New York: Mulberry Books.

Cowley, J. (1986). *Up in a tree.* Ill. V. Biro. Bothell, WA: The Wright Group.

Cowley, J. (1987). *Wake up, mom!* Ill. E. Fuller. Bothell, WA: The Wright Group.

Cowley, J. (1987). *The smile.* Ill. C. Bowes. Auckland, NZ: Learning Media Limited.

Cowley, J. (1990). *Dan the flying man.* Ill. A. Dickinson. Bothell, WA: The Wright Group.

Cowley, J. (1983). *Mouse.* Bothell, WA: The Wright Group.

Hutchins, P. (1986). *Rosie's walk.* New York: Simon & Schuster.

Klein, A. (1994). *I love music.* Ill. M. Taylor. San Diego, CA: Dominie Press, Inc.

Kraus, R. (1971). *Leo the late bloomer.* Ill. J. Aruego. New York: Windmill Books.

Martin, C. (1993). *My bike.* Auckland, NZ: Learning Media Limited.

Randell, B. (1995). *The waving sheep.* Ill. L. McClelland. Petone, NZ: Nelson Price Milburn.

Randell, B. (1996). *Hot dogs.* Ill. E. Papps. Crystal Lake, IL: Rigby.

Rice, E. (1977). *Sam who never forgets.* New York: HarperTrophy.

Scott, Foresman and Company. (1979). *A bird can fly.* Glenview, IL: Author.

Scott, Foresman and Company. (1979). *Hats.* Glenview, IL: Author.

The ability to use a wide variety of assessment tools and practices to understand students' literacy development is a crucial element of teacher professional knowledge in the elementary grades. Equally important is the ability to

> Use assessment information to plan, evaluate, and revise effective instruction that meets the needs of all students, including those at different stages and those from different cultural and linguistic backgrounds. (International Reading Association, 2004, Standard 3.2)

The population of students learning English as a new language in U.S. schools is rising dramatically, affecting all states in the nation. In the 2003–2004 school year, 13.3% of enrolled elementary public school students were classified as limited English proficient (Strizek, Pittsonberger, Riordan, Lyter, & Orlofsky, 2006). As more students bring diverse linguistic backgrounds to the classroom it becomes even more imperative that teachers understand and are prepared to build on the knowledge that students bring with them to literacy learning.

Tailoring Instruction for José and Khamtay: How Literacy Assessments Guide Teaching with English Language Learners

Lori A. Helman
University of Minnesota

109

Teachers throughout the elementary grades are accustomed to using a variety of formal and informal assessments in their classrooms to monitor student progress, identify individuals in need of extra help, and plan lessons that address next steps in students' literacy development. Most classroom teachers, however, have received little training in how to analyze assessments with an eye to what they show about the specific progress of English language learners (ELLs). In fact, "one size does *not* fit all" when it comes to using assessment results to guide instruction. Tailoring instruction with ELLs requires taking a deeper look at the types of errors students make, in addition to noting the numerical score at the top of the assessment page (Rogers & Helman, 2009).

This chapter provides an overview of various language and literacy assessments currently used to inform teachers about the literacy development of their students. After describing literacy development and the use of particular assessments at each stage, I (a) share information that may be gleaned from assessment results when working with ELLs, (b) describe aspects of second language literacy learning that may be uncovered through these common assessments, and (c) share patterns in literacy development that have surfaced from my research with colleagues. The final section of the chapter provides suggestions for using results of literacy assessments to plan instruction with students like José and Khamtay, who are learning to read in English as they simultaneously learn to speak it.

A Developmental Model of Literacy Learning

Learning to read and write is a major accomplishment in the lives of children. The journey begins at a young age as children experience text in the world — hearing it read and making their first attempts to read it on their own. Children see writing used in their world and experiment with creating their own messages. From these initial touchstones in emergent literacy, scholars have noted a fairly predictable series of behaviors that students take on as they develop advanced proficiency (Clay, 1991; Ehri, 1997; Henderson, 1981). In this section, I describe characteristics of students as they progress through developmental levels of literacy acquisition. Although children may take different paths to literacy, a teacher benefits from an overview of changes to watch for along the way. Students' development has major implications for the types of literacy assessments that will be helpful at a given point in time, as well as how teachers plan for the most-effective classroom instruction.

Emergent Literacy

Emergent readers and writers are coupling their learning from the world with their new learning of texts. They are developing an awareness of the form and purpose of print. Students are trying out reading and writing behaviors such as pretending to read a storybook or scribbling a note to an important person (Bear, Helman, Templeton, Invernizzi, & Johnston, 2007). Chue, a Hmong-speaking student in the fall of first grade, would be classified as an emergent literacy learner when he wrote IYAPPI AePPI to tell a story about his family. While his writing

> As more students bring diverse linguistic backgrounds to the classroom it becomes even more imperative that teachers understand and are prepared to build on the knowledge that students bring with them to literacy learning.

consisted of two strings of letters with no sound-symbol correspondence to the story he was telling, he shows that he is learning about the shapes of letters, that letters represent spoken words, and that print moves from left to right.

Important steps through the emergent literacy stage include an ongoing expectation that things will make sense, learning about books, and acquiring concepts about print, alphabet knowledge, phonological awareness, and a beginning bank of known words (Clay, 1991; Ehri, 1997; National Institute of Child Health and Human Development, 2000). Students discover the alphabetic principle — that letters represent the individual phonemes that are part of spoken words. When students put together what they are learning in the emergent stage to read simple and predictable texts, they are practicing one-to-one correspondence or *concept of word* (Morris, Bloodgood, Lomax, & Perney, 2003). Opportunities for learning about and using oral language are vital to students' progress in reading and writing. Typically, emergent learners are students of preschool or kindergarten age, but ELLs with limited formal schooling may be emergent learners at higher grade levels.

Beginning Literacy

Beginning readers use their knowledge of the world, as well as what they know about print (e.g., letter sounds, words they can retrieve automatically) to read simple texts. They use alphabetic as well as other options to make meaning during reading.

Important benchmarks for beginning readers include control over letter-sound correspondences when reading and writing and accumulating a set of about 200 automatically known words. Although beginners read word-by-word in staccato fashion as they are attending closely to print, they become more fluent in their reading—approaching 70 words per minute (Bear & Smith, in press). They are beginning to put the reading process together and use multiple sources of information more effectively and efficiently.

Writing ranges from partial to fully alphabetic; for this reason, they are called *letter name-alphabetic spellers* (Bear et al., 2007). An early letter name-alphabetic speller may write the word *white* as YT, using the name of the letter *y* (wie) to spell out the first sounds heard in the word. Later a student will likely be fully alphabetic — representing each sound heard in a word by a distinct grapheme, such as in the spelling of *train* as TRAN. Beginning readers are still cracking the code of the English writing system, and the more practice they have with texts they can read, the more automatic and fluent they will become. Beginning readers are typically found in kindergarten to early third-grade classrooms, but newcomers to the country may be beginning readers at later grades as well.

Transitional Readers

Transitional readers are able to read longer texts with greater ease; they are now reading early chapter books and writing texts of one or

Tailoring instruction with ELLs requires taking a deeper look at the types of errors students make, in addition to noting the numerical score at the top of the assessment page.

two paragraphs with fluency. Students make great strides in reading fluency during this stage, accelerating from approximately 70 to about 100 words per minute, and come to prefer silent reading (Bear & Smith, in press). Because students are much more automatic and fluent as they read, they have access to a wider range of reading materials. They are no longer focused on the mechanics of the decoding process; rather, since the texts are accessible through students' decoding skills, the limits to proficient reading are set by the vocabulary and conceptual understandings that students bring to the texts.

By around age 8, a child with a firm foundation would be

- tuned to the meanings of texts,
- eager to talk and read and write,
- able to compose and write simple texts, and
- able to read narrative and non-narrative texts.

(Clay, 1991, p. 10)

The child would have learned how to use a range of strategic activities for understanding texts such as

- monitoring and correcting errors in both reading and writing,
- using a reading and writing vocabulary rapidly,
- knowing and using ways of getting to new words in reading and writing from words already known,
- using a variety of cognitive processes to learn more about reading and writing, and
- using equivalent processes in each language if a bilingual child.

(Clay, 1991, pp. 10–11)

While transitional readers' writing may not be totally accurate, it is usually easy to read. In other words, these students are *transitioning* from the alphabetic spellings to more-correct spellings (Gentry, 1982). Transitional readers are typically *within-word pattern spellers*; that is, they make errors relating to the vowel patterns within single-syllable words. They learn to spell more-complex vowel patterns such as the long vowels (e.g., *make* or *sweet*), other vowel patterns (e.g., *chew* or *fight*), and diphthongs (e.g., *shout* or *boil*).

Second grader Sashitorn, a Karen-speaking student, showed that she is learning more-complex vowel patterns even though she does not spell them all correctly when writing this message:

WHEN IT IS TORNADO DRILL EVEYBODY NEAT TO GO TO THE BESTMEST OR DOWN DEEP UNDER THE GROUND

for

When it is tornado drill everybody need to go
to the basement or down deep under the ground.

> Because transitional students are much more automatic and fluent as they read, they have access to a wider range of reading materials.

Sashitorn was able to correctly spell *down, deep,* and *ground,* although she confused *need* (NEAT) and *base* (BEST) in *basement.* Her errors show that she was operating at the within-word pattern level of orthographic development (Bear et al., 2007).

Intermediate and Advanced Readers

Students who have passed the transitional stage of literacy development look much more like adult-level readers. These students use reading in purposeful ways to learn about the world and increase their vocabulary knowledge. Students read with good fluency — about 110 words per minute and up for intermediate readers, and 180 words per minute and up for advanced readers (Bear & Smith, in press).

Intermediate and advanced readers are reading silently in longer texts. They are expanding their horizons to multiple genres of texts and more-complex academic vocabulary; they use writing for numerous and varied purposes. Intermediate and advanced readers are typically in the upper elementary grades and secondary schools. ELL students who have come more recently to English reading instruction may demonstrate these reading and spelling behaviors at a slightly older age (Bear et al., 2007).

Intermediate readers are typically *syllables and affixes spellers.* This means that they are gaining proficiency in spelling multisyllabic words in which consonants need to be doubled or vowels dropped. A typical error for a student at this stage might be ATEND for *attend,* or CARRYS for *carries* (Bear et al., 2007). Advanced readers tend to be *derivational relation spellers;* they are working on examining the spelling-meaning connection that is evident across many Greek and Latin word roots (Templeton, 2004). A typical derivational relations spelling error is OPPISITION for *opposition* (Bear et al., 2007).

Why is Development an Important Factor in Literacy Assessment?

Understanding development is important for several reasons. First, when teachers have a handle on the typical process of development, they are able to understand their students in a more holistic way — an emergent student is likely to exhibit certain reading behaviors, and in turn, related writing behaviors. What students grasp about how words work, their pool of orthographic knowledge, influences both their reading proficiency and writing proficiency at any given point in time. In other words, there is a *synchrony* among reading, writing, and spelling (Bear & Templeton, 2000). When teachers learn what a student understands about how words are spelled, they also get a glimpse into the student's reading skills. Marie Clay (1991, 2001) refers to the *reciprocity* of reading and writing. The two processes support each other and provide indications of the knowledge sources a child uses to read or write. This information is useful in planning appropriate instructional activities in the classroom.

Understanding development is also important because it helps teachers select the most-appropriate types of assessments at various points in stu-

What students grasp about how words work, their pool of orthographic knowledge, influences both their reading proficiency and writing proficiency at any given point in time.

dents' literacy journeys. For example, students who are fully representing the sounds within words do not need to be assessed for phonological awareness — they are already demonstrating that understanding. Students who are struggling to decode high-frequency and phonetically regular words do not need to be assessed for reading fluency; that will be absent at this stage. Instructional time in the classroom is limited; it is important that teachers are able to select the appropriate assessment tools to match each student's developmental needs.

Finally, it is crucial to use the lens of development when evaluating students who may be experiencing some difficulties in their reading development. It is normal for students to be able to read harder text than they can spell, but if there is asynchrony between the reading and spelling behaviors at a given stage of development as outlined above, that may be a sign to evaluate the student's literacy development in greater depth.

Informal Assessments to Measure Literacy Learning

Informal assessments are the ongoing tasks used in the classroom to measure growth, catch students before they fail, and help teachers adjust their instruction. In this section, I outline several common and useful literacy assessments that are frequently used in elementary classrooms (see Table 1). I describe information that teachers can glean from these assessments and discuss special considerations for ELLs. This discus-

---

Table 1
Examples of Assessments to Help Teachers
of English Language Learners

Oral language proficiency assessments
- Standardized
- Classroom observation

Home language proficiency assessments

Writing samples

Qualitative spelling inventories

Systematic observation tasks such as Clay's (2002, 2006) *An Observation Survey of Early Literacy Achievement* that assesses Letter Identification, Word Knowledge, Concepts About Print, Hearing and Recording Sounds in Words, Writing Vocabulary, and Text Reading

Running records of text reading to analyze a child's reading behaviors on connected text and to examine the child's progress over time (see Clay, 2002, 2006, or Johnston, 1997)

Informal comprehension assessments (tasks such as retellings, questioning, discussion, organizers, listening comprehension, etc.)

Informal reading inventories

Word tests

---

sion sets the stage for the rest of the chapter where I explore patterns that have surfaced in observing the literacy development of ELLs, and make suggestions for how teachers can use assessment results to tailor their literacy instruction.

Assessments of Oral Language Proficiency and Home Language Literacy

One of the first things teachers want to know is what language and literacy resources students bring with them to the classroom. Standardized measures of oral language proficiency such as the Language Assessment Scales-Oral (DeAvila & Duncan, 1994) may be administered in your district as part of the registration process for students with a home language other than English. If possible, look at the results of a child's language proficiency assessment and note the kinds of strengths and challenges that each child may have in English.

Whether or not your school has administered a formal language proficiency assessment, take time to observe ELL students in interactions in the classroom. For each student, take notes.

- Does the student use English?
- How often and in what forms?
- Do you notice oral fluency in social interactions?
- How does the student do when more-formal, academic language is called for?

Remember, a student may appear to be fluent in English but have many gaps in the academic language needed at school (Cummins, 2003).

Teachers can learn a lot about their students by collecting a simple writing sample. If students are bilingual, ask them to write what they can in both English and their home language. This will give you a preliminary idea of the literacy background that students bring to the classroom.

If you have access to bilingual personnel, more-formal assessments of home language literacy can be used such as reading with students in texts from their home language, or asking them to write a set of progressively more-difficult words. Knowing which students have home language literacy skills or are biliterate is useful information for tailoring future instruction.

José is a first-grade student who recently arrived from Mexico. When he enrolled in his new classroom, the first thing his teacher did was ask him to draw a picture and write a story. From this simple exercise, the teacher learned that José had a few letter-sound correspondences in Spanish and that he was comfortable talking about his drawing in his home language. While he does not speak at all in English, the teacher knows that if she works with him to develop oral language skills in English, she will be able to transfer some of what he knows of the Spanish alphabet to his English literacy development. In the meantime, she also allows him to write his stories using Spanish.

> One of the first things teachers want to know is what language and literacy resources students bring with them to the classroom.

Assess Developmental Level Using a Qualitative Spelling Inventory

One of the best ways for teachers to quickly understand their students' literacy development is to administer a qualitative spelling inventory (QSI). These informal assessments ask students to write a series of words that include increasingly difficult orthographic features. Depending on the grade level of the student, a range of words is presented with features such as beginning and ending consonant sounds, short vowels, long vowels, other vowel patterns, inflected endings, affixes, and derivational spellings (Bear et al., 2007). When a spelling stage is determined for a student, information about reading can be inferred.

Figure 1 shows a developmental spelling inventory for Khamtay, a Lao-speaking student in January of his second-grade year. Khamtay demonstrates full alphabetic spelling skills in his work; he has chosen a grapheme to represent each sound in words.

Khamtay used the graphemes PH, A, and N to represent the three sounds in *fan;* graphemes S, L, A, and D to represent the four sounds in *sled.* Even though he is not spelling all of the words correctly, he is demonstrating letter name-alphabetic understandings. Knowing this, we can estimate that Khamtay is a beginning reader and predict some of the reading behaviors we might expect to see.

A student's level of spelling development may also be determined by evaluating a piece of unedited writing according to the criteria in a qualitative checklist. Teachers will note if students are using behaviors associated with the emergent, letter name-alphabetic, within-word pattern, syllables and affixes, or derivational relations stage (Bear, Invernizzi, Templeton, & Johnston, 2008).

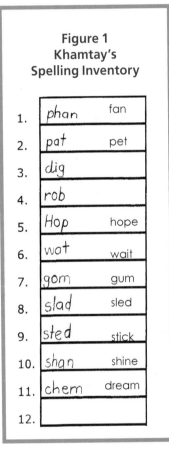

**Figure 1
Khamtay's
Spelling Inventory**

1.	phan	fan
2.	pat	pet
3.	dig	
4.	rob	
5.	Hop	hope
6.	wat	wait
7.	gom	gum
8.	slad	sled
9.	sted	stick
10.	shan	shine
11.	chem	dream
12.		

Select Literacy Assessments that Match a Student's Developmental Level

When teachers have a sense of a child's strengths and challenges, individual assessments of reading and writing will be easier to select. For example, a student like Khamtay, who is using fully alphabetic spelling, may be assessed on the milestones of beginning readers such as reading connected text in leveled books, knowledge of automatic sight words, and letter-sound correspondences (including digraphs and blends). See Table 2 for an overview of the kinds of information that informal literacy assessments can yield at each developmental level.

When a student is unsuccessful on an assessment at a particular level, teachers should take a step back. Try to determine where the student is finding success instead of assessing the student at a frustration level. If you notice an asynchrony, that is, a student's spelling and reading behaviors seem to be radically different than those outlined on the chart and in this chapter, that may be a sign that further child study may be in order.

Table 2
Examples of Useful Literacy Information by Developmental Level

Development		What to Assess
Reading	**Spelling**	
Emergent	Emergent Assess with a writing sample to see if students are using scribbles, letter-like figures, or letters. Assess directionality. If letters are used to represent words, are students using alphabetic strategies?	• Concepts About Print • Letter recognition • Letter-sound knowledge • Phonological awareness (rhyming, beginning sounds, blending) • Phonemic awareness (segmentation of sounds) • Concept of word (Can students finger point to the printed words in an easy text in a one-to-one manner?)
Beginning	Letter-Name Alphabetic Assess for the use of beginning consonants, ending consonants, and representation of vowel sounds using letter name strategies.	• Letter-sound knowledge • Phonemic awareness (segmentation of sounds) • Automatic sight words • Accuracy, comprehension, reading behaviors used, and beginning phrasing while reading leveled books
Transitional	Within-Word Pattern Assess for the use of long vowel markers such as silent e and vowel teams; assess how students represent more-complex "other vowel patterns."	• Accuracy, comprehension, reading behaviors used, and fluency in connected texts
Intermediate	Syllables and Affixes Assess the use of inflectional endings such as –ed and –ing; and the spelling of the junctures in words. (e.g., hopping/hoping)	• Accuracy, comprehension, and fluency in reading multiple genres and textual materials
Advanced	Derivational Relations Assess the spelling of multisyllabic words, the unaccented schwa sound in words, and words that are related derivationally to more-common words. (e.g., recite/recitation)	• Comprehension of multiple genres of textual materials

Assess Vocabulary and Language Structures to Support Comprehension

It is not enough to know that students are learning the isolated pieces of reading and writing. Teachers need to observe how children read and write connected text: Are they focusing on the meaning of the text while using visual information from the print, vocabulary, and language structures? Do they have a repertoire of ways to problem solve new words? Teachers need to be confident that students can understand what they read as well as decode it.

When students are reading at the late beginning- to early transitional-level, the texts they read can become the source of discussions and comprehension activities in class. But emergent and early beginning reading materials use a limited number of words and often represent very simple concepts. How then might teachers assess students' understanding of the texts they read? Consider these suggestions:

1. Administer and analyze a running record of text reading (Clay, 2002, 2006). You can learn from the child's errors and self-corrections if he is reading for meaning, using language structures, attending to the print, and learning ways to figure out new words. You will also get information about the pacing, phrasing, and fluency of the oral reading.

2. Use the same types of comprehension assessments you use with more-advanced readers (e.g., comprehension questions, retellings, discussions, graphic organizers) with material that has been read aloud to novice readers. In this way, the teacher is assessing listening comprehension in the same ways that reading comprehension will later be assessed. This strategy serves two very useful purposes: First, teachers learn whether the material they are using with students is making sense. Second, students are guided to see comprehension as an essential goal of the reading process.

3. Informal assessments of students' vocabulary and syntactical knowledge in English provide important information to help teachers create instruction that is comprehensible and builds on what students know. Consider taking informal notes as students participate in small-group activities. These anecdotal records will provide an in-depth look into the vocabulary strengths and gaps of the students in your class in relation to the language they need to know to succeed (Garcia & DeNicolo, in press).

Patterns in Literacy Development with English Language Learners

From the discussion up to this point, it is clear that much can be learned from using informal literacy assessments with ELLs. In this section, I share some of the patterns that have surfaced in my collegial work with fellow researchers as we have evaluated informal assessments of develop-

> Teachers need to be confident that students can understand what they read as well as decode it.

mental spelling and reading with ELLs across the elementary grades. In our studies, we have noted the following:

1. There is an interaction between the student's home language and English in reading and spelling behaviors. The sound system of a student's home language may influence the ease or difficulty of distinguishing particular sounds and representing them in writing. For example, Spanish-speaking students often confuse the spelling of the /sh/ sound, because that sound does not exist in Spanish (Helman, 2004a). Similarly, when students' home languages do not have certain grammatical properties such as inflected endings, students will often read the text and skip these endings (e.g., reads "the puppy tail" for *the puppy's tail*, or "camp" for *camped*).

2. ELLs may substitute whole words for unknown words in their spelling and reading. This is probably because the student is attempting to make the task meaningful by inserting a similar-sounding word into the literacy task based on his or her background knowledge, such as when a student substituted BORDER for *broadcast* (Helman & Bear, 2007).

3. ELLs often do more sounding out in their spelling. For example, Spanish speakers are much likely than native English speakers to represent two sounds in a diphthong such as the vowel sound in the word *blade* (ay-ee). Spanish speakers at the letter name-alphabetic level more frequently represent two sounds for the long a diphthong, as in BLEID or BLEYD.

4. ELLs show evidence of progressing through the same set of developmental stages as native English speakers, but this development often takes longer (Helman & Bear, 2007). For example, in a statewide literacy initiative in Nevada for "at-risk" schools, 27.9% of Spanish-speaking students were performing at a beginning reading level as compared to 6.6% of native English speakers in the spring of third grade (Helman, 2004b).

5. ELLs may be able to decode and read fluently but still lack comprehension of what is being read. As has been noted by other researchers (e.g., Garcia, 2000), we have seen that simply being able to decode text at a reasonable oral reading rate does not ensure that students are able to comprehend what they are reading. The assumption that fluent oral reading is equivalent to comprehension does not hold up in our work. We found that fluency and comprehension did not significantly correlate for ELLs in a sample of second-through fifth-grade students (McIntyre, 2006).

> ELLs may be able to decode and read fluently but still lack comprehension of what is being read.

Informal literacy assessments provide important information about children that may be used to guide instruction with ELL students. In the next section, I share ideas about using what you learn from informal literacy assessments to tailor your instruction to meet the needs of students like José and Khamtay.

Using Assessment Results to Guide Instruction

As is evident throughout this chapter, students' literacy development is a crucial source of information for tailoring instruction. After evaluating where students are in their literacy development, teachers can form leveled groups of proximal students to work with them at their instructional level in reading and word study (Bear et al., 2008). Many of the literacy assessments described in this chapter will also help teachers use assessment data to identify and meet students' individual literacy needs.

In addition to assessment data, other considerations must be taken into account for ELLs. The following suggestions build on the patterns of literacy development for ELLs that were outlined above:

- Because there is a connection between what students know in their home languages and how they interpret the English

Teachers use students' writing samples
to assess individual needs and plan instruction.

writing system, teachers will find it helpful to learn about the background languages of the major linguistic groups in their classrooms. When teachers understand something of the sound and grammar systems of their students' languages, they are more likely to recognize the logic of reading and writing miscues in students' work. A helpful resource is *Learner English* (Swan & Smith, 2001), a book that provides an overview of major world languages and how their sounds, syntax, and morphology compare with English. Although teachers in classrooms with dozens of languages will not be able to study each one, beginning with one of the most-common languages in the class will be a good start and will likely teach you about more than just that one language.

- As you learn more about your students' languages, build in opportunities for practicing the sounds, words, grammatical structures, and other elements of English that are very different from students' home languages.

- Teachers who assess their students' home literacy are in a position to use that information to modify instruction for those who already have literacy in a home language. Students' progress can be accelerated by showing them similarities between literacy skills in English and their home language. Invite community members who speak students' languages to share with students their insights for transferring skills from the home language to English.

- Remind students that reading and writing are meaning-making processes, and ensure that no literacy activity is ever done without attention to understanding the message. Even word study activities should provide opportunities for students to use the words in meaningful conversations, ask questions about their meanings, and so on. If students come to believe that skills presented in their reading and writing instruction in class do not relate to making sense of text, they will not gain language and comprehension benefits from the activities.

- Because students learning English may take longer to progress through the continuum of literacy learning, it is important that teachers at the upper-grade levels understand the process of reading development. Upper-grade teachers may find more students in their classrooms who are reading and spelling at lower developmental levels. Teachers might look to professional development opportunities such as courses, study groups, or professional learning communities to discuss their concerns. Upper-grade teachers might seek to consult with colleagues from the lower grades who have more-extensive experiences working with developing readers.

- Because English learners can sometimes learn to decode text with adequate oral fluency rates and still not understand the meaning of what is being read, it is important for teach-

It is important for teachers at all developmental levels to provide rich instruction that encourages language and concept development.

ers at all developmental levels to provide rich instruction that encourages language and concept development. Effective teachers frequently check for student understanding of the reading material and use effective second language instruction teaching methods to communicate information and learn vocabulary (c.f., Echevarria, Vogt, & Short, 2008). ELLs need to know that they are expected to understand the texts they engage with and to self-monitor their own comprehension. There are many things that teachers can do to structure opportunities for students to discuss, apply, analyze, question, and personalize what they are reading and writing in social interactions every day in the classroom.

> When these tools are used along with good observational skills and a quest to understand the background languages and literacy strengths of students, teacher professional knowledge grows exponentially.

This chapter began with the aspiration, stated in the standards of the International Reading Association, that all teachers are prepared to use assessments to tailor instruction for students of diverse linguistic backgrounds and developmental levels. Teachers have much to learn from informal literacy assessments. When these tools are used along with good observational skills and a quest to understand the background languages and literacy strengths of students, teacher professional knowledge grows exponentially. Many more students like José and Khamtay are heading into our classrooms in the years to come. They have much to teach us about literacy development and effective instruction if we are ready to take the time to explore what they can do.

References

Bear, D. R., Helman, L., Templeton, S., Invernizzi, M., & Johnston, F. (2007). *Words their way with English learners: Word study for phonics, vocabulary, and spelling instruction.* Upper Saddle River, NJ: Pearson/Merrill Prentice Hall.

Bear, D. R., Invernizzi, M., Templeton, S., & Johnston, F. (2008). *Words their way: Word study for phonics, vocabulary, and spelling instruction,* (4th ed). Upper Saddle River, NJ: Prentice Hall.

Bear, D. R., & Smith, R. (in press). The literacy development of English learners: What do we know about each student's literacy development? In L. Helman (Ed.), *Literacy development with English learners: Research-based instruction in grades K–6.* New York: Guilford Press.

Bear, D. R., & Templeton, S. (2000). Matching development and instruction. In N. Padak & T. Rasinski, et al. (Eds.), *Distinguished educators on reading: Contributions that have shaped effective literacy instruction* (pp. 334–376). Newark, DE: International Reading Association.

Clay, M. M. (1991). *Becoming literate: The construction of inner control.* Portsmouth, NH: Heinemann.

Clay, M. M. (2001). *Change over time in children's literacy development.* Portsmouth, NH: Heinemann.

Clay, M. M. (2002, 2006). *An observation survey of early literacy achievement.* (2nd ed., rev. 2nd ed.). Portsmouth, NH: Heinemann.

Cummins, J. (2003). Reading and the bilingual student: Fact and friction. In G. G. García (Ed.), *English learners: Reaching the highest level of English literacy* (pp. 2–33). Newark, DE: International Reading Association.

De Avila, E. A., & Duncan, S. E. (1994). *Language assessment scales.* Monterey, CA: CTB Macmillan/McGraw-Hill.

Echevarria, J., Vogt, M. E., & Short, D. (2008). *Making content comprehensible for English learners: The SIOP model* (3rd ed.). Boston: Allyn & Bacon.

Ehri, L. C. (1997). Learning to read and learning to spell are one and the same, almost. In C. A. Perfetti, L. Rieben, & M. Fayol (Eds.), *Learning to spell: Research, theory, and practice across languages* (pp. 237–269). Mahwah, NJ: Lawrence Erlbaum Associates.

Garcia, G. E. (2000). Bilingual children's reading. In M. L. Kamil, P. B. Mosenthal, P. D. Pearson, & R. Barr (Eds.), *Handbook of reading research, volume 3* (pp. 813–834). Mahwah, NJ: Lawrence Erlbaum.

Garcia, G. E., & DeNicolo, C. P. (in press). Making informed decisions about the language and literacy assessment of English language learners. In L. Helman (Ed.), *Literacy development with English learners: Research-based instruction in grades K–6.* New York: Guilford Press.

Gentry, J. R. (1982). An analysis of developmental spelling in GNYS AT WRK. *The Reading Teacher, 36*(2), 192–200.

Helman, L. (2004a). Building on the sound system of Spanish: Insights from the alphabetic spellings of English language learners. *The Reading Teacher, 57*(5), 452–460.

Helman, L. (2004b). Spanish-speaking students' development as beginning readers in English: Results from a statewide assessment of early literacy. Unpublished doctoral dissertation, University of Nevada, Reno.

Helman, L. A., & Bear, D. R. (2007). Does an established model of orthographic development hold true for English learners? In D. W. Rowe, R. Jimenez, D. L. Compton, D. K.Dickinson, Y. Kim, K. M. Leander, & V. J. Risko (Eds.), *Fifty-sixth yearbook of the National Reading Conference* (pp. 266–280). Chicago: National Reading Conference.

Henderson, E. H. (1981). *Learning to read and spell: The child's knowledge of words.* DeKalb, IL: Northern Illinois Press.

International Reading Association (2004). *Standards for reading professionals.* Newark, DE: International Reading Association Professional Standards and Ethics Committee.

Johnston, P. H. (1997). *Knowing literacy: Constructive literacy assessment.* York, ME: Stenhouse.

McIntyre, A. (2006). *The fluency-comprehension relationship for English language learner students.* Unpublished master's thesis, University of Minnesota, Twin Cities.

Morris, D., Bloodgood, J. W., Lomax, R. G., & Perney, J. (2003). Developmental steps in learning to read: A longitudinal study in kindergarten and first grade. *Reading Research Quarterly, 38*(3), 302–328.

National Institute of Child Health and Human Development. (2000). *Report of the National Reading Panel. Teaching children to read: An evidence-based assessment of the scientific research literature on reading and its implications for reading instruction: Reports of the subgroups* (NIH Publication No. 00-4754). Washington, DC: U.S. Government Printing Office.

Rogers, C., & Helman, L. (2009). One size does not fit all: How assessment guides instruction in word study with English learners. *New England Reading Association Journal (NERAJ), 44*(2), 17–22.

Strizek, G. A., Pittsonberger, J. L., Riordan, K. E., Lyter, D. M., & Orlofsky, G. F. (2006). *Characteristics of schools, districts, teachers, principals, and school libraries in the United States: 2003–04 schools and staffing survey I* (NCES 2006-313 Revised). U.S. Department of Education, National Center for Education Statistics. Washington, DC: U.S. Government Printing Office.

Swan, M., & Smith, B. (2001). *Learner English.* New York: Cambridge University Press.

Templeton, S. (2004). The vocabulary-spelling connection: Orthographic development and morphological knowledge at the intermediate grades and beyond. In J. F. Baumann & E. J. Kame'enui (Eds.), *Vocabulary instruction: Research to practice* (pp. 118–138). New York: Guilford Press.

How does the quality of thought change with a refined, deepened vocabulary?

How does self-perception change?

How is *language* a part of thinking?

Teaching Essential Vocabulary to English Language Learners

Susan O'Leary

Madison (Wisconsin) Metropolitan School District

Imagine a favorite English language learner (ELL) student of yours, some years from now in middle school. How well do you think that student knows content area vocabulary? Stop for a moment and consider: Without that vocabulary, or strategies for learning it, how likely is that student to engage in science? In history? In math? Do you think this lack of engagement might lead this student, or other students of yours, to start skipping class? Skipping school? Without essential vocabulary, students can't think the essential thoughts. Who are they in school then?

The work in this chapter draws on the years I taught, both as an English as a second language (ESL) teacher and literacy coach, at Lincoln Elementary School in Madison, Wisconsin.[1] The questions above are some that we kept coming back to as we intentionally focused on teaching content area vocabulary in classes where almost half of the students were learning in a second language. Some of these students came from Africa, Mexico, and South America. Others had grown up in the United States in families that spoke Spanish, Hmong, or Cambodian.

Lincoln teachers, like many teachers in the last decade, were profoundly affected by the ideas in *Mosaic of Thought* (Keene & Zimmermann, 1997), *Non-Fiction Matters* (Harvey, 1998), and *Strategies that Work* (Harvey & Goudvis, 2000). But at the same time as we were purposefully teaching comprehension strategies in literacy lessons, our students continued to be stymied by key understandings in the content areas. Fifth-grade teachers were frustrated that students still confused city and state, or state and country. Students studied bones and water in Full Option Science System[2] (FOSS) science units and did wonderful hands-on experiments, but by the end of a unit had not understood the key principles they had studied. We worked with the comprehension strategies in the content areas. But we soon found that students couldn't apply them well because they simply didn't have the words they needed in order to think about what they were studying.

We turned our attention to conscious, specific teaching of essential vocabulary. Margaret Mooney helped to guide our first explorations of what it would mean to have a whole-school focus for teaching vocabulary.[3] A year into our work, teachers formed a study group around *Bringing Words to Life* (Beck, McKeown, & Kucan, 2002), and then *Teaching with the Brain in Mind* (Jensen, 1998). ESL teachers brought to the conversation the understanding of Cummins' Basic Interpersonal Communicative Skill (BICS) and Cognitive Academic Linguistic Proficiency (CALP). As our students began to acquire essential vocabulary, we brought Margaret Mooney's (2001) work on *who, what, when, where, why,* and *how* questions together with Don and Jenny Kilgallon's (2000) sentence composing, in order to support especially our ELLs in writing at the level they were thinking. Marie Clay's abundant respect for every child's learning and Thich Nhat Hanh's (2004) explanation of deep listening held the heart of our continuing work. As a result of this sustained collaborative focus by teachers, learning, reflection, and involved exploration of unknown topics opened up for our students.

Understandings from Brain Research and Linguistics that Shaped Our Teaching

Attention to Brain Research

Three aspects of brain research guided our work:

1. Emotional connection and a sense of safety increase the ability to learn.

2. Learning and understanding take place through multiple, simultaneous processes.

3. Learning is a constructive process.

Emotional connection and a sense of safety increase the ability to learn

Vocabulary study that draws children in, that is done in a community and encourages curiosity, is much more likely to be remembered and later used than learning that is assigned, individual, and rote. When

> At the same time as we were purposefully teaching comprehension strategies in literacy lessons, our students continued to be stymied by key understandings in the content areas.

students are asked to become curious about words, their relation to both words and learning changes. When it is understood that wrong guesses will be a part of learning—and that the practice of guessing is a good thing—children become willing both to think more and to know more about words. A sense of safety enhances learning and deepens thought.

Learning and understanding take place through multiple, simultaneous processes

We don't just learn in one way. We access and simultaneously use multiple memory pathways in the brain. Understanding is created in part through pathways connected to the senses and emotions. There are also discrete neural pathways for episodic information (related to events, circumstances, and locations); semantic information (having to do with words, symbols, and abstractions); procedural information (learning physical skills); and reflexive information like conditioned responses (Jensen, 1998). Designing vocabulary instruction that accesses multiple ways of learning increases the likelihood that students will understand and remember. It engages more than one memory system and thus uses and connects more of the brain.

Learning is a constructive process

"When children learn a concept, they are able to self-organize and independently generalize the learned concept to another context or situation" (Lyons, 2004, p. 6). Content area instruction that begins with students as a class coming up with their own oral definitions of essential words creates the conditions for students to then work with this vocabulary and make it their own. When students apply these definitions in experiments, discussions, and in reading and writing, they increasingly solidify and deepen their thought. Through repeated engagement, they create their own learning.

Attention to Linguistic Elements

Our teaching of vocabulary relied on these three linguistic elements:

1. Certain word knowledge is essential to content area learning and thought.
2. Word knowledge takes place along a continuum.
3. Knowledge of linguistic categories helps in investigating words at a strategy level.

Certain word knowledge is essential to content area learning and thought

Meaning holds thought. And an understanding of certain core vocabulary is essential to engaged content area learning. When a class of first graders (over days and weeks) thinks about, defines, and discusses the direction *north,* they develop tools for talking about and reflecting on cultural, geographic, and topical subjects. When as a class fifth graders define and then deepen their understanding of what *government* is, the students can think differently and ask different questions about

> Designing vocabulary instruction that accesses multiple ways of learning increases the likelihood that students will understand and remember.

democracy. The ELLs in this class, having the opportunity to repeatedly return to and become flexible with a few essential words, gain the opportunity to think about and explore abstract concepts.

In our work with students, we learned what is seemingly counter-intuitive. When we taught only a few words in depth—rather than introducing and defining many words—our students gained a much deeper grasp of content. (They also incidentally learned many more words than when we had tried to *teach* more words.) Because we came back to these few words often in discussion, experiment, drawing, note taking, and written reflection, students became fluent in and conscious of their use of these few words. It seemed that the students' fluency with these words became the context that facilitated learning and remembering secondary words that connected to them.

Word knowledge takes place along a continuum

Word knowledge is a range of knowledge. It is relational, qualitative, and quantitative (Beck, McKeown, & Kucan, 2002). You don't just know or not know a word, and this understanding—that word knowledge is not binary—becomes a condition of learning for many ELLs.

One of our Hmong-American students was quite tentative about her learning and had difficulty recalling or maintaining meaning. As she came to understand that knowing that she had seen a word—even if she didn't know its meaning—meant that she had partial knowledge of that word, she began learning in a new way. When looking at a new focus word she would say, "I know I've seen it…" and then pause. She allowed herself to consider what she might remember, rather than withdrawing and tuning out as she had in the past because she couldn't define the word.

Some gradients in word knowledge are

- knowing a word as an expert does;
- knowing a word and being able to define it easily;
- feeling like you know a word, but not really being able to explain it;
- being aware that you have seen or heard a word, but not knowing its definition;
- not knowing a word itself, but knowing what parts of the word mean; and
- not knowing the word.

Students who learn to think along this continuum become more flexible in acquiring word knowledge and seem to learn words more quickly. Through the lens of the continuum, being aware that you have seen or heard a word—even though you don't know its definition—is now part way to knowing a word. Realizing you know a part of a word leads to learning to take words apart by their morphology or structure (for example, unlocking *perfectionist* through *perfect + tion + ist*). It becomes

> You don't just know or not know a word, and this understanding—that word knowledge is not binary—becomes a condition of learning for many ELLs.

a strategy that students can use on the run, much as they take words apart visually in reading. For the ELL, this way of knowing words is an opening to academic success.

The power of this approach for a classroom teacher is that it benefits not only the beginning or intermediate ELL. The very top students in the class also become much more involved with a careful and deep investigation of essential words, for expert knowledge is often created through repeated consideration of simple questions or ideas (Csikszentmihalyi, 1997). Einstein kept inquiring into what energy was, and his revolutionary thought is represented as $E = mc^2$. (It means simply, energy is equal to mass times the speed of light squared.) It is a culture-shifting realization, yet all words in the definition, aside from equal, are one-syllable words. Think how deeply Einstein considered what energy really is and what mass really is. Profound, developed thought often plays with and springs from simple words and givens. Teaching a few words deeply rather than lists of words for passive, surface understanding invigorates whole-class learning.

Knowledge of simple linguistic categories helps in investigating words at a strategy level

Morphology and etymology are two branches of linguistics that students easily learn to use as they investigate new words. *Morphology* is the study of the structure of words by their meaningful parts. *Etymology* is the study of word origins.

Recognizing and using prefixes and suffixes is using morphology, but all students need to learn about the roots of words, too. In asking the powerful question, "Do I know a word like this or what a *part* of this word means?" students learn to apply a morphological approach to the whole word. It is with this analogical questioning, "How is this word like a word I already know?" that students' awareness of words—and awareness of themselves as learners—shifts.

Upper-elementary students who read below grade level often simply gloss over long words when they read, not pausing to consider their meaning. Ana taught us how important teaching and reteaching the strategy of thinking about what you might know about a word's meaning when she suddenly exclaimed in the middle of class that she knew what *mathematics* was because she knew the word *math*. Through years of schooling, she had had no idea that the words were related. Her prior lens on the words had been that one was long and one was short.

Exploring etymology, or word origins, heightens students' curiosity about words. In studying Wisconsin's first peoples, our fourth-grade students learned that *cultivate* and *culture* come from the same root. Why would a word that means to grow food and one that means the beliefs and behaviors of a group of people have the same origins? How do you think these words might have been related long, long ago? In exploring questions like this through oral discussion, and then reflecting on the same questions in open-ended writing, students become

> Teaching a few words deeply rather than lists of words for passive, surface understanding invigorates whole-class learning.

more curious about and connected to what they are reading. They begin to notice words in a different way.

You don't need a background in etymology to teach students this strategy. Keep a good etymological dictionary like *The American Heritage Dictionary of the English Language* (2006) in a quickly accessible place for your teaching. (Find classroom copies at a used bookstore.) Model your curiosity about words and pause in class discussion to see where they came from by looking up word origins in the dictionary. With your guidance, students studying science can learn that *tendon* and *tension* both come from the Latin root *ten*, which means to stretch. Thinking analogically through these simple words, they might wonder, 'How are tendons connecting bones somehow like the surface tension of water? Why is a word that in part means to stretch important for such different scientific topics?' It's not the right answer that matters here; it's the engagement in learning at a higher, more-abstract level, the curiosity about a classroom topic. This kind of learning is too commonly not expected of ELLs.

Teaching from These Understandings
An Example from Fourth-Grade Science

If you don't know the words *bone, joint*, and *tendon,* how can you ask curious questions about how our skeleton is structured and functions? If surface tension is a phrase your teacher uses but you don't really get, how well can you engage in and perform experiments about surface tension?

Essential vocabulary deepens understanding by giving access to learning to students who don't come to school with academic vocabulary. Many students learning in a second language master difficult content

---

Figure 1
Student Assessment of Essential Words

	I know this word and I can tell what it means	I know this word, but I can't really explain it	I think I've heard it or seen it	I know a word like it or what a *part* of the word means	I don't know this word
bone					
joint					
opposable thumb					
skeleton					
tendon					

Adapted from Beck, McKeown, & Kucan (0000)

---

in that second language and pursue advanced studies. But many more don't. There are cultural and economic reasons for this, as well as reasons having to do with gender. But ELLs often are denied access to learning because they don't have a secure understanding of the words needed to guide their thinking. Focusing on essential vocabulary gives them those words and makes possible that learning.

For the FOSS unit on bones, we began by having students assess what they already knew about essential words. (See Figure 1.) The chart is drawn from Beck, McKeown and Kucan, but some category descriptions were changed by our students to reflect their understanding and language. We determined these words to be the essential ones for students to learn.

We also taught as secondary vocabulary the words *cartilage, skull, torso, immobilize, ligament,* and the three kinds of joints: *ball and socket, hinge,* and *gliding.*

In a fourth-grade class where half of the students were intermediate to advanced ELLs, students could describe *bone* and *skeleton.* Many had heard of *joint,* but didn't know what it meant. Almost all of the students had not seen or heard *tendon* before, and none knew *opposable thumb.*

We began investigating the meaning of joint by asking, "Do you know a word like this?" Looking for words in words or words like words is a powerful strategy for learning more words, but it doesn't always lead to the right meaning. The first answer students gave when asked, "Do you know a word like *joint*?" was *point.* We validated the guess, but told students it wasn't related in meaning to *joint.*

Throughout the year, I used the analogy of shooting free throws with our students. When you practice shooting free throws, you know you won't make all the baskets. But in practicing over and over, you come to know more about how to throw a basketball, about the detail and feel of it, and you make more baskets. Becoming curious about word origin and meaning is similar. In making guesses about the meaning of words, students will make mistakes. Since there is a similar word in Spanish for roughly a third of English words, Spanish speakers can easily draw on their first language in learning new English vocabulary. Sometimes, however, they will relate words that take them down the wrong path like the English *language* and Spanish *lengua* (tongue). Though these words have some meaning in common, they aren't synonyms. (You don't move your language to help you swallow.) But in continuing to make analogies and to guess, students will learn more about words and eventually make more right guesses. When we explored new words and students offered incorrect guesses, I would say as a compliment, "Practicing free throws," and then move to another student's guess.

So we came back to the question, "Do you know a word like *joint*?" The next student said *join,* and we investigated the meaning of that word.

> Throughout the year, I used the analogy of shooting free throws with our students. When you practice shooting free throws, you know you won't make all the baskets.

Students came up with the following:

- Join our group
- Join After School Safe Haven
- Become a part of
- Come together

With the students' knowledge of *join* foregrounded, it was easy for them to think of a *joint* as a place where bones come together; where two bones join each other. They then could hold on to the *meaning* of the word joint, and could consider joints in terms of this open-ended question: "What happens where bones join one another?"

Relying now on their background knowledge (a scientific background knowledge they had been unaware they had), thinking conceptually about joints, students understood the function of joints in terms of movement. Joints allow the elaborated movement of the body and its bones.

Notice how simple the language is in the question, "What happens where bones join one another?" and that I had made sure through class discussion (not teacher knowledge imparting) that *join* and *joint* were both understood and in the foreground of student thinking.

Stop and think about what it is like for students to consider this large question in an experiment when the word *joint* is clear to them. And what it's like to be in a classroom where you're doing this experiment, but you don't really know what a joint is or why you are doing the experiment. Too often, that is the experience of ELLs in school.

A further experiment in the series had students explore the usefulness and mechanics of the human opposable thumb. Again, we began with a study of the words before doing the experiment.

Fourth-grade students work together to complete their experiments.

The students knew the word *thumb*, so we started with *opposable*. "Do you know a word like that?" took us to oppose (which only some of the students knew). We then had our class discussion, creating our meaning of the word. Students brought up *opposite*, too, as being a word like *opposable*. We talked about how both mean *against*. Our class working definition became, "If you oppose something, you're against it." Everyone understood that.

We then talked about how the human opposable thumb can come up against or oppose our fingers. Touch the rest of your hand with your thumb. Touch your finger with your thumb. What can you do with it? See how because it *opposes* the rest, because we can put it *against* the rest of your hand, you can use it differently than other joints. The students' experiment was performed with their thumb taped against their hand so the thumb was immobile — in essence, they lost their opposable thumb. Again, because they all were well aware of the meaning of opposable as they performed their experiment, they could think about and be curious about their experiment. They could wonder and ask questions. They could determine what was important in this experiment. They could infer structural information and synthesize their learning. All these strategies opened up for them because they were secure in using the one word they needed to think conceptually.

A class definition will not always be an exact, precise definition. It should be in students' words and reflect student understanding. It can always be modified as student understanding grows. Our mantra for *surface tension*, "Water will try to stay in the smallest space it can," described more specifically how water reacts in space. But implicit in this definition was the students' understanding of the elasticity of the surface of water. It captured what was important for students to keep reflecting on as they performed experiments and investigated properties of water. The day after our discussion of surface tension, Miguel, a Spanish-speaking ELL, pulled me over to tell me, "Ms. O'Leary, yesterday I didn't know what surface tension was, and now I know it here." He looked at me seriously, covering his heart.

With definitions of essential words secure, we then encouraged students to consciously use the *who, what, when, where, why* and *how* questions (5 Wh + H), to learn more about the words and concepts they were studying. In science this became, "Why does condensation form near the window but not near the heater?" "Where does water go when it evaporates?" In social studies, we created 5 Wh + H graphic organizers to help them to read specifically to find and summarize 5 Wh + H information.

Margaret Mooney (2001, p. 9) points out that students need to become conscious of and flexible in using these strategies across content domains. In social studies, *who, when,* and *why* will often (but not always) be the most-important questions. In science, *how* and *why* are often the most-useful questions and understandings. If we teach ELLs to ask 5 Wh + H questions in all areas of study, we deepen their under-

> With definitions of essential words secure, we then encouraged students to consciously use the *who, what, when, where, why* and *how* questions (5 Wh + H), to learn more about the words and concepts they were studying.

standing of the usefulness of those words as organizing principles for learning. My ELLs much more easily use *who* and *what happened* than character and plot in understanding and discussing what they read. *Who* and *what happened* are transferable to the study of social studies and science, and lead to analogical thinking. Character and plot are limited to literary study.

Once again, all students—not only the ELLs—benefited from our focus on 5 Wh + H questions. These are the questions of inquiry.

We encouraged students to use ways of learning that best helped them to know and understand. ELL Andrew regularly synthesized his knowledge in drawings. His drawing below showed how well he had understood the *what*, *why*, and *how* of a surface tension experiment.

Other students became aware that it was talking, writing, or doing (or a combination of these) that best helped them to make sense of the content and its vocabulary. During this year of study, science was presented by first helping students to use a linguist's tools to understand and define new words, and then encouraging students to use their definitions to question and learn. By the end of this year, students were so engaged that they wanted to create a class website of their study of water.[4] The students' written descriptions and detailed drawings of their experiments showed a grounded understanding of what they had studied, why they had studied it, and what it meant.

For some ELLs, using drawings is a helpful tool to synthesize their knowledge.

When they see themselves as active creators of the definitions of words, students become much more involved in learning and discussing words.

Andrew and Ramon wrote about condensation.

> We learned that water vapor makes condensation. When water vapor can't go anywhere, it condenses into water and becomes condensation on the surface it can't go through. We learned that when you come inside when the weather is cold and you have on glasses, they get fogged up with condensation. We also learned that a change to a warmer temperature can make condensation. We discovered that condensation was sort of like fog.

Julian and Manuel summarized what they had learned about evaporation.

> We learned that evaporation is caused by atoms drifting away from each other. We also learned that water vapor goes up because it is less dense than air. We learned that when water vapor has nowhere to go, it turns back into a liquid again. We learned that water vapor evaporates pretty darn fast at high temperatures. It can also evaporate at room temperature, too.

Ashante and Carmen described how water reacts to different surfaces.

> We did this experiment to see how water reacts to different surfaces. We learned about and saw firsthand how water can bead on various surfaces and be absorbed on others. Beading means the water goes all over into little circles on top of the surface. It is not absorbed. Absorb means to soak into a material.

Our students vividly taught us in this year that when they see themselves as active creators of the definitions of words, they become much more involved in learning and discussing words. They realize the excitement of learning. They confidently understand that in discussing and using essential words, they solidify their word knowledge and their conceptual understanding.

Children learn and practice abstract concepts like north, south, east, and west on a large outdoor playground map.

An Example from K–1 Geography

In determining Lincoln K–5 essential vocabulary, Lincoln teachers chose direction words as essential words to teach in first-grade geography. Carolyn Konkol and I planned instruction for her K–1 class to address this vocabulary. Because Wisconsin is in the far north of the United States, we used *north* as our focal word to introduce direction in varied ways and contexts for the students.

Carolyn grounded her instruction about direction in the class study of the migration of butterflies (linked to the study of the caterpillar metamorphosizing in the room), and introduced, along with *north*, these other content area words: *south, east, west, country, map, Wisconsin,* and *United States.* Gail Gibbons' 1991 book, *Monarch Butterfly,* provided the visual introduction to the larger migration question, "Where are the butterflies going and why?"

To make an abstract concept like *north* more concrete, Carolyn encouraged her students to be the word. She took them to a large map of the United States on the playground and gave group directions, "North! South! Wisconsin! Texas!" The students ran as a group from the north to the south, back and forth, loving learning the words.

Carolyn read *Zoom* (Banyai, 1998) with the class, and over days they created a class book based on it, starting with their classroom in Madison, Wisconsin. This book easily reinforced the vocabulary that Carolyn had introduced. She then encouraged students to draw their own maps of the classroom, which now contained the directions north, south, east, and west. First grader Brenda understood her world like the drawing at the top of the next page.

Students also orally explained their maps to volunteers who worked in the room. By the end of this unit of study, K–1 students had explored essential geography vocabulary words through shared reading of texts, repeated class discussions using the words, a game in which they became different directions, class construction of a book full of maps and vocabulary, individual writing and mapping, and discussion of

This first grader's drawing reveals her understanding of her classroom world.

their work with teachers and volunteers. Content area work was tied to literacy, and literacy was tied to content area work. Through repeated use, concepts that would be difficult in the abstract became part of their active vocabulary.

How We Chose Essential Words

You can be aware without words, but can you *think* without words?

How do you know what you know?

What is essential in the content areas? What are the words that lead to understanding of key concepts? To determine which words we would focus on, classroom, ESL, Title I, and learning disabilities teachers came together to identify the words that would most impact student learning. From kindergarten through fifth grade, we started with content area standards and asked,

- What words occur over and over, across grades?
- What words are necessary for thought?
- What words can be built on for deeper understanding?

As we entered the discussion of essential vocabulary, what quickly surfaced was the need to clarify what we believed really matters in each content area. Why are you teaching, say, geography or history? What are the large ideas you want students to understand? We created essential understandings for each part of the standards that answered the question, "Why teach this?" For geography, we agreed that it is important to teach geography so that students

- can visualize and understand that the world is bigger than just here;
- understand causal relations — that our actions in the U.S. affect others in the world; that actions by others in the world affect us. If students don't know where countries are, and don't know the difference between a continent and a country, how deep can their understanding of world events be?;
- develop a sense of stewardship; and
- can use it as a tool for understanding the political and the historical.

Believing this is why we teach geography, we then carefully chose the words from K–5 geography standards. Each word was puzzled out and agreed on by the representative group of teachers as important to teaching the essence of geography. But in our first year, we came up with far too many words. After 1 year of using this list, teachers were demoralized (we were never able to teach all of them), and students' learning had only somewhat improved. We spent days the following summer going over our word lists, culling words by asking again and again, "What few words would my students who struggle the most need to be able to actively use to understand this topic? What words do we want them to be able to walk out the door at the end of the year still actively using?"

These questions shifted our focus from accepting a passive, receptive understanding of words—seeming to know them and at least recognizing them when reading—to an active productive one where the words became the students' tools for thinking about and understanding large ideas. Previously, we had been trying to cover important words. Now we were truly teaching them.

This is when we found that teaching a few words well meant that students learned more words, more easily. And that students became truly curious about learning as much as they could about essential words and about the concepts connected to the words. What exactly *is* water? What kinds of joints am I using right now, holding this pencil?

With a specific, clear focus for just a few words for each grade level, we found that finally most of our students *did* know the meaning of words like city, state, and country. Because each year teachers and students focused on only a few concept words, it meant that those words didn't need to be retaught the following year. But more importantly, the shift to only a few words opened up a new kind of learning for *all* of our

> This is when we found that teaching a few words well meant that students learned more words, more easily.

students. The advanced ones, as well as those who struggled, became more actively involved in their learning.

Beck, McKeown, and Kucan (2002) describe three tiers of words. Tier 1 words are common, spoken language words. Tier 2 words are more-sophisticated words, those found in written texts and used by persons with large vocabularies. Tier 3 words are lower-frequency words, or those used only in specific domains such as mathematics, science, and history. Beck, McKeown, and Kucan encourage teachers to focus on teaching Tier 2 words.

Jim Cummins' (1979) seminal work in English language acquisition clarified the difference between functioning fluency in a language—Basic Interpersonal Communicative Skills or BICS — and the actual vocabulary needed for academic success and intellectual thought — Cognitive Academic Language Proficiency or CALP. In identifying essential content area vocabulary, we found that cognitive academic language came from all three tiers. At times ELLs and other students would not necessarily fluently understand Tier 1 words like *city, state,* or *country.* At times, a Tier 2 word like *exchange* was crucial to understanding a historical era. And at times understanding of a Tier 3 word like *artifact* would be necessary to explore our history textbook's resources. We learned it was more helpful to reflect on what words were essential for learning than to stick to tiers. Still, it was much easier to create lists of important words than to choose the truly essential ones for understanding. We learned to prioritize two levels of words we would teach. One was the essential — the words we wanted every student to know. The second was words we thought were important and would introduce and use, but we would not expect that all students would fully learn them. For geography, our prioritized list after a few years of work became that shown in Table 1.

In teaching direction words and focusing on *north*, Carolyn taught other important words that were not on this list. But *north* was the focus, the word and concept we wanted all students to learn well so that it could hold other understandings. Notice that in starting so very

> This study of essential vocabulary changed us as teachers. We had more—and more in depth—conversations with colleagues.

Table 1
Prioritized List of Geography Words to Teach

Kindergarten	First Grade	Second Grade	Third Grade	Fourth Grade	Fifth Grade
address	N, S, E, W	symbol	capital	state	relief map
map	water	oceans	city	region	physical map
	land	the seven continents	NE, SE, NW, SW	county	political map
	globe		country	migration	historical map
	earth		borders	river	population
			urban/rural	latitude	landforms
				longitude	location

simply, we reached a point by fifth grade where students were expected to learn and work with fairly sophisticated levels of words.

We recognized that many of our students came to their grade already knowing most of the essential words for that year. This method of inquiry allowed them to gain a deeper knowledge of the word — to study or map countries on a continent, or to really work with latitude and longitude in describing varied locations in the world.

The teachers benefited from this specific attention now to teaching vocabulary, because in teaching many fewer words in depth, we could much more clearly see and reflect on the difficulties students had in learning certain words. We were surprised to find that *population* was hard for many of our fifth graders. But think for a moment about what is involved in understanding the word *population*. It means the number of people living in a certain area. In American history, it also has to do with immigration, ethnicity, tensions between native peoples and Europeans, religion, urban and rural distinctions, landforms, and place value understanding. (If you don't understand the difference between 100,000 and 1,000,000, you won't be able to understand a modern population map.)

What We as Teachers Learned

This study of essential vocabulary changed us as teachers. We had more—and more in-depth—conversations with colleagues. We learned the power of teaching vocabulary specifically and with focus. Our nonfiction lessons in literacy could no longer be how to read an informational text. We now purposively taught content area texts in literacy, and literacy in the content areas.

We learned a framework for addressing the detail of standards simply. We learned how to become more carefully aware of what our students didn't know, why they didn't know it, and what we as teachers didn't know about our students. One of our most-meaningful extended conversations centered around a timeline assessment that fifth-grade classroom, ESL, and Title I teachers had created, and that students failed miserably. It showed us that most of our students had no concept of historical time, which led us to realize, "Why would they?" We hadn't given them the tools for understanding it. We started thinking about how, just as students need an internal number line to understand numbers and operations, they needed an internal historical timeline to understand history. And school-wide, we needed to give them the tools to create it. Before, we knew very well that our students didn't know or understand many, many content area concepts. Now we had a way of getting at them.

We built on three important ideas in *Bringing Words to Life* (Beck, McKeown, & Kucan, 2002): the concept of tiers of words, the continuum of word knowledge, and the importance of oral definitions.

> Before, we knew very well that our students didn't know or understand many, many content area concepts. Now we had a way of getting at them.

Because ELLs may often not know high-frequency or Tier 1 words well or be able to use them in academic contexts, we learned that the words we chose came from all three tiers of Beck, McKeown, and Kucan's work. But it was the concept of tiers that helped us to begin to separate important academic words from essential academic words. While we used and introduced both kinds of words, it was the essential ones that we carefully and repeatedly taught and used to plan instruction.

From Beck, McKeown, and Kucan, we learned that you can know a word ever-increasingly well. This understanding helped us to articulate what we wanted for all of our students, but especially our ELLs and other students with limited academic vocabulary. We learned that in teaching a few academic words deeply, we could help our students to develop a child's expert knowledge of a concept. One reason that ELLs perform as a group below their monolingual peers is that expectations are commonly lower for them. Those lower expectations mean that they don't always have the same access to higher-order thinking as other students. We searched for the ways for our ELLs to experience not just knowing academic content in school, but knowing it as Miguel needed to tell me he knew surface tension — in his heart. Our expectation became that our students would be involved in learning as an expert would, with continuing curiosity and reflection, fluent use of analogy, and deepening understanding. Our study of vocabulary was based in security, close investigation, multiple processes and pathways for learning, high expectations, and an invitation to question and reflect.

Last year in Kari Petre's class, we began a year-long study of Wisconsin by investigating Wisconsin's earliest people. Students read about, discussed, took notes on, and drew the tools, art, and shelter of peoples who lived here 12,000 to 500 years ago. We talked about how there wouldn't have been formal schooling or education at that time as we know it now, but still, wouldn't you have to in some way teach things in order for your group to survive?

On the last day of the chapter study, I asked students to write about or draw what they wanted to remember. The room was absolutely still. As I walked around, Gustavo made eye contact with me. I went over to look in his notebook, and he whispered to me quietly and surely, "I think they must have played in the snow with their children." In those short simple words and his intense involvement as he spoke was an understanding of climate and culture, of tradition, commitment, necessity, and love. How better to teach your children to survive harsh winter and to keep your family close than to take pleasure in teaching your children as they learn necessary skills? You could see on Gustavo's face how deeply involved he was in this thought. We had framed this study with essential words. And Gustavo brought his essential understandings to the task.

> Our study of vocabulary was based in security, close investigation, multiple processes and pathways for learning, high expectations, and an invitation to question and reflect.

Endnotes

[1] Allison Vincent, Kari Petre, Suzanne Welles, Marc Kornblatt, and Carolyn Konkol are the classroom teachers with whom I collaborated in teaching vocabulary. Lincoln Title I teachers Barb Bickford, Andreal Davis, and Barb Laughon and ESL teachers Lori Gustafson and Amy Niesen, along with Patty Schultz and Eileen Potts-Dawson, were part of this teaching with other students and classroom teachers. We shared regular conversation about vocabulary over these years. Donal Maccoon, at the University of Wisconsin-Madison Waisman Laboratory for Brain Imaging and Behavior, answered each question I had about current brain research.

[2] FOSS (Full Option Science System) is a K–8 science curriculum developed at the University of California-Berkeley. http://www.lawrencehallofscience.org/foss

[3] Lincoln School had the immense pleasure of working with Margaret Mooney during her 2-week long residences with us.

[4] http://www.madison.k12.wi.us/midlinc/vincent.html

References

American Heritage Dictionary of the English Language (4th ed.). (2006). New York: Houghton Mifflin.

Beck, I., McKeown, M., & Kucan, L. (2002). *Bringing words to life: Robust vocabulary instruction.* New York: The Guilford Press.

Cummins, J. (1979). Cognitive/academic language proficiency, linguistic interdependence, the optimum age question and some other matters. *Working Papers on Bilingualism*, No. 19, 121–129.

Csikszentmihalyi, M. (1997). *Creativity.* New York: Harper Perennial.

Harvey, S. (1998). *Nonfiction matters.* Portland, ME: Stenhouse.

Harvey, S., & Goudvis, A. (2000). *Strategies that work.* Portland, ME: Stenhouse.

Jensen, E. (1998). *Teaching with the brain in mind.* Alexandria, VA: Association for Supervision and Curriculum Development.

Keene, E. O., & Zimmermann, S. (1997). *Mosaic of thought: Teaching comprehension in a reader's workshop.* Portsmouth, NH: Heinemann.

Kilgallon, D., & Kilgallon, J. (2000). *Sentence composing.* Portsmouth, NH: Heinemann.

Lyons, C. (2004). Applying principles of brain research to maximize every child's learning potential. *The Journal of Reading Recovery, 4*(1), 1–11.

Mooney, M. (2001). *Text forms and features: A resource for intentional teaching.* Katonah, NY: Richard C. Owen Press.

Nhat Hanh, T. (2004). *Creating true peace.* New York: Free Press.

Vincent, A. (2005). *Water, water everywhere.* Retrieved January 18, 2008, from http://www.madison.k12.wi.us/midlinc/vincent.htm

Children's Books Cited

Banyai, I. (1998). *Zoom.* New York: Puffin.

Gibbons, G. (1991). *Monarch butterfly.* New York: Holiday House.

Programs of bilingual education, especially those using Spanish and English as mediums of instruction, have been widely implemented in the U.S. for the past 40 years. Recent syntheses of research have established the efficacy of these programs, particularly as they relate to teaching literacy to the nation's large and growing population of English language learners (ELLs) (August & Shanahan, 2006; Genesee & Riches, 2006; Slavin & Cheung, 2003).

While these research syntheses have reaffirmed the desirability of using a child's native language as a medium of instruction, they include several caveats and areas in need of further research and investigation. For example, while consensus abounds on the value of the child's first language as a medium of instruction, less consensus exists about best practice with regard to teaching methods (Slavin & Cheung, 2003). In fact, all of the above-named syntheses call for renewed focus in research and practice on the quality of instruction as a means of enhancing bilingual program effectiveness. These research syntheses specifically suggested the need for (a) programs that address and examine the efficacy of simultaneous literacy instruction (Slavin & Cheung), and (b) programs that prioritize explicit and direct teaching and formal opportunities for children to make cross-language connections (Genesee & Riches, 2006).

Using Writing to Make Cross-Language Connections from Spanish to English

Kathy Escamilla
Diana Geisler
Susan Hopewell
Wendy Sparrow
Sandra Butvilofsky
University of Colorado, Boulder

In an attempt to address the research needs outlined above, authors of this chapter created, and are currently implementing, a 5-year research project called Literacy Squared® (Escamilla, Hopewell, Geisler, & Ruiz, 2007). This program is based on the fundamental understanding that for Spanish-speaking emerging bilinguals, literacy instruction in Spanish serves as a positive scaffold to literacy in English. However, the Literacy Squared intervention differs from more-traditional bilingual programs in several significant ways:

1. Instruction in literacy in both Spanish and English beginning in first grade (simultaneous or paired instruction)
2. Promotion of literacy acquisition as a single trajectory to biliteracy rather than viewing literacy acquisition as two separate and distinct processes
3. Development of intervention lessons with the intent of providing examples of concrete ways in which teachers can assist children in making explicit cross-language connections between Spanish and English

The authors of this chapter suggest that learning to read and write in two languages differs from learning to read and write in only one (Bernhardt, 2003). Further, helping students understand how to draw on all of their linguistic resources as they become biliterate is a charge unique to bilingual teachers. These teachers, however, are often led to believe that simply applying the theories and strategies that are effective in monolingual literacy environments will result in effective biliteracy development. We contend that biliteracy differs from literacy in just one language in significant ways, and that attending to these differences thoughtfully will increase the overall academic performance of bilingual students.

This chapter will focus on cross-language connections from Spanish to English. As our knowledge of developing trajectories toward biliteracy has emerged, we have created lessons involving two types of cross-language connections. The first area we refer to as *cross-language methods*, the second as *cross-language strategies*. We will define each of these terms in the following pages and then provide examples of a cross-language teaching method (The Dictado*)* and a cross-language teaching strategy (Así se dice). It is our view that the utilization of cross-language connections can improve the writing skills of ELLs in both bilingual and English medium classrooms.

The issue of cross-language transfer has been studied much more extensively in reading than in writing (August & Shanahan, 2006). Researchers agree that learning to read in Spanish is highly and positively correlated to learning to read in English (August & Shanahan; Escamilla et al., 2007). Our Literacy Squared research has also found that high and positive correlations exist between writing in Spanish and writing in English in areas of content (.65), punctuation (.55), and overall writing (.67). However, we have found that spelling in Spanish does not correlate highly to spelling in English (.35) (Escamilla et al.). We

> A cross-language method is the utilization of a particular teaching methodology in two languages. For example, shared reading and read-alouds are methodologies that can be implemented in either Spanish or English.

submit that these findings support the utilization of cross-language connections in the teaching of writing in English and Spanish, as children actively apply what they know in one language when they are learning another. Teaching approaches that focus on cross-language connections in the teaching of writing enhance and utilize what children know in one language to assist them in learning a second language.

Cross-Language Method: The Dictado

A cross-language method is the utilization of a particular teaching methodology in two languages. For example, shared reading and read-alouds are methodologies that can be implemented in either Spanish or English. In this chapter, we will discuss *The Dictado* as a method of teaching writing that can be used in both Spanish and English. Because this method is widely used in Mexico and Latin America, the utilization of it in English, as well as Spanish, qualifies it as a cross-language methodology. The Dictado is likely most effective when used in bilingual classrooms where children are learning to read and write in both Spanish and English. We suggest that it can also be used in English medium classrooms as a component of English as a second language (ESL) instruction.

> As a tool for language analysis, this cross-cultural methodology invites focused scrutiny of linguistic similarities and differences across languages.

Definition of The Dictado

The title of the method used, The Dictado, is intentionally bilingual because it recognizes that we have adapted a methodology that is used extensively throughout Mexico and Latin America to meet the linguistic and pedagogical needs of teachers and students in the U.S. bilingual context. The title also reflects the knowledge that translation rarely completely captures the purpose, the meaning, or the process being considered. In fact, in this instance, a literal translation would be misleading. We concur with those who caution that teachers should not import methods wholesale from one country and apply them entirely in the new country (Smith, Jiménez, & Martínez-León, 2003), as their effectiveness depends on context and purpose.

The term, The Dictado, was chosen to distinguish this strategy from the English term *dictation*. As it is applied and discussed in most scholarly literature in the U.S., dictation serves two primary purposes: to diagnose and measure students' knowledge about the alphabetic principle of sound-symbol correspondence (Clay, 1993; Oller, 1972; Oller & Streiff, 1975) and to extend and expand children's ability to participate more fully in their literacy environments by having them dictate their original stories to their teachers (Cooper, 2005; Dorr, 2006). Often referred to as *language experience approach*, this second function asks students to dictate to teachers the texts that they will use to learn to read. The method ensures that the vocabulary is within students' oral repertoires and that the texts are personally meaningful. Originally conceived as a means to teach reading to monolingual speakers of English, this methodology has been widely incorporated into ESL environments as a means of connecting written language to students' oral competencies (Peregoy & Boyle, 2006).

Insights, Assessment, Instruction

Conversely, *el dictado*, as used in Mexico and other Spanish-speaking countries, is a technique in which the teacher dictates a series of words or sentences to the students (Secretaria de Educación Pública, 1996). The students and teacher then collaborate to create a corrected model of the focus text. Students amend their sentences using a two-color system to draw attention to errors. The same dictation is repeated throughout the week, giving students multiple opportunities to practice and learn the target linguistic applications. Students are taught to attend to proper conventions and form, as part of the lesson focus is perfecting grammar and spelling (Cassany, 2004). We believe that with consistent application of this methodology throughout the primary grades, it is a particularly effective didactic tool.

Our use of The Dictado draws heavily on the Mexican methodology, but expands the purpose from primarily internalizing the orthography and writing conventions of an academic language, to also formulating a basis for analyzing both the surface and deep structures of learning two languages simultaneously. As a tool for language analysis, this cross-cultural methodology invites focused scrutiny of linguistic similarities and differences across languages.

The strength of this methodology depends upon a metalinguistic discussion about language and punctuation and the opportunities students have to read and correct their passages (Saunders & Goldenberg, 1999; Saunders, O'Brien, Lennon, & McLean, 1998). It provides a format for deepening students' metalinguistic awareness and it broadens students' opportunities to focus by integrating aural, visual, and kinesthetic modes of communication (Jafarpur & Yamini, 1993). Our conviction about the importance of focused, explicit, repeated practice analyzing the semantic, syntactic, and visual representation of ideas in writing across two languages comes from our experience reading and analyzing thousands of bilingual students' writing samples over the course of our study.

Throughout the study, we have noticed that students' approximations across languages often remain the same. The words students were misspelling in first grade are the same words they are misspelling in third and fourth grade. For example, the word *because*—spelled as *bicus* or *becuz* in first grade—may continue to be spelled the same way by the same child in third or fourth grade. Such misspellings and their occurrence across languages have been observed in both Spanish and English. Further, in both languages, the unique syntactical variations that appear in the early grades continue to persist into the upper grades.

We must take responsibility for providing guided and focused practice attending to the written, linguistic, and communicative needs of our students, and we must abandon our fear of teaching them standard ways to record their thinking (Delpit, 1995; Reyes, 1992). We are not arguing for the wholesale adoption of the standard form at the expense of another equally valid language variation. In fact, we oppose language

> While The Dictado is an important cross-language methodology, it is not meant to be the entire language arts program. In fact, we suggest that it be done no more than 10–15 minutes at a time for 3–5 days a week.

eradication. Rather, we argue in favor of guiding children to know that they can draw upon multiple communicative registers. Knowing the standard academic register is critical to their continued academic success.

While The Dictado is an important cross-language methodology, it is not meant to be the entire language arts program. In fact, we suggest that it be done no more than 10–15 minutes at a time for 3–5 days a week.

Procedures for Implementing The Dictado

The Dictado can be used with an entire class or with small groups. One focus dictado is given each week in each language. It is important to note that the Spanish and English dictados are not the same. What students know and control in one language will be very different from what they know and control in the other. The effectiveness of this methodology depends upon using it to address students' developmental linguistic needs.

Weekly routine

The weekly routine for The Dictado approach is detailed in Table 1.

Table 1
The Dictado: Weekly Procedures

Day	Procedures
1 — The Dictado	• The teacher reads through The Dictado at a normal rate, with normal expression. • Together the teacher and children count the number of words in The Dictado. • The teacher tells the children to get ready to write. The children write in pencil. • The teacher begins by saying, "First word, first sentence." The teacher proceeds through the first sentence word-by-word. At the end of the first sentence the teacher says, "End of sentence." Then, "First word, second sentence" and so on.
1 — The Talk-Through	• The children change their pencils for pens or red pencils. • The teacher and the children talk through The Dictado linguistically, grammatically, and metalinguistically in an interactive and explicit manner. • As the talk-through progresses, the teacher is slowly constructing a correct model on the board, asking children to contribute to the construction of the correct model on the board. The students self-correct their own papers with a red pencil, and **they do not erase.**
2	Students dictate in pairs. Then, corrections are made and compared to Day 1. (Note: This is optional.)
3	The teacher dictates again, emphasizing any issues that she notes in the children's writing. Corrections are made and compared to Days 2 and 1.
4	Repeat Day 2. (Note: This is optional.)
5	The teacher administers the final dictado, collects students' work, and grades it.

The talk-through steps are crucial because these are the points when teachers

- make explicit, direct teaching points including language, grammar, and spelling;
- model and generate meta-language; and
- help students make cross-language connections.

Talk-through

Following is a segment of a classroom example of a talk-through. The sentence being corrected is "Do you want to come?" The conversation below picks up at the point where "Do you want to come" has been written on the board.

Teacher:	And what comes next?
Jorge:	A period.
Marco:	No, it needs a question mark!
Teacher: (to Marco)	Why does it need a question mark?
Marco:	Because it's asking. (The teacher hands the chalk to Marco and he writes the question mark after the word *come*.)
Teacher:	We write questions differently in English than we do in Spanish.
Marco:	Yeah, in Spanish we have to write two question marks, one in front and one in back.

Standard marking code

The teacher or school will need to develop a standard marking code to be used for self-corrections and teach it to the children. For example, children will need to know how to mark an omitted or incorrect letter, omitted or incorrect punctuation, and anything else that may need revising. Consistency in this marking code is important, and it is very helpful if a standard marking code is used across the grades within a school. Many of the schools in the Literacy Squared research study have chosen to use marking codes that match the Colorado Student Assessment Program (CSAP) or the Texas Assessment of Knowledge and Skills (TAKS) state exams. Several sources for writers' editing marks can be found online. (e.g., http://thewritingsite.org/resources/managing/)

In Figure 1, The Dictado consisted of two sentences: "Recess is fun. We like to play." The student wrote, *Rises es fun Jui laik tu plei* without punctuation. During the talk-through, the student made self-corrections without erasures. The marking codes used illustrate strike-through for

> By explicitly teaching what does and does not transfer across languages, and by teaching for cross-language connections, teaching can become more efficient.

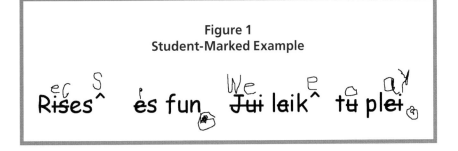

Figure 1
Student-Marked Example

incorrect letters, carets when letters needed to be inserted, and circles with periods in them when the periods were omitted.

Suggestions for getting started

The Dictado can take many forms and address multiple learning objectives. So, how do teachers get started? Of course, state and local standards and objectives must be addressed, but how can teachers teach specifically and work in their students' zones of proximal development?

We strongly suggest that teachers begin by analyzing their students' writing in both languages if students are in bilingual programs and in English if students are in English medium programs. What are the students' strengths and weaknesses in Spanish and in English? If writing in English, what is transferring from Spanish, and conversely if writing in Spanish, what is transferring to English? What do the students need to know in English that cannot be learned in Spanish? Deep analysis is required with consideration of more than spelling and conventions. The quality, variety, complexity, and pragmatics of the students' language should be considered. Over time, the teacher should attempt to incorporate increasingly sophisticated vocabulary and grammatical structures so that The Dictados address vocabulary and language structures students have yet to acquire.

Similarities and differences across languages should be emphasized. By explicitly teaching what does and does not transfer across languages, and by teaching for cross-language connections, teaching can become more efficient, as many objectives do not need to be taught twice. Furthermore, it is important to note that cross-language transfer is bidirectional. That is, Spanish transfers to English and vice versa. If teachers are teaching in English medium classrooms, emphases can be placed on English structures, grammar, and spelling, and less on cross-language transfers.

Spanish Dictados

To help determine appropriate Spanish learning objectives, we have found the scope and sequence of the language arts program, "Español," from the Secretaría de Educación Pública (1996) in Mexico informa-

Table 2
The Dictado in Spanish: Sample Lessons

The Dictado	Anticipated Talk-Through Teaching Points
Grade 1: El perro y el ratón corren. *The dog and the rat run.*	• Capitalization: first word in a sentence • Spaces separate words • Punctuation: final period • Spelling and phonemic distinction: *rr, r* • **Cross-language connections: In English the first three points above are also true.**
Grade 3: Es un día precioso en México. Raúl y yo vamos a ir al Museo de Arte Contemporáneo. ¿Quieres venir? *It is a beautiful day in Mexico. Raul and I are going to the Museum of Contemporary Art. Do you want to come?*	• Punctuation: question marks ¿? • Proper/common nouns • Capitalization: proper nouns • Spelling: words with *c* and *s* • **Cross-language connections: In English, only one question mark is used and proper nouns are capitalized in both languages.**
Grade 5: Mañana iremos al Museo de Historia Natural. Acuérdense que deberían de traer sus almuerzos, el permiso, sus chamarras, y el dinero. ¡Los autobuses partirán a las 9:00 en punto! ¡Así es que, sean puntuales! *Tomorrow we will go to the Museum of Natural History. Remember to bring your lunches, your permission slips, your jackets, and money. The buses will leave at 9:00 pronto! Be on time!*	• Punctuation: two uses of commas, exclamation marks • Text structure: reminder note • Capitalization: proper names • Formatting: indent the first word of each paragraph • Spelling: plural commands • **Cross-language connections: In English, only one exclamation mark is needed; cognates (*museo, historia, natural, permiso, puntuales*); the first word of each paragraph is indented in both languages.**

tive. However, teachers are also encouraged to use children's own writing and oral language to generate The Dictado.

The lesson ideas for Spanish dictados in Table 2 were generated by Literacy Squared teachers as they participated in professional development sessions. These lesson ideas include teaching for cross-language connections, as well as Spanish conventions and spelling.

English Dictados

Often, the teaching emphases in English will differ from those in Spanish. This is because what students know and control in each language most likely differs. Teachers need to know how to use the theoretical construct of transfer to accelerate linguistic development. The challenge for our students in learning to read and write in ESL settings is mostly a language challenge, not a reading/writing challenge (Escamilla et al., 2007) since Spanish literacy learning acquisition leads to ESL literacy acquisition. In The Dictado in English, attention must be given to language development. We suggest that children's writing is a good source of information for what children should be taught to write in a standard way. Based on our preliminary examination of the English writing of bilingual children in first, second, and third grade, some of their common writing behaviors when writing in English are listed below.

1. The use of Spanish graphemes to encode words in English: *jui laik tu pley* (*We like to play*).

2. Approximations in spelling high-frequency words are common to both emerging bilinguals as well as native English speakers: *wen* for *when*; *dat* for *that*; *wud* for *would*. Frequent inclusion of these high-frequency words into The Dictado is strongly recommended.

3. Use of Spanish syntax when writing in English: a) possessive structures: *the chair of the baby* instead of *the baby's chair*; b) the past tense verb form: *he want to eat* instead of *he wanted to eat*; and c) adjective/noun placement: the *truck blue* instead of the *blue truck*.

4. Code-switching: At times, children code-switch from English to Spanish or vice versa because they may not have

---

Table 3
The Dictado in English: Sample Lessons

The Dictado	Anticipated Talk-Through Teaching Points
Grade 1: I like to play with my cat.	• Prepositional phrase • Spelling: high-frequency words — I, like, play • **Cross-language connections: Capitalize first word, spaces between words, and final period are the same as in Spanish**
Grade 3: This is Ana's pencil. Don't take hers. Please take Jorge's pencil instead. I don't think he will mind.	• Spelling: high-frequency words — don't, have, take • Possessives and possessive pronouns • Use of apostrophe for possession and for contractions • **Cross-language connections: Syntax differences (the pencil of Ana vs. Ana's pencil)**
Grade 5: Colorado got its name for its reddish dirt. Many rivers run through Colorado. Over millions of years, the rivers have cut breathtaking canyons in the red rock. The wind, sun, and water have taken their toll on the land. That is called erosion.	• Vocabulary: erosion, breathtaking • Past perfect tense (have cut, have taken their toll); over millions of years • Spelling: that, breathtaking • **Cross-language connections: Colorado is a Spanish word; cognate—canyon**

had an opportunity to learn vocabulary or structures in the target language. The Dictado can be used to help teach these structures and vocabulary.

5. Punctuation: Punctuation rules vary across languages. The Dictado provides a structure to teach cross-language differences.

6. Run-on sentences: In Spanish, sentences are often so long that from an English perspective the sentences would be viewed as run-ons. So, Spanish writers learning to write in English may need to learn acceptable grammar in English.

Based on what we saw children doing in our research project, we worked with Literacy Squared teachers to create some ideas for using The Dictado as a part of the ESL component as shown in Table 3.

In addition to cross-language teaching methods, there are several cross-language teaching strategies that we have found to be useful in helping emerging bilingual children in their writing development. In contrast to cross-language methods, cross-language strategies are focused on teaching children the metacognitive linguistic skills of cross-language expression. One such strategy, Así se dice (That's how you say it), is discussed below.

A Cross-Language Teaching Strategy: Así Se Dice

Students learning to read and write in two languages have the advantage of being able to interpret, create, and process text by accessing multiple linguistic resources. The most-successful bilingual readers and writers instinctively incorporate unique bilingual strategies into their text-processing repertoire. These strategies include recognizing cognates, judiciously using translation, and drawing upon background knowledge acquired across languages (Jiménez, García, & Pearson, 1996). Some students, however, need to be explicitly taught how their knowledge in and about each language can be accessed to aid in text creation, comprehension, and interpretation. Teachers can support this process by establishing a linguistically rich classroom environment and by explicitly teaching cross-language strategies. We suggest that this strategy can best be employed beginning in third grade.

Cross-language teaching strategies posit that two languages used strategically can enhance and advance students' intellectual and linguistic growth (Kenner, 2004; Zentella, 1997). Regardless of the program model, students can be encouraged to draw upon their first language while acquiring a second. Classrooms should be equipped with resources such as bilingual dictionaries and first- and second-language thesauri to help students problem solve across languages. Additionally, students should be encouraged to deepen their conceptual and procedural knowledge by discussing, debating, and negotiating meaning with peers who share their home language.

> The most-successful bilingual readers and writers instinctively incorporate unique bilingual strategies into their text-processing repertoire.

Care must be taken, however, to be sure that cross-language strategies are taught and employed thoughtfully. Creating a space for students to be deliberately and strategically bilingual is fundamentally different from the persistent or spontaneous use of concurrent translation. Many researchers have documented that concurrent translation results in students 'tuning out' (Faltis, 1996; Ovando & Collier, 2003) because they come to rely on the translation. The practice of repeating or emphasizing key concepts through regular concurrent translation teaches students that they need not attend to information presented in the second language. It eliminates an authentic need to engage with, and practice, the newly acquired language. Cross-language strategies should not be confused with concurrent translation.

One powerful cross-language strategy that we have developed is called *Así se dice*. Así se dice validates translation as a constructive and worthwhile endeavor and engages students in a complex, sophisticated scrutiny of language that emphasizes the subtleties and nuances of communicating messages across cultures and languages. Accurate translation requires sophisticated linguistic and metalinguistic knowledge that not only involves understanding the words being used, but also knowing the underlying concepts and the ways in which those concepts might be interpreted and conveyed differently across cultures and languages. Employed thoughtfully, Así se dice promises to be a catalyst for vigorous and spirited classroom discussion.

Procedures for Implementing Así Se Dice

The procedure for this strategy is as follows:

- Present and discuss a carefully chosen short passage.

- Have students translate the passage in pairs.

- Encourage students to consult resources and to discuss the text with each other.

- Provide time for each pair to share its translation of the text.

- Facilitate a discussion in which the class constructs a final version using the individual interpretations.

- Compare the class version to an 'official' translation, if such a translation exists. Be prepared for the fact that the students may vehemently judge the official version to be inferior to the one that they have created.

Teaching students how to draw upon all of their linguistic resources as they interpret and translate material requires the establishment of a safe place to flow in and out of two languages. This multilingual environment recognizes that bilinguals are not two monolinguals in one head (Grosjean, 1989), and that the constant compartmentalization of languages is unnatural.

Así se dice validates translation as a constructive and worthwhile endeavor and engages students in a complex, sophisticated scrutiny of language that emphasizes the subtleties and nuances of communicating messages across cultures and languages.

We suggest that this strategy can best be employed beginning in third grade.

Así se dice is a multi-day activity that takes advantage of this newly sanctioned bilingual space. It requires students to visit and revisit the same text multiple times in an effort to generate an accurate translation. The procedures for this strategy are demonstrated in Table 4.

After all of the translated texts are shared, the students engage in a critical conversation not only about the texts they have created, but also about the processes they used, the insights they generated, and the difficulties they encountered. Through their articulation and negotiation, students develop a sophisticated ability to attend to both meaning and metalinguistic knowledge.

We have found that it is best to begin by choosing a short, personally meaningful text. Many have used poetry as a rich starting point. This is especially effective and engaging if the poem has been officially translated. Initially, it will be important that all students are translating the same material, but as the students' skills in this area develop, you may want to have students translate and present different texts, always explaining how they arrived at the final version. Other good sources for this activity include idioms, figurative language, and text related to content themes. It is better to engage deeply in the translation of a short but complex text than to translate long passages that preclude extensive discussion.

Because this task may be unfamiliar to students, it is best to begin by modeling how you might approach the translation:

- Using a think-aloud procedure, demonstrate how you read and reread the text to maintain the meaning of the piece.
- Explain how you evaluate different alternatives, ultimately accepting or rejecting a particular version.
- Particularly critical is that you illustrate that word-for-word translation is often inadequate.

Table 4
Así Se Dice Procedures

Day	Procedures
1	Students either read, discuss and/or interpret a text chosen by the teacher. They may also write their own text that will later be translated by their classmates.
2	The students work with a partner to translate the assigned text.
3	Students share their translated version in small groups while the teacher circulates, intervening when students encounter difficulties or to celebrate their growing abilities to work accurately across languages.
4	Students share their work with the whole group.

- Discuss how consideration of the communicative function and context are as important in accurate translation as the words themselves.

- Consider consulting classroom resources to model how students can help themselves when they think they have arrived at an impasse.

- After you have modeled the procedure, orchestrate an interactive whole-group Así se dice activity so that the group jointly practices how to talk and negotiate while translating.

- When you are sure that the students understand how to negotiate meaning by affirming or disaffirming translation attempts, release them to work in pairs or small groups.

While it may take a few attempts to create a respectful space in which to generate, interpret, and translate text collectively, the effort will be substantially rewarded by the metalinguistic advances your students make. This cross-language strategy teaches students to attend differently to meaningful communication across languages. You will find them negotiating not just how to communicate ideas across languages, but also how best to interpret a text in the first language. This cross-language strategy purposefully requires students to focus on, and attend to, meaning. It advocates sophisticated analyses and celebrates socially constructed and negotiated interpretation.

Student examples of Así se dice

After reading a variety of legends in both Spanish and English literacy, one fifth-grade bilingual teacher chose a passage from a legend about the origin of the two Mexican volcanoes, Ixtaccíhuatl and Popocatépetl, as the basis for an Así se dice language investigation. The passage was related to a genre study required by the school district, but the chosen legend was culturally relevant to the students, as all of them were of Mexican heritage. It is important to note that the teacher did not begin the Así se dice activity until she was convinced that the students were very familiar with the story and all of its various versions. The students translated and discussed several passages related to this theme, though we have only chosen one sentence to discuss.

The students worked in pairs to translate the phrase, *Le exige a Popo que encabece el ejercito del imperio para derrotar el enemigo*. See Table 5 for a sample of the variety of translations the students generated.

While the variety of translations is fascinating, it primarily serves as a point of departure for an extended conversation about how to translate concepts and ideas across languages. In this instance, the students held a lively debate about the difference between the words *told, commanded*, and *demands*. They also vehemently argued about the difference between an *enemy* and an *opponent*, finally settling on the idea that an opponent was someone you faced on a soccer field, but an enemy might merit war. When no group translated *el ejercito del imperio* as the

This cross-language strategy purposefully requires students to focus on, and attend to, meaning. It advocates sophisticated analyses and celebrates socially constructed and negotiated interpretation.

Table 5
Así Se Dice: Fifth-Grade Example

Original Spanish Text	English Translations
Le exige a Popo que encabece el ejercito del imperio para derrotar el enemigo	He told Popo to be the leader of the army and beat their enemy.
	He commanded Popo to take lead of the army to the empire to destroy the enemy.
	He demands to be the leader of the empire's army so he could destroy all the opponents.
	He tells Popo to switch the ejércit to derrotate the enemy.

---

imperial army, the teacher guided them to think about how this phrase might be appropriate, and whether the term imperial was important and/or necessary. Was it enough to simply say the army?

The class not only engaged in analysis of how to translate text from English to Spanish, but they also dissected the words in Spanish to understand how the roots of those words could better inform their understanding. In this instance, the word *encabece* was explicitly linked to *cabeza* (head) and the idea of "heading up" an army. From heading up, the class was able to agree on the terms lead and leader. As illustrated in these examples, the teacher can gain valuable information about the students' bilingual language development. These exercises provide yet another source for identifying appropriate foci for The Dictado. For instance, the teacher could create an appropriate dictado that acknowledges the students' need to practice understanding when and how to choose English prepositions.

It is particularly important to examine the final translation. We would argue that a child writing this in an English-only environment might be labeled as having difficulty distinguishing between his/her languages. The child's bilingualism might be viewed as a source of interference or confusion rather than as a resource. In fact, we would argue that this child is making sophisticated generalizations about the way Spanish and English interact. The use of the word *ejercito* for *army* illustrates this student's knowledge that sometimes the removal of the final vowel on a Spanish noun results in its English equivalent.

Consider, for example the following:

Carro becomes *car; rancho* becomes *ranch*

Knowing this, is it not too much of a stretch to think that *ejercito* might be *ejercit.*

Additionally, Spanish verbs ending in *ar* can sometimes be anglicized by replacing *ar* with *ate,* such that *interrogar* becomes *interrogate*; and *celebrar* becomes *celebrate.*

Knowing this, it is not a stretch to go from *derrotar* to *derrotate.*

The teacher's role in advancing these students' linguistic strategies and understandings is critical. Monolingual teachers might not understand the complexity of their bilingual students' writing development and would therefore benefit from working with their bilingual colleagues who have an understanding of both languages.

Conclusion

In concluding this chapter, it is important to reiterate that current research call for teachers to help children make explicit cross-language connections (Genesee & Riches, 2006). Teachers can help children make these cross-language connections in bilingual classrooms, as well as English medium classrooms. We have provided a method, The Dicatdo, and a strategy, Así se dice, that teachers can easily implement in bilingual and English medium classrooms. By utilizing these suggestions, teachers can provide their emerging bilingual students with the necessary tools to improve their writing skills, ultimately creating a positive trajectory toward biliteracy.

> The teacher's role in advancing these students' linguistic strategies and understandings is critical.

References

August, D., & Shanahan, T. (2006). *Developing literacy in second-language learners: Report of the National Literacy Panel on language-minority children and youth.* Mahwah, NJ: Lawrence Erlbaum & Assoc.

Bernhardt, E. (2003). Challenges to reading research from a multilingual world. *Reading Research Quarterly, 38*(1), 112–117.

Cassany, D. (2004). El dictado como tarea comunicativa. *Tabula Rasa, 2,* 229–250.

Clay, M. M. (1993). *Reading Recovery: A guidebook for teachers in training.* Portsmouth, NH: Heinemann.

Cooper, P. M. (2005). Literacy learning and pedagogical purpose in Vivian Paley's storytelling curriculum. *Journal of Early Childhood Literacy, 5*(3), 229–251.

Delpit, L. (1995). *Other people's children.* New York: New Press.

Dorr, R. E. (2006). Something old is new again: Revisiting language experience. *The Reading Teacher, 60*(2), 138–146.

Escamilla K., Hopewell, S., Geisler, D., & Ruiz, O. (2007, April). *Transitions to biliteracy: Beyond Spanish and English.* Paper presented at the annual conference of the American Educational Research Association, Chicago, IL.

Faltis, C. (1996). Learning to teach content bilingually in a middle school bilingual classroom. *Bilingual Research Journal, 20*(1), 29–44.

Genesee, F., & Riches, C. (2006). Literacy: Instructional issues. In F. Genesee, K. Lindholm-Leary, W. Saunders, & D. Christian, (Eds.), *Educating English language learners: A synthesis of research evidence* (pp. 109–175). Cambridge, England: Cambridge University Press.

Grosjean, F. (1989). Neurolinguists beware! The bilingual is not two monolinguals in one. *Brain and Language, 36(1),* 3–15.

Jafarpur, A., & Yamini, M. (1993). Does practice with dictation improve language skills? *System, 21*(3), 359–369.

Jiménez, R., García, G. E., & Pearson, P. D. (1996). The reading strategies of bilingual Latina/o students who are successful English readers: Opportunities and obstacles. *Reading Research Quarterly, 31*(1), 90–112.

Kenner, C. (2004). Living in simultaneous worlds: Difference and integration in bilingual script-learning. *Bilingual Education and Bilingualism, 7*(1), 43–61.

Oller, J. W. (1972). Dictation as a test of ESL proficiency. In H. B. Allen & R. R. Campbell (Eds.), *Teaching English as a second language: A book of readings* (pp. 346–354). New York: McGraw-Hill.

Oller, J. W., & Streiff, V. (1975). Dictation: A test of grammar-based expectancies. *ELT Journal, 30*(1), 25–36.

Ovando, C. & Collier, V. (2003). *Bilingual and ESL classrooms.* New York: McGraw-Hill.

Peregoy, S. & Boyle, O. (2005). *Reading, writing and learning ESL.* New York: Longman.

Reyes, M. (1992). Challenging venerable assumptions: Literacy instruction for linguistically different students. *Harvard Educational Review, 62(4),* 427–445.

Saunders, W. M., & Goldenberg, C. (1999). Effects of instructional conversation and literature logs on limited- and fluent-English proficient students' story comprehension and thematic understanding. *The Elementary School Journal, 99*(4), 277–301.

Saunders, W., O'Brien, G., Lennon, D., & McLean, J. (1998). Making the transition to English literacy successful: Effective strategies for studying literature with transition students. In R. M. Gersten & R. T. Jiménez (Eds.), *Promoting learning for culturally and linguistically diverse students* (pp. 99–132). Belmont, CA: Wadsworth.

Secretaria de Educación Pública (1996). *Español: Sugerencias para su enseñanza, primer grado.* México, D.F.: La Dirección General de Materiales y Métodos Educativos de la Subsecretaria de Educación Básica y Normal.

Slavin, R., & Cheung, A. (2003). *Effective reading programs for English language learners: A best-evidence synthesis.* Washington, DC: Center for Research on the Education of Students Placed at Risk (CRESPAR).

Smith, P. H., Jiménez, R. T., & Martínez-León, N. (2003). Other countries' literacies: What U.S. educators can learn from Mexican schools. *The Reading Teacher, 56(8),* 772–781.

Zentella, A. (1997). *Growing up bilingual: Puerto Rican children in New York.* Boston: Blackwell Publishing.

Let's walk into a classroom where English learners (ELs) are actively engaged. What makes this classroom tick? In the following excerpt, a group of ELs are discussing a landform while reading a text called *Amazing Landforms* (Brian, 1991).

Estefanía: What's a camel?

Marisol: They live in the desert and have humps on their backs.

José: Un camello. (A camel)

Estefanía: Oh, I know it now!

Jetzabel: She didn't know what a camel means in English but she does in Spanish. But I don't think it looks like a camel. It doesn't have a tail or a face.

Marisol: It kind of looks like it is sitting down cause it doesn't have legs.

José: It's a camel that can't walk.

Estefanía: Poor camel! (said with humor)

Engaging English Learners Through Effective Classroom Practices

Joan A. Williams
Sam Houston State University

Claudia Christensen Haag
Texas Woman's University

The above conversation comes from a study (Williams, 2003) of ELs' language using reciprocal teaching (Palinscar & Brown, 1984). This group of fourth-grade ELs is actively engaged using academic language in a conversational format. What is important to note is that the teacher's voice is absent because students have taken over the responsibility of responding and building meaning collaboratively. As an example of the gradual release of responsibility model (Pearson & Gallagher, 1983), these students take on the role of active language learners.

In this chapter, the authors share their experiences from elementary bilingual, dual language, and English as a second language (ESL) perspectives. They also describe effective practices that support ELs' engagement and academic needs. Let's begin by laying a foundation for a learning environment that not only builds strong academic language, but also promotes active engagement.

Engaging the English Learner

We often hear researchers extolling the importance of student engagement for ELs (Cummins, 2001; Mohr & Mohr, 2007; Solis & Grayson, 2007), but what does that entail? First, the teacher needs to value what the student brings to the table. All children possess "funds of knowledge" and it is our job to use what they already know to build to new understandings (Moll, Amanti, Neff, & Gonzalez, 1992).

What's in the EL's toolkit already? They

- talk and/or write about a topic in their first language,
- use cognates (words similar in both languages) to expand vocabulary,
- expand academic experiences by using their cultural knowledge,
- think about language in more than one language (metalinguistic abilities),
- use their own motivation and purpose in learning the English language,
- solve problems related to learning in two worlds,
- use nonverbal abilities to "read" body language and intonation,
- use humor as a coping mechanism, and
- transfer language and literacy abilities from one language to another.

Creating a supportive learning environment involves a teacher who understands the necessity of building upon what the students bring in the door—their language, their culture, and their identity—to promote active student engagement. Such a community begins with a student-centered classroom where teacher-student interactions demonstrate respect. There is a strong link between cognitive engagement and stu-

> Creating a supportive learning environment involves a teacher who understands the necessity of building upon what the students bring in the door—their language, their culture, and their identity—to promote active student engagement.

dent identity, and human relationships play a significant role in whether students choose to engage in classroom activities (Cummins, 2001). Gutiérrez, Baquedano-Lopez, Alvarez, & Chiu (1999) state, "The goal, then, is to create rich zones of development in which all participants learn by jointly participating in activities in which they share material, sociocultural, linguistic, and cognitive resources" (p. 88).

The Importance of Academic Language

Academic language proficiency has enormous impact on the learning opportunities for ELs (Collier, 1987, 1989; Collier & Thomas, 1989; Cummins, 1981, 2001; Krashen & Biber, 1988). Academic discourse is the language of textbooks, and success in school depends on proficiency at this cognitive level. Many educators focus on the distinction between academic and social competence as described in seminal research by Cummins (1981). Another framework by Cummins (2001) can give teachers a way to thoroughly *develop* language proficiency. This perspective builds academic language through three key concepts: meaning, language, and use.

Meaning

It is no accident that *meaning* is the first category in Cummins's (2001) framework. Without understanding, students will not be able to benefit from the other two areas of language focus. Cummins shares a continuum of meaning that begins with literal knowledge and progresses toward creative understanding. From beginning levels of language proficiency, students are able to share high levels of comprehension when they are given alternate formats for response (Mohr & Mohr, 2007).

For example, in Claudia's ESL classroom, Tanya, a second grader and recent immigrant from Russia, is enacting a scene out of Eleanor Roosevelt's picture biography (Adler, 1991). As Tanya 'becomes' Eleanor, she proceeds to scrunch up her face. When Claudia asks Tanya why she is doing this, she smiles and says, "The book say she ugly!" Although Tanya is on a very beginning level of language development, she understands the content and is able to creatively express her understandings. The addition of drama in this case gave Tanya the ability to use her nonverbal responses to creatively share her understandings.

Language

The second focus area, *language*, is multifaceted and extends from a study of structure to a comparison of languages. The language component seeks to develop an awareness of how language functions in different social situations and includes the often-confusing figurative language.

For example, the idiom that many teachers use, "Put your thinking caps on," may be met by a look of total confusion by ELs. The language component also includes the teaching of form and function with an exploration of root words, suffixes, prefixes, and cognates. A teacher who offers

> A teacher who offers explicit instruction in the form and function of language will empower all students to become active in their own language development.

explicit instruction in the form and function of language will empower all students to become active in their own language development.

Use

Finally, the third focus area concentrates on *use*. Teachers need to provide opportunities for students to use language, play with language, and acquire language through multiple formats and strategies. Drama and role-playing are two examples of authentic activities that promote language learning.

Three Effective Strategies

Taking academic language and student engagement into consideration, the authors share three effective strategies to promote meaning, language, and use: *student as questioner, student as language detective,* and *student as performer.*

Student as Questioner

A challenge for all students, but especially for ELs, is the ability to feel confident in asking questions to clarify vocabulary and content confusions. Consider this example from Joan's experiences as a third-grade bilingual teacher. A former student, Leonel, felt comfortable as a fourth grader coming back to visit his teacher from the previous year. Leonel appeared at her classroom door every afternoon to ask her questions. Joan realized that he evidently didn't feel comfortable in asking these questions within his new classroom and that she hadn't explicitly taught him how to ask questions when his comprehension broke down. "Mrs. Williams, what does *Loch Ness* mean?" "Can you tell me what a *circuit* is?"

Day after day, Leonel came to Joan's classroom to ask similar questions after school. This experience with Leonel sent Joan to professional readings to find strategies to help her students develop questioning skills. In her research, she studied a well-known strategy, *reciprocal teaching* (Palinscar & Brown, 1984), that not only addresses learning how to ask important questions but also how to ask for clarification when comprehension breaks down.

In Joan's next year of teaching, she used the reciprocal teaching strategies (predicting, questioning, summarizing, and clarification) during small-group guided reading. She found some effective ideas for implementing reciprocal teaching in a book by Oczkus (2003).

After all four strategies were thoroughly modeled and practiced for more than a month in small groups, students were observed transferring these skills from small- to whole-group settings. Using the clarification strategy, students were given a format to ask questions and monitor when their own comprehension broke down. For example, fourth grader Noemi in a whole-group discussion about government, said, "I need clarification on something. What does *legislation* mean?" Noemi now had the vocabulary to clarify and practice monitoring her own

> A challenge for all students, but especially for ELs, is the ability to feel confident in asking questions to clarify vocabulary and content confusions.

comprehension. Although teaching and modeling these strategies were critical, the foundational piece was Noemi's comfort and engagement in her learning community.

Student as Language Detective

A significant part of transitioning from one language to another is vocabulary and concept development. In both authors' experiences, the more they were able to build on the students' prior knowledge of concepts and vocabulary, the more powerful the students' learning became.

A strategy that Joan found especially effective when she began to teach in a third-grade dual language classroom was to explicitly teach the meaning of cognates — words that look similar and have the same meaning in both languages. For example:

- Spanish *enfermo* (sick) and English cognate *infirm*
- Spanish *proceso* and English *process*
- Spanish *océano* and English *ocean*
- Spanish *números* and English *numbers*

Cognates can account for from one-third to one-half of active vocabulary (Nash, 1997) and their use can increase the students' comprehension of academic language. Both English and Spanish share a bond with Latin, which explains the existence of these cognates. Many of the academic words in English tend to be everyday words in Spanish.

Students become 'detectives' — looking for cognates that support and enhance their English development.

Cognate Box

Caja de Cognados

After students in Joan's class understood the concept of cognates, they then became detectives looking for cognates in English and Spanish during shared, guided, and independent reading. Students placed these cognate "treasures" (written on sticky notes) in a box labeled "Caja de Cognados/Cognate Box." Once a week this box was opened, and several cognates were drawn out for discussion and then placed upon an appropriate word wall.

Students' metalinguistic abilities flourished as they found hundreds of cognates and began to realize how Spanish and English are connected. These cognates also began to appear in the students' writing and oral language. Joan considered these cognates to be diamonds in the rough because of their ability to transfer across languages. What seemed to be a very obvious connection between Spanish and English for Joan was now made transparent and explicit for her ELs.

It is also important to call students' attention to how language is used and how it works (Wong Fillmore, 2002). With ELs, teachers often need to go beyond interpretation of texts and focus attention on actual words, phrases, and grammatical devices. Consider the excerpt below taken from one of Joan's reciprocal teaching lessons (Williams, 2003).

The students were reading and talking about the book titled *Graeme Base: Writer and Illustrator* (Curtain, 2001). Marisol did not understand the implied comparison in the gerund phrase *prefer drawing to writing* even when it was translated into Spanish by another student.

> With ELs, teachers often need to go beyond interpretation of texts and focus attention on actual words, phrases, and grammatical devices.

Marisol:	I don't understand this part here: *I prefer drawing to writing.*
José:	El prefirió dibujar a escribir. (He preferred drawing to writing.)
Marisol:	Yeah, but I get *I prefer drawing,* but I don't get it when it says *to writing*.
Jetzabel:	Like I like better to draw than to write.
Teacher:	Yes, and the *than* isn't there and that makes it confusing.
Marisol:	Oh, I see.

Marisol was able to ask for clarification when her comprehension broke down.

Other examples of confusion or misuse by native Spanish-speaking students involve prepositions, which may possibly be explained by an examination of some verbs in Spanish. Many Spanish verbs have the preposition built in (Wong Fillmore, 2002). Examples include *poner* (to put on), *salir* (to go out), *bajar* (to come down). Because many verbs in Spanish contain the idea of the preposition within them, it is understandable that native Spanish speaking students may become confused with some verb/preposition combinations in English. Additional confusion can be created by the frequency of phrasal verbs in English (*drop off, drop in, drop by*), and the study of these verb combinations is another essential part of word study for ELs.

Combining cognate study with a study of Greek and Latin root words may also be beneficial because many Spanish/English cognates have these common origins. An example is the Latin root *dicere*, which means *say*; in Spanish the verb *decir* means *to say*. The Latin root *dicere* is the basis for cognates like *predecir/predict, predicción/prediction, dictado/dictation* and *diccionario/dictionary*. A focus on word parts can promote *semantic agility* (McWilliam, 1998). Part of semantic agility includes an awareness of how root words combine with prefixes and suffixes to generate an extensive assortment of words and word derivations (e.g., *predict, prediction, predictable, predictably*).

Once again, Joan found that the students needed explicit instruction to see and understand the connections between words and their derivations. For example, in Joan's dual language class, her fourth graders readily understood the words *mountain* and *sticky* in an informational text, but became confused and needed further explanation when suffixes changed these words to *mountainous* and *stickiness*. A resource titled "Nifty Thrifty Fifty" from *Month-by-Month Phonics (*Cunningham & Hall, 1998) proved to be valuable in promoting semantic agility for Joan's students. These 50 words formed the basis for activities that helped the students to access the multisyllabic words of their academic texts (e.g., *classify, forecast, irresponsible, signature*). Not only did these words go on to the word wall, but spelling chants with movement and/or music (d-i-s-c-o-v-e-r-y) made the learning engaging and the students had a constant visual reminder of how the words looked.

This kind of focus on language can propel students to go beyond the communicative level of language they can easily achieve as they interact with other children. It is important to center this kind of language focus on the texts the students and teachers are actually reading and not on isolated skills. Language-rich environments like these are found in classrooms where students have ample time and opportunity to experiment with and develop their academic language.

In her role as an ESL/bilingual specialist, Claudia was invited to work with ESL teachers and decided to use another word detective strategy. One teacher in particular had the challenging task of abruptly transitioning a bilingual fourth-grade classroom into all English and to prepare them for the state writing assessment. The teacher sent Claudia several writing examples with a plea for help on how to move them forward. The first writing from a student named Miguel was a challenge to understand due to his combined use of Spanish and English

> It is important to center this kind of language focus on the texts the students and teachers are actually reading and not on isolated skills.

orthography. One of Miguel's first narratives shared a story about a friend playing soccer:

> *gi escor 1. The next day and rices, Felipe tolme to play basketball guet gim.* (He score 1. The next day, and recess, Felipe told me to play basketball with him.)

Miguel's writing showed strengths in sharing a meaningful storyline, using punctuation and capitalization effectively, and showing some knowledge of within-word spelling. His writing borrowed substantially from his knowledge of Spanish orthography. Bear, Templeton, Helman, & Baren (2003) state that

> …many bilingual learners bring substantial knowledge to the writing process in English. Based on their knowledge of Spanish spelling, they attach the closest letter name in Spanish to the unknown vowel sound and the results look different than they would for English-only letter-name spellers. (p. 81)

For a teacher without knowledge of Spanish orthography, however, Miguel's spelling errors made little sense and made his work almost impossible to read. Miguel's teacher was trying hard to understand his writing, and her comments to Claudia were heartfelt while sharing her frustration: "Good luck reading this. This is the boy that I'm working with on phonics. He also has a limited vocabulary."

In looking at the example, Claudia sent back a copy with some of the correlations from Spanish to English (e.g., *gi* for *he*) and talked about how Miguel was using his ability to hear sounds in both languages and his ever-growing list of important words that were spelled correctly over and over again (*basketball, day, play*, etc.). She suggested that the teacher use a language detective activity where her bilingual students could peer review each others' drafts and find examples of words where their knowledge of Spanish orthography had been used. They could then share what they knew with their teacher about their own metalinguistic abilities.

The ESL teacher demonstrated the process and had the students work in pairs to look for their own examples. The class created a language detective T-chart in order to examine words in both languages. They titled their graphic organizer "How We Used Our Spanish Knowledge." The chart soon became filled with examples of how they used their Spanish knowledge on one side of the T, with the standard English spelling on the other side (See Figure 1).

When Claudia was invited to visit the class, all students enjoyed sharing words that came from their personal work and what they had learned. Spelling errors were seen as windows into the transition process for their teacher and the students were able to share their personal toolkits. This writing workshop soon became a time for collaborative, purposeful engagement.

Figure 1
T-Chart Using Spanish Knowledge

Our Spelling Using Our Spanish Knoweldge	Standard English Spelling
gi	he
guer	here
guet	with
git	hit
gim	him
escor	score
espechus	specials
gu	you
gus	was
den	then
ban	van
lunche	lunch
oder	other
dem	then
dis	this
den	then
tolmi	told me

In Miguel's writing sample, he found that *gi* was spelled *he* and *escore* was spelled *score*. He was empowered by his teacher's comments about how smart he was to use what he knew about language (his orthographic knowledge and metalinguistic abilities) in two languages, and the chart also inspired students to ask questions about language. Two months later this teacher sent a new batch of writing samples with the message … "I'm so proud." Below is an excerpt of Miguel's writing:

> This Chirsmas, I when with my friend to play video games in his house.

Although his English standard spelling was still developing, Adrian's teacher was able to expand her view of his language and celebrate his current progress in spelling and writing abilities. Seeing what children know in two languages should be used to inform our teaching; we should start analyzing what they know about both languages and how they are using this knowledge (Escamilla, 2000). The teacher's emphasis on phonics changed to an emphasis on idea development and explicit word study. Both sides (student and teacher) won.

Student as Performer

Drama yields positive benefits for both language and literacy development (Clay, 1986; Haag, 1998; Holdaway, 1979; Pellegini & Galda, 1993; Wolf, 1994). For the English learner, drama allows an alternate way of showing what is understood within the classroom and encourages more active engagement. "The arts encircle learning with meaning and thereby make comprehension and engagement fundamental for participation" (Heath, 2004, p. 339). Using a read-aloud activity followed by dramatic expression, students are challenged to listen carefully, ask questions for clarification, and step into the story to bring it to life. For all students, but especially important for ELs, the sheer act of being able to use nonverbal gestures and facial expressions allows them to show what they know.

> For all students, but especially important for ELs, the sheer act of being able to use nonverbal gestures and facial expressions allows them to show what they know.

An example of Claudia's ESL K–5 classroom dramatization sessions started early in the school year with predictable books that were repeatedly shared. Students were encouraged to add actions and gestures as they chimed in with the text. Books such as *The Little Old Lady Who Was Not Afraid of Anything* (Williams, 1986) and *Hattie and the Fox* (Fox, 1992) were all-time favorites. (See Appendix A — Teacher's Toolkit for other examples.)

In the beginning weeks of school, Claudia found that a scaffolded model where the students were given explicit directives proved effective. With structure and guidance, Claudia created a community safety zone that allowed the class to discuss how to use body gestures without invading each other's space. This important procedural lesson set the stage for future, more-independent performances, which soon transitioned from teacher-led dramatizations to student choice of text, actions, and props.

Research on using drama, particularly choral reading and readers theater, reveals the importance of repeated readings of text (McCauley & McCauley, 1992; Martinez, Roser, & Strecker, 1999; Shepard, 1994; Wolf, 1993). Repeated reading gives emergent, early, and struggling readers much-needed reading practice leading to proficiency in fluency and comprehension. To scaffold her students into the reading process, Claudia moved her story enactments into individual or choral readings of favorite poems.

For example, during a November unit that encompassed learning about Thanksgiving and Native Americans, students were encouraged to choose their own favorite poems to enact with their own choice of props and reading formats. Some chose a shared reading format and performed their poems in groups, while others wanted to individually share their poems with their chosen props. All performances were videotaped, and one of the students' favorite parts of the week was getting to watch their own presentations.

Self-assessments of language and literacy skills were noted by students as they commented on their performances. Asael, a fourth grader from Brazil, enjoyed watching his presentation of Jack Prelutsky's (1982) Thanksgiving poem, "When Daddy Carved the Turkey," and was congratulated by all peers on his wonderful homemade props (a finger bandaged with a tissue and tape showing red magic marker for blood to be held up as he read).

One line from his performance yielded an excellent self-evaluation learning opportunity for Asael. He read…"He yells as loud as tunder (thunder) right before the bird is through, for when Daddy carves the turkey, Daddy carves his finger too." After viewing his videotaped presentation, Asael asked for help with the word "thunder" as he realized his pronunciation, "tunder" didn't sound right to him. He was able to assess his own language and set his own learning goals. Reading and fluency skills grew with each repeated reading and engagement stayed high due to ownership and an expanded "choice" format.

Another drama layer may be added by including the rewriting of fiction and nonfiction text into scripts. This practice allows teachers to model (through shared writing) the writing process, to help students continually practice reading together the cocreated text, and to split the text into parts to practice and present. Fables work well as a first script-writing practice as they are short and humorous, and their sometimes abstract morals become comprehensible through the addition of talk and problem solving.

For example, in rewriting the fable, "The Dragon King" taken from Demi's *A Chinese Zoo* (1987), Claudia's first-grade English learners were able to problem solve what the main character should do to impart the moral: "No great thing is created suddenly." Since the main character

---

Another drama layer may be added by including the rewriting of fiction and nonfiction text into scripts.

had been commissioned to draw a beautiful picture of the Dragon King's wife, the students talked about how this meant he had to practice a lot. They decided to show this by having several attempted drawings crumpled up and around the artist's feet as he worked at his artist table. Typing the scripts and allowing for multiple opportunities to try out different parts led to final performances. The repeated readings resulted in a definite increase in fluency and clearer understandings of vocabulary and meaning in context. Students were also seeing their own reading abilities (fluency/comprehension) grow.

One young first grader, Donnie, from Vietnam, shared how important these shared writing and repeated reading experiences were for his own growth and confidence. He literally bounced into ESL class several days after practicing his class script and loudly declared with a broad smile on his face, "Guess what Mrs. Haag (Claudia); I'm a READER!" Through helping to write and repeatedly read his script, he became confident in his emerging reading abilities, and both his classroom teacher and ESL teacher saw a breakthrough in his language and literacy development.

Children learn about language and literacy as they share the joy of drama.

The zone of proximal development that is created within drama activities may allow a student to act "as though he was a head taller than himself" (Vygotsky, 1978, p. 102) and stretch his own understandings and learning.

> Stories have yet another magical quality; fully developed sentences borrowed from someone else. The dialogue can change a child from inarticulate embarrassment to confidence, as if by a magic wand. (Paley, 1981, p. 122)

These benefits of drama were seen as powerful motivation to continue to scaffold the drama process and allow students to experience expanded formats for developing language and literacy skills.

Conclusion

So, what makes these classrooms tick? It is the teachers who know how to set up learning environments that

- scaffold language learning through effective literacy practices that allow students to develop their language and literacy skills while focusing upon meaning, use, and form;
- provide a community environment and activities that value the language and culture that students bring in the door; and
- use students' current language, literacy, and cultural knowledge as a bridge to English learning.

English learners need diverse response opportunities. Students who are engaged in literacy events as questioners, language detectives, and performers experience a broader educational canvas. They will be able to play with, practice, and refine their language and literacy skills. Such an environment promotes respect for what our ELs bring to the table, while carefully crafting the academic language so necessary for success in school.

> Students who are engaged in literacy events as questioners, language detectives, and performers experience a broader educational canvas.

Appendix A — Teacher's Toolkit

Resources to Promote Engagement and Word Study

Reciprocal Teaching	Ozkus, 2003
Cognate Dictionary	Nash, 1997
Using Cognates to Develop Comprehension in English http://www.colorincolorado.org/introduction/cognates.php http://www.cognates.org	
Month-to-Month Phonics (Nifty Thrifty Fifty)	Cunningham & Hall, 1998
Interactive Read-Alouds	Hoyt, 2007

Books that Beg to be Dramatized

Hattie and the Fox	Fox, 1992
A Chinese Zoo	Demi, 1987
Chato's Kitchen	Soto, 1995
King Bidgood's in the Bathtub	Wood, 1993
The Little Old Lady *Who Wasn't Afraid of Anything*	Williams, 1986
Amazing Grace	Hoffman, 1991
Dancing Teepees	Sneve, 1991
From Seed to Plant	Gibbons, 1993

Drama Resources

Literacy and the Arts *for the Integrated Classroom*	Cecil & Lauritzen, 1994
Dramatizing Literature *in Whole Language Classrooms*	Stewig & Buege, 1994
Story Drama: Creating Stories *Through Role Playing, Improvising,* *and Reading Aloud*	Booth, 2005

References

Bear, D., Templeton, S., Helman, L., & Baren, T. (2003). Orthographic development and learning to read in different languages. In G. Garcia (Ed.), *English learners: Reaching the highest level of literacy* (pp. 71–95). Newark, DE: International Reading Association.

Booth, D. (2005). *Story drama: Creating stories through role playing, improvising and reading aloud.* Portland, ME: Stenhouse Publishers.

Cecil, N. L., & Lauritzen, P. (1994). *Literacy and the arts for the integrated classroom.* White Plains, NY: Longman.

Clay, M. (1986). Constructive processes: Talking, reading, writing, art, and craft. *The Reading Teacher, 39*(8), 764–770.

Collier, V. (1987). Age and rate of acquisition of second language for academic purposes. *TESOL Quarterly, 25*(4), 509–531.

Collier, V. P. (1989). How long? A synthesis of research on academic achievement in a second language. *TESOL Quarterly, 23*(3), 509–531.

Collier, V. P., & Thomas, W. P. (1989, Fall). How quickly can immigrants become proficient in school English? *Journal of Educational Issues of Language Minority Students, 5,* 26–38.

Cummins, J. (1981). The role of primary language development in promoting educational success for language minority students. In *Schooling and language minority students: A theoretical framework.* Office of Bilingual Education, 3–49. Los Angeles: California State University, Evaluation, Dissemination, and Assessment Center.

Cummins, J. (2001). *Negotiating identities: Education for empowerment in a diverse society* (2nd ed.). Los Angeles: California Association for Bilingual Education.

Cunningham, P., & Hall, D. (1998). *Month-by-month phonics for upper grades.* Greensboro, NC: Carson-Dellosa Publishing Company.

Escamilla, K. (2000). Bilingual means two: Assessment issues, early literacy and two language children. In *Research in literacy for limited English proficient students* (pp. 100–128). Washington, DC: National Clearinghouse for Bilingual Education.

Gutiérrez, K., Baquedano-Lopez, P., Alvarez, H., & Chiu, M. (1999). Building a culture of collaboration through hybrid language practices. *Theory Into Practice, 38*(2), 87–93.

Haag, C. (1998). *Exploring participation in a first grade multicultural classroom during two literacy events: The read aloud and the literature dramatization.* Unpublished doctoral dissertation, Texas Woman's University, Denton, TX.

Heath, S. B. (2004). Learning language and strategic thinking through the arts. *Reading Research Quarterly, 39*(3), 347–366.

Holdaway, D. (1979). *The foundations of literacy.* New York: Ashton Scholastic.

Hoyt, L. (2007). *Interactive read alouds, grades 2–3.* Portsmouth, NH: Heinemann.

Krashen, S., & Biber, D. (1988). *On course: Bilingual education's success in California.* Sacramento, CA: California Association for Bilingual Education.

Martinez, M., Roser, N., & Strecker, S. (1999). "I never thought I could be a star:" A readers theatre ticket to fluency. *The Reading Teacher, 52*(4), 326–334.

McCauley, J. K., & McCauley, D. S. (1992). Using choral reading to promote language learning for ESL students. *The Reading Teacher, 45*(7), 526–533.

McWilliam, N. (1998). *What's in a word? Vocabulary development in multilingual classrooms.* Stoke on Trent: Trentham Books.

Mohr, K., & Mohr, E. (2007). Extending English-language learners' classroom interactions using the response protocol. *The Reading Teacher, 60*(5), 440–450.

Moll, L., Amanti, C., Neff, D., & Gonzalez, N. (1992). Funds of knowledge for teaching: Using a qualitative approach to connect homes and classrooms. *Theory Into Practice, 31*(2), 132–141.

Nash, R. (1997). *NTC's dictionary of Spanish cognates thematically organized.* Lincolnwood, IL: NTC Publishing Group.

Oczkus, L. (2003). *Reciprocal teaching at work: Strategies for improving teaching comprehension.* Newark, DE: International Reading Association.

Paley, V. G. (1981). *Wally's stories.* Cambridge, MA: Harvard University Press.

Palinscar, A. S., & Brown, A. L. (1984). Reciprocal teaching of comprehension-fostering and comprehension-monitoring activities. *Cognition and Instruction, 1*(2), 117–175.

Pearson, P. D., & Gallagher, M. C. (1983). The instruction of reading comprehension. *Contemporary Educational Psychology, 8*(3), 317–344.

Pellegini, A. D., & Galda, L. (1993). Ten years after: A re-examination of symbolic play and literacy research. *Reading Research Quarterly, 28*(2), 163–174.

Shepard, A. (1994). From script to stage: Tips for readers theatre. *The Reading Teacher, 48*(2), 184–186.

Solis, A., & Grayson, K. (2007). You can't win if you don't get to play: Effectively engaging all English language learners. *IDRA Newsletter.* Retrieved April 4, 2007 from http://www.idra.org/IDRA_Newsletters/March_2007

Stewig, J. W., & Buege, C. (1994). *Dramatizing literature in whole language classrooms.* (2nd ed.). New York: Teachers College Press.

Vygotsky, L. (1978). Mind in society. In M. Cole, V. John-Steiner, S. Scribner, & E. Souberman (Eds.), *The development of higher psychological processes.* Cambridge, MA: Harvard University Press.

Williams, J. (2003). *Talk about text: Examining the academic language of English language learners.* Unpublished doctoral dissertation, Texas Woman's University, Denton, TX.

Wolf, S. (1993). What's in a name? Labels and literacy in readers theatre. *The Reading Teacher, 46*(7), 540–545.

Wolf, S. (1994). Learning to act/acting to learn: Children as actors, critics, and characters in classroom theatre. *Research in the Teaching of English, 28*(1), 7–44.

Wong Fillmore, L. (2002, October). *The development of academic language through early literacy experiences.* Paper presented at the Texas Woman's University Early Literacy Conference, Dallas, TX.

Wood, A. (1993). *King Bidgood's in the bathtub.* New York: Scholastic.

Children's Books Cited

Adler, D. (1991). *A picture book of Eleanor Roosevelt.* New York: Holiday House.

Brian, J. (1991). *Natural disasters.* Mission Hills, CA: Australian Press.

Curtain, E. (2001). *Graeme Base: Writer and illustrator.* Littleton, MA: Sundance Publishing.

Demi. (1987). *A Chinese zoo: Fables and proverbs.* San Diego: Harcourt Brace Jovanovich.

Fox, M. (1992). *Hattie and the fox.* New York: Simon & Schuster.

Gibbons, G. (1993). *From seed to plant.* New York: Holiday House.

Hoffman, M. (1991). *Amazing grace.* New York: Dial Books for Young Readers.

Prelutsky, J. (1982). *It's Thanksgiving.* New York: William Morrow & Company Inc.

Sneve, V. (1991). *Dancing teepees: Poems of Indian youth.* New York: Holiday House.

Soto, G. (1995). *Chato's kitchen.* New York: Putnam.

Williams, L. (1986). *The little old lady who wasn't afraid of anything.* New York: Harper & Row Publishers.

Sandra Butvilofsky is a research assistant and doctoral candidate at the University of Colorado, Boulder. Her research interests include classroom-based research with a focus on the writing development of emerging bilingual Latino elementary students.

Ester J. de Jong is an associate professor in ESL/bilingual education at the University of Florida. A native of the Netherlands, she received an Ed.D in literacy and culture studies from Boston University. She moved to the University of Florida in 2001 after several years as an assistant director of bilingual education in the Framingham Public Schools, Massachusetts. Her research interests include bilingual education with a particular focus on two-way immersion programs, educational language policy, and teacher preparation for standard curriculum K–12 teachers working with bilingual students. She has published in *Educational Policy, Journal of Adolescent and Adult Literacy, Urban Education*, and other teacher education texts.

Kathy Escamilla is a professor in education at the University of Colorado, Boulder. She does research on biliteracy development and assessment of Spanish-speaking Latino children. She has over 35 years of experience in the field of bilingual/ESL education as a teacher, researcher, and school administrator. She served two terms as president of the National Association for Biingual Education.

Diana Geisler is a bilingual teacher of young bilinguals, a mentor teacher of their teachers, and an emerging researcher and author. Dr. Geisler's research centers on language and literacy acquisition of young bilingual children in the United States, with an emphasis on Spanish-English bilinguals. She is particularly interested in the interrelationship between oracy and literacy.

Claudia Haag is an assistant professor at Texas Woman's University in the Department of Reading. Her research interests include effective literacy practices for the English learner, multicultural literature, drama, and culturally responsive pedagogy. She has collaborated on book chapters and presented her research at national conferences. Dr. Haag has taught in three states in mainstream and ESL classrooms, taught at three universities, and recently stepped back into the ESL classroom to do teacher research.

Candace Harper is an associate professor in ESL/bilingual education at the University of Florida. Her research and teacher education interests include second language literacy development, the professional expertise of specialist language teachers, and the preparation and

About the Contributors

collaboration of general educators and ESL/bilingual educators to provide effective instruction for English language learners. Dr. Harper has been an ESL/EFL teacher and teacher educator in the U.S., Australia, Bosnia, and France. She has published in the *TESOL Quarterly, Journal of Teacher Education, Journal of Adolescent and Adult Literacy*, and other teacher education texts. She also co-authored a resource book on cross-age literacy tutoring for English language learners.

Lori A. Helman is an assistant professor in literacy education in the Curriculum and Instruction Department at the University of Minnesota, Twin Cities. Her research investigates literacy development and effective teaching practices for English learners at the elementary school level. In addition to numerous published research articles, she has written chapters, texts, and curriculum support materials that guide teachers to apply second language literacy research in their classrooms.

Susan Hopewell is a doctoral candidate at the University of Colorado, Boulder. Her research focuses on strengthening biliteracy education for Spanish-English bilingual children in the United States. Her K–12 teaching experience includes 8 years as a classroom teacher in a dual language elementary school and 4 years as the literacy coach in a maintenance bilingual program.

Patricia R. Kelly is a professor in the College of Education at San Diego State University, where she is currently interim associate dean for faculty development and research. She has been an elementary school teacher, a reading specialist, and a teacher educator. In her role as a Reading Recovery trainer, she was director of the Reading Recovery program at SDSU and also served as director of the SDSU Literacy Center. Her recent research and publications have examined early literacy practices, early intervention, and effective instruction for English language learners.

Judith Chibante Neal is a professor of education at California State University, Fresno. She received post-doctoral certification as a Reading Recovery trainer from The Ohio State University, earned a doctorate in education from University of the Pacific, and holds three California service credentials. Her experience includes 20 years of university teaching, 14 of which were dedicated to training Reading Recovery teachers and teacher leaders and directing the Central California Reading Recovery Project (CCRRP). Dr. Neal's professional contributions include over 80 presentations on international and national levels; published articles in *Journal of Reading, Reading & Writing Quarterly, Literacy Teaching and Learning: An International Journal of Early Reading and Writing*, and *ERS Spectrum*; consulting services to 65 education entities in 15 states; and service on the editorial boards of five academic journals. She is founding editor of *The Journal of Reading Recovery* and served as its editor-in-chief for 5 years.

Susan O'Leary is the author of several books, including the Reading Recovery-based books *Five Kids: Stories of Children Learning to Read* (The Wright Group) and *You Can Make a Difference: A Teacher's Guide to Political Action* (Heinemann). She taught Reading Recovery for 8 years and has since served as a schoolwide facilitator, literacy coach, ESL teacher, and consultant. Most recently, she was the literacy advisor to the Wisconsin Historical Society in its development of the fourth-grade history book, *Wisconsin: Our State, Our Story*, and co-authored the book's teachers' guides.

Cynthia Rodríguez-Eagle is a lecturer in the Department of Reading at Texas Woman's University. She has been a trainer for Reading Recovery and Descubriendo la Lectura since 2005. Her previous roles include Reading Recovery/Descubriendo la Lectura teacher leader and bilingual/ESL classroom teacher. Dr. Rodríguez-Eagle's research interests include early intervention for bilingual students and English language learners literacy development.

Rudolfo (Rudy) Rodríguez recently retired as a professor at the University of North Texas College of Education. He previously served as a faculty member of the Texas Woman's University teacher education program and as department chair of reading and bilingual education. He continues to influence the lives of teachers, children, and adolescents as a member of the Denton Independent School District Board of Trustees. Dr. Rodríguez has received several service awards, including the Ted Booker Award for contributions to Texas teacher education and the Texas Council for Reading and the Bilingual Child for meritorious service in the areas of reading and bilingual education. He has numerous awards from the National and Texas Associations for Bilingual Education in recognition of his work in support of English language learners and bilingual/ESL teacher education.

Wendy Sparrow is a doctoral candidate at the University of Colorado, Boulder. Her research interests include bilingual literacy development (Spanish/English) and examining issues related to fidelity of program implementation in bilingual/ESL and dual language programs.

Joan A. Williams is an assistant professor at Sam Houston State University in the Department of Language, Literacy, and Special Populations. Her research interests center on academic language, classroom language, and English learners. She has published articles, collaborated on book chapters, and made national presentations on these topics. Dr. Williams also has 20 years of experience in elementary and middle school mainstream, bilingual, and dual-language classrooms.

Bogum Yoon began her career as an English teacher in Seoul, Korea. She has also worked at the University of Buffalo, New York, and is currently an assistant professor in the Department of Reading at Texas Woman's University. Her research interests include critical literacy, cultural and social identity, and teacher education on English language learners. Her most-recent articles are published in *The Reading Teacher* and *American Educational Research Journal*.

Yvonne and David Freeman

Dr. Yvonne Freeman is a professor of bilingual education and Dr. David Freeman is a professor of reading/ESL at The University of Texas at Brownsville. Both are interested in literacy education for English language learners. In addition to doing staff development with school districts across the country, they present regularly at international, national, and state conferences. The Freemans have published numerous books, articles, and book chapters jointly and separately on the topics of second language teaching, biliteracy, bilingual education, linguistics, and second language acquisition.

Our Vision
We open doors to a literate future for children who initially struggle in learning to read and write.

The Reading Recovery Council of North America (RRCNA) is a not-for-profit association dedicated to serving Reading Recovery and early literacy professionals throughout North America. Established in 1996, the Council provides a wide variety of programs and services including advocacy, publications, conferences, online learning, and professional resources. These activities strengthen Reading Recovery implementation and provide opportunities for professional development and leadership.

Members include Reading Recovery professionals and partners who are classroom teachers, Title I teachers, early literacy educators, school principals and other administrators, scholars, parents, and community members. Governed by a board of directors, membership is open to anyone interested in Reading Recovery and early literacy.

The Council meets national standards developed for nonprofit organizations. *Standards for Excellence: An Ethics and Accountability Code for the Nonprofit Sector* certifies that an organization's governance and management policies, practices, and procedures meet the highest ethics and quality standards.

For more information about Reading Recovery and RRCNA, please visit our website. www.readingrecovery.org